# I Can't Give You Anything but Love, Baby

*Dorothy Fields and Her Life in the
American Musical Theater*

Kristin Stultz Pressley

**APPLAUSE**
THEATRE & CINEMA BOOKS
Guilford, Connecticut

Applause Theatre & Cinema Books
An imprint of The Rowman & Littlefield Publishing Group, Inc.
4501 Forbes Boulevard, Suite 200, Lanham, Maryland 20706
www.rowman.com

Distributed by NATIONAL BOOK NETWORK

British Library Cataloguing in Publication Information Available

**Library of Congress Cataloging-in-Publication Data Available**

ISBN 978-1-4930-5094-9 (hardcover)
ISBN 978-1-4930-5095-6 (e-book)

∞™ The paper used in this publication meets the minimum requirements of American National Standard for Information Sciences—Permanence of Paper for Printed Library Materials, ANSI/NISO Z39.48-1992.

Printed in the United States of America

www.applausebooks.com

*to Jeremy*
*"I know why my mother taught me to be true.*
*She meant me for someone exactly like you."*

*to Jones, Freddie, and the Four I Adore*

*to Mom, Daddy, and Sissy*

# Contents

Contents

# Acknowledgments

It is unbelievably daunting to attempt to remember everyone whose million-and-one small helps have been so beneficial as I've undertaken the work of writing a book. There are the women from my church, who've prayed for and encouraged me; there are the dear, sweet friends who have understood why I couldn't spend as much time on the telephone as I usually do. There are the folks at the local cafe who let me park in their shop, computer before me, half-milk/half-coffee beside. I'm terrified of neglecting to include even one name, so to the legion of you who have been so gracious and patient and kind to me as I've gone through this process, thank you. Your incredible goodness has not gone unnoticed, nor is it unappreciated.

Thank You also to God, my Help, my Strength, and the Giver of "every good and perfect gift" (James 1:17, ESV), Who not only made me with a passion for theater but continues to give me the opportunities to pursue it. "I will sing to the Lord, because He has dealt bountifully with me" (Psalm 13:6).

Thank you to my husband and sons: you three have borne the brunt of my exhaustion and frustration throughout this writing journey. Thank you for that. Thank you, Jeremy, for telling me at the outset, "Just go through the process." You have no idea how repeating that to myself helped to center me when I'd start feeling frazzled. To Jones and Freddie, thank you for entertaining yourselves all summer long when you'd much rather have had Mama's undivided attention.

Thank you to my parents, my first and greatest fans. Thank you, Daddy, for walking me through contracts, for loaning me the SkyMiles to take those research trips, for asking every single night if I had another chapter for you to read. Thank you, Mom, for all of your help with the boys. Had you not stepped in to help in such significant ways, I never, ever could have completed this task that you've been trying to get me to do for nearly twenty years now.

Thank you to Dr. Rhoda-Gale Pollack, professor emeritus at the University of Kentucky and the adviser for my master's thesis. You were on the other end of all those hours of conversation that led to the revelation of the topic I'd spend the next seventeen years of my life studying. Thank you for listening and for being as excited about my discoveries as I was. To the theater faculties at Furman University, the University of Kentucky, and the University of Georgia, thank you for allowing me to make every single research paper about one musical or another. To David Lahm, who's patiently answered email after email of questions about his mother's life, thank you. To the incredible teams at both the New York Public Library for the Performing Arts and the Library of Congress, thank you. To Jane Klain, who let me camp out in her office, watching sixty-year-old television broadcasts, thank you. To Ronn Carroll, your first-person accounts of interacting with so many of the people in this book make me want to write another biography—about you! To the team at Rowman and Littlefield, including Barbara Claire, Jessica Thwaite, and Emily Hatesohl, the copy editor who saved my neck one line at a time, thank you. Particular gratitude goes to acquisitions editor Carol Flannery: I never, EVER thought you'd respond to that unsolicited email pitch, but you did, and you made my dream come true. Thank you.

Finally, to Dorothy Fields, when I think about the joy I have found in researching your life, I can't help but recall one of your *Seesaw* song-titles, "Poor Ev'rybody Else." For the woman you were, for the life that you led, for the inspiration that you continue to be, thank you.

# Introduction

Dorothy Fields was not the first woman to make a successful career out of writing songs. In fact, she'd be the first to admit as much. In an interview conducted by Henry Kane for his 1962 book *How to Write a Song*, Dorothy corrected Kane when he suggested she was some sort of an anomaly. "Oh, but women *do* write songs," she insisted, listing just a few of her female contemporaries: "Anne Caldwell, Dorothy Donnelly, Carrie Jacobs Bond, Kay Swift, Mabel Wayne, Betty Comden, Mary Rodgers."[1] She could have gone on and on. Perhaps part of the motivation behind her correction was Dorothy's tendency to be self-effacing. In interview after interview, she routinely diverted attention from herself to her colleagues. The other part, however, was a simple statement of fact. Since the advent of American popular music, women have been writing songs. Working as either composer or lyricist (or, in a handful of cases, both), women have always contributed to the nation's songbook, albeit in significantly smaller numbers than their male counterparts.

Take the case of Maude Nugent. In 1896, the popular vaudevillian wrote both music and lyrics to "Sweet Rosie O'Grady." The song sold more than a million copies. Mabel Wayne, a composer, sold more than a million copies of two different songs—1927's "In a Little Spanish Town" (lyrics by Sam M. Lewis and Joe Young) and 1928's "Ramona" (lyrics by L. Wolfe Gilbert).[2] Ann Ronell was a composer and lyricist. In addition to the classic "Willow Weep for Me," her "Who's Afraid of the Big, Bad Wolf," written for a Walt Disney cartoon, has become synonymous with the telling of "The Three Little Pigs." Kay Swift wrote musical comedies like *Fine and Dandy* (1930). She was later a staff composer for Radio City Music Hall and The Rockettes. Vee Lawnhurst (music) and Tot Seymour (lyrics) combined to form the first female songwriting tandem. Together, they wrote four of the top one hundred songs of 1935.[3] Dana Suesse was the so-called "Girl Gershwin." Perhaps best known for her composition of jazz and film

1

scores, her beginnings were on Tin Pan Alley, where she composed such songs as "Whistling in the Dark" and "You Ought to Be in Pictures."

Finally, when *Billboard* magazine—then called *The Billboard*—published its first National List of Best-Selling Retail Records, it was Ruth Lowe's music and lyrics that sat atop the inaugural chart. As performed by Tommy Dorsey and His Orchestra (featuring a vocalist named Frank Sinatra), "I'll Never Smile Again" held the top spot for three months.[4] For every woman whose work is acknowledged here, there are a handful of others. Their numbers were admittedly small when compared to the scores of men writing, but their output was remarkably successful.

None, however, was more successful than Dorothy Fields. Her career as a lyricist began in 1927 and ended with her sudden death forty-seven years later. Along the way, she wrote the lyrics for hundreds of songs, working with eighteen different composers to pen much of the soundtrack of the century. Titles like "I Can't Give You Anything but Love, Baby," "On the Sunny Side of the Street," and "The Way You Look Tonight" earned Dorothy the distinction of being the first woman ever inducted into the Songwriter's Hall of Fame. She also wrote librettos. The monumentally successful *Annie Get Your Gun*, one of the most beloved shows in the canon of Golden Age musicals, was Dorothy's brainchild. *Redhead*, the Gwen Verdon vehicle and Bob Fosse's directorial debut, was too. Nearly forty years after her first million-selling song, Dorothy collaborated with Cy Coleman on the songs for *Sweet Charity*. Edgy phrases like those from 1966's "Big Spender" sprang from the same well of genius that had brought forth a more demure idea in 1936's "Pick Yourself Up."

While Dorothy Fields was not the first woman songwriter, she was definitely the most prolific. Still, just as she recognized the work of her female peers, her female peers recognized the work of Dorothy. "She was *the* woman songwriter," said Betty Comden, whose long career as Adolph Green's co-lyricist began with 1944's *On the Town*. "But man or woman, it made no difference either in her work or in the esteem in which she was held by her colleagues."[5] Suesse expressed similar sentiments: "I can't think of any other woman who reached [Fields's] preeminence as a lyricist or book writer . . . No one could touch Dorothy. She had scores of hits."[6]

"Scores of hits," an Academy Award, a Tony Award, and a catalog that one-time ASCAP president Stanley Adams called "the most important and significant of any woman writer ever in the history of ASCAP"[7]—these are just a few of the professional accolades Dorothy Fields collected in a career that spanned nearly five decades.

This is a book about who she was, what she did, and how she did it.

# Chapter 1
## "Hello, Daddy"

On July 21, 1974, a group of Broadway luminaries gathered in the John Drew Theatre at Guild Hall in East Hampton, New York. They weren't there to celebrate the opening of a new show. Rather, they came together to commemorate the closing of one of the great careers in American theater history. Their honoree was Dorothy Fields. Dorothy referred to herself as a "playwright and lyric writer,"[1] but for one whose output and impact was as significant as hers, that seems like an understatement. A playwright? Yes. Collaborating with her brother Herbert Fields, she wrote the librettos for eight Broadway musicals. A lyric writer? Without a doubt. Dorothy wrote with eighteen composers and amassed a collection of popular hits hundreds of songs long. To those who gathered in the Hamptons that day, however, she was far more than a major contributor to the canon of the Golden Age American musical. Dorothy was a much-beloved colleague, "a lyricist's lyricist,"[2] whose sudden death on March 28, 1974, left a hole in the hearts of all who knew her. "Neither glamorous nor physically imposing, nor a prima donna in her behavior, [Dorothy Fields] was reliable, respectful, and professional," wrote Caryl Flinn in her biography of Dorothy's friend, Ethel Merman. "The Broadway community was united in its adoration of Dorothy, responding not only to her talent but also to her wit, generosity, and warmth. Everyone knew her as a good egg."[3]

They came from far and wide to remember their friend that summer. Arthur Schwartz, a composer with whom Dorothy collaborated on the scores to *A Tree Grows in Brooklyn* and *By the Beautiful Sea*, flew in from London. Gwen Verdon arrived from Las Vegas. She'd worked with Dorothy on both *Redhead* and *Sweet Charity*. Richard Kiley, who'd starred opposite Verdon in *Redhead*, came in from the Midwest. Whether they'd worked with Dorothy or not, though, theater folk flocked to be a part of the so-called "Tribute to Dorothy Fields." Cy Coleman, who'd spearheaded the affair, was Dorothy's final collaborator. "We want to give her the greatness, the recognition she deserves," he said. "People who do great things should be recognized by their peers, and this show, we hope, will show how she contributed so much to the theater and to all of us."[4]

Dorothy Fields's story began 160 miles southwest of East Hampton as Lew and Rose Fields summered with their three children: daughter Frances was ten and sons Joseph and Herbert were nine and almost seven, respectively. Based in New York City for most of the year, the Fields family made a tradition of spending summers at the shore. The summer of 1904—in spite of Rose's heavily pregnant condition—was no different. Their "home away from home" was a spacious rental house near the intersection of Main Street and Corlies Avenue in the newly incorporated community of Allenhurst, New Jersey.

Fewer than ten years earlier, Allenhurst had been no more than a family farm. Bordered to the south by Deal Lake and to the east by the Atlantic Ocean, the 120-acre Allen Estate was prime property for developers looking to establish a seaside retreat for New York elites. The Coast Land Company made quick work of the transition. Within a year, there were dozens of massive homes on wide avenues. No modern convenience was spared. Paved streets, electric lights, a pavilion on the beach, and, soon after, an oceanfront casino added to the appeal of the idyllic community just sixty miles due south of Manhattan. With home costs ranging from $12,000 to $100,000,[5] Allenhurst catered to "only the best class of refined Summer residents."[6] One advertisement promised "favorable prices and terms to desirable parties, while undesirable parties cannot buy at any price."[7]

This was a community of vacationers into which the Fields family made a comfortable fit. Residents like Hubert T. Parson, the president of the F. W. Woolworth Company, and John Augustine McCall, head of the New York Life Insurance Company, rubbed elbows with the likes of former New York congressman James J. Belden. While Lew Fields was not a head of industry or of state, he was a captain of comedy. *The Billboard* referred to him as "one of the foremost employers of prominent comedians in the theatrical life of today."[8] Not just an "employer of prominent comedians," Fields was a comedian of the utmost prominence himself. Knowing Lew Fields is an essential component to knowing Dorothy Fields.

Born in Poland in 1867, Lew Fields was then known as Moses Schoenfeld. The son of Solomon and Sarah, Moses was five years old when the family immigrated to the United States. They came, of course, to New York City. Settling, as so many others did, on the Lower East Side, Solomon Schoenfeld imagined his four young sons (and the others that followed after the family's arrival in the United States) would be helpful in the family business. Solomon was a tailor by trade and soon established a sweatshop in the Schoenfeld's three-room home on Division Street; it quickly became clear, however, that Moses's talents lay elsewhere. As a student in New York City's public school system, he received an Americanized name— "Moses" became "Lew"; "Schoenfeld" became "Fields"—and a crash course in the idiosyncrasies of the many ethnicities by which he was surrounded in an immigrant-rich neighborhood.[9] He also received a best friend named Joe Weber.

There are several stories as to how the two boys, born just months apart in 1867, met. Each possible scenario reads like a bit from the massively popular vaudevillians the pair would become. What actually happened is difficult to discern, yet each possibility offers insights into the boyhood beginnings of a duo that would someday be known as "the two most heartily-loved comedians in this country."[10] Weber once told it this way: he was being chased by a gang, having bought a cake that the gang wanted. To keep the gang from getting it, Weber stuffed the cake in his mouth, making his mouth so full that he couldn't talk. Seeing this, members of the gang assumed he was mute. "They thought deaf and dummies were terrible strong," Weber said. Fields, also a part of the interview, continued, "Yes. You were foxier than I. I yelled, and they got my cake, but when I saw what you did, I came up and spoke to you." "But I did not answer you, until we got out of sight of that bunch of loafers," finished Weber, who'd been intent on keeping up his ruse.[11]

In its obituary of Lew Fields, the *New York Times* offered another possible scenario for the boys' introduction: both Weber and Fields were expelled from school for doing handstands instead of arithmetic. The resulting days off gave the pair plenty of time to develop a relationship, while studying "the dime a dozen 'stars' of the neighborhood halls" and "mimic[ing] them on the sly."[12] A third account of Lew Fields meeting Joe Weber is offered in *From the Bowery to Broadway: Lew Fields and the Roots of American Popular Theater*. This remarkably exhaustive tome was written by two of Fields's nephews, who suggest Lew Fields met Joe Weber while watching their classmates clog: "To impress Joe, Lew . . . bragged that . . . he could dance on a plate without breaking it." Of course, he couldn't. His willingness to destroy the family china, though, intrigued Weber enough for a lifelong friendship to begin.[13]

Whatever the genesis of the boys' camaraderie, their beginnings would change the course of each child's life, and, by extension, set a course for the lifestyle to which Lew's four children would become accustomed (Joe Weber and his wife, Lillian, did not have children). Together, the precocious pair roamed the crowded Lower East Side streets. Not knowing each day's "play" was, in fact, research for what would become their life's work, Weber and Fields—a label they wouldn't wear professionally for several more years—absorbed the cacophony of cultures and dialects that provided the soundtrack to their section of the city. (Interestingly, a hallmark of Dorothy Fields's lyrics is her mastery of the vernacular.) The notorious Bowery area was their stomping grounds. Once a fashionable downtown district that was home to some of the city's finest theaters, the Bowery eventually became known for its "rowdy saloons, notorious brothels, and dangerous street gangs."[14] This was the Bowery the boys knew, loved, and longed to be a part of.

Though each performed odd jobs in order to contribute to his family's income, they nonetheless made time to practice their craft. They rehearsed "on cellar doors, in empty basements, and in the haylofts of nearby stables" until they finally booked their first gig.[15] Weber and Fields were barely ten years old. Under the name "the Dutch Senators,"[16] they took the stage at Turn Hall on East Fourth Street and performed in blackface for the Elks Serenaders Social Club. They were not a hit; they were, however, determined to keep trying and eventually landed gigs at several of the oddity museums that bordered the Bowery. The Chatham Square Museum paid the boys three dollars a week to do nine shows a day; later, the Globe Museum offered twenty-five dollars a week.

Constantly massaging their routine—"We never wrote out our parts," Lew said. "Lines that got a laugh, we kept; others, we dropped."[17]—Weber and Fields eventually landed on the schtick that would become their bread and butter. Weber would be Mike, "short, meek, and well-stuffed with pillows," the straight man to Lew's "tall and domineering" Meyer.[18] With Mike and Meyer, Weber and Fields had found their niche. Their alter egos were German immigrants whose heavy accents led to many misunderstandings. Audiences, many of whom were new to this country and could, thereby, relate to the fictional duo's difficulties, found routines like these side-splitting.

> MIKE: I am delightfulness to meet you.
> MEYER: Der disgust is all mine.
> MIKE: I receivedid a letter from mein goil, but I don't know how to writtenin her back.
> MEYER: Writtenin her back! Such an edumacation you got? Writtenin her back! You mean rottenin her back. How can you answer her ven you don't know how to write?
> MIKE: Dot makes no never mind. She don't know how to read![19]

Together, Weber and Fields took Mike and Meyer on the road. Now bigger than the Bowery circuit, the entertaining tandem toured the country; they'd organized their own road show by the time they'd turned twenty-two. Five years later, they were earning a whopping $400 per week. When Oscar Hammerstein I, grandfather of the Oscar Hammerstein who'd become Richard Rodgers's songwriting partner, invited Weber and Fields to play his massive Olympia Theatre compound at Forty-Fourth Street and Broadway, they couldn't resist. It was during this run that they developed their concept of lampooning shows of the current theatrical season. These burlesques—the first of which was a satire of David Belasco's *Heart of Maryland* renamed *The Art of Maryland*—were as outrageously popular as Mike and Meyer had been. *Cyrano de Bergerac* became *Cyranose de Bric-a-Brac*; *The Stubbornness of Geraldine* became *The Stickiness of Gelatine*. With these and others like them, an American tradition of satire—one continued more recently by writers like Gerard Alessandrini, who produced his *Forbidden Broadway* parodies from 1981 to 2014—was born.

The demand for these types of entertainments was so great, in fact, that many producers sent their scripts to Weber and Fields, asking the pair if they'd burlesque the show. Turns out, the spoof material made for great marketing. To accommodate audience demand for more, Weber and Fields leased a space at Broadway and Twenty-Ninth Street. The six-hundred-seat Weber and Fields Music Hall made a happy home for the company's successful send-ups and the musical comedies that followed. To have a show parodied by Weber and Fields was a feather in the cap of any producer; to perform in a show produced by Weber and Fields was equally as career-affirming. As was noted in *Variety*, "Virtually every famous performer around the turn of the century and later at one time or another starred in Weber & Fields musicals." Members of the regular company included Fay Templeton, DeWolf Hopper, William "Willie" Collier, and Lillian Russell, who was paid $1,000 a week—"the most fabulous stipend of the time."[20]

It was this sort of lavish spending, though, that contributed to the demise of Weber and Fields's nearly thirty-year professional association. As a producer, Lew spared no expense. The best of performers, the best of productions—money was no object to his way of thinking. Weber was, fiscally, more conservative. As production costs rose, he was concerned that the company's growth was unsustainable in a relatively small house for which all tickets were $2.50 or less.[21] When a new fire ordinance mandated that they either close the Music Hall or rebuild it, the pair couldn't agree on what to do. Instead, Weber and Fields went their separate ways.[22] It was May of 1904. Weber, who'd saved a huge portion of his massive earnings, maintained control of the Music Hall, which was renamed the Weber Music Hall and later turned into a movie house. Fields, driven by a desire to remain a major force in the American theater and a need to stay ahead of a pretty significant gambling habit, partnered with Julian Mitchell, his stage manager, and Fred Hamlin, a producer. They formed the firm Hamlin, Mitchell, and Fields and planned to produce entertainments similar to those Lew had staged with Weber. To this end, Lew leased a newly built facility at 254 West Forty-Second Street; he named it the Fields Theatre. He also made plans to spend the summer with his growing family in the chic retreat of Allenhurst, New Jersey.

There was nothing out of the ordinary about Lew, Rose, and the children summering at the sea. Allenhurst was a short train ride from New York, making the city easy to reach, should Lew's work require him to return home; it frequently did. Very pregnant, Rose spent her days preparing to deliver a fourth child; Frances, Joseph, and Herbert took advantage of all the up-and-coming town had to offer. By 1904, the town's amenities had grown to include a saltwater pool and a boardwalk modeled on the one in Atlantic City. Then came July 15. "I must have arrived ahead of time," said Dorothy Fields. "I've always heard how Lee Shubert and Willie Collier, the actor, who were both good friends of my father (and who were spending the weekend with the Fields family) . . . ran through the streets looking for a doctor or midwife."[23]

Whether professional help eventually arrived is uncertain. Dorothy once said, "I'm told everybody assisted in the birth. A newspaperman acted as midwife."[24] What is known is that, on July 15, 1904,[25] Rose Fields delivered a baby girl at their Allenhurst summer rental. News of the birth spread quickly. Telegrams of congratulations—more than sixty of them, according to one newspaper—poured in from friends of the family and colleagues of Lew Fields. Naming the baby took several days. When asked what the new addition would be called, Lew responded, "Don't know yet. Jury is still out, and Mrs. Fields is foreman. It is up to her."[26]

This is typical of how the Fields family functioned. Lew's space was the stage; Rose, who'd worked as a toy buyer at Brooklyn's A.I. Namm & Son department store prior to marrying Lew, handled the home life.[27] A few days after her newborn daughter's birth, Rose decided to name the baby Dorothy; it can't be known for certain whether this had an impact on her decision, but it is worth noting, as other biographers have suggested, that L. Frank Baum's *The Wonderful Wizard of Oz* was published in 1900. In response, American homes were flooded with little girls who shared the name of Baum's heroine, Dorothy. Lew Fields's new partners had been responsible for bringing a stage adaptation of the book to Broadway in 1903 and again in the year of Dorothy Fields's birth. It is not difficult to imagine that one or all of these events may have played into Rose's decision.

Regardless, the family settled back into its New York City home at 334 West Eighty-Eighth Street. Life returned to business as usual. That meant that Lew Fields was often away. Theirs was a happy home life, and he tried to stay as connected with Rose and the children as possible; it proved difficult, however, given the professional demands placed on the time of a man who had become one of the largest employers of theatrical talent in the world. In order to fulfill his many commitments, Fields engaged as many as two thousand theater artists across the country.[28] He was gone so often, in fact, that the story is told of a two-year-old Dorothy screaming in fear when the man she believed to be a stranger showed up for dinner.[29]

For the next several years, Lew Fields was producing theater in New York and on the road at a frenetic pace. There were several spans of time in which he had multiple shows running on Broadway. Later, he also acquired a stake in—and lent his name to—Chicago's Lew Fields American Music Hall. There were touring companies he managed, as well as productions in which Lew himself starred. He was careful, however, to keep his professional life completely distinct from his personal one. "My job is that of a comedian," he said. "I come here in the theater and do my job with the tools of my profession, which I keep here, just as a mechanic goes to his work and uses his tools. I do not carry my work of the theater into my home life."[30] A large part of this was at his wife's insistence. As the "foreman" of the home, Rose Fields appreciated the lifestyle which her husband's work afforded the family, but she was aware of the stigma that some attached to those who worked in the theater. Both she and Lew wanted more "respectable" lives for their children. They also had no interest in exposing Frances, Joseph, Herbert, and now Dorothy to the instability of show business. Except for a night or two a year—Lew's birthday, for instance—the children were intentionally sheltered from the people with whom their father worked. Lew Fields is said to have told the children things like, "If I hear of any one of you getting messed up in [theater], I'll call the cops"[31] and "Lay off show business. It's lousy. Even if you're lucky, it's here today, gone tomorrow. The Waldorf today, cafeteria the next."[32]

**Lew Fields and family in front of their New York City home: Dorothy, Mr. Fields, Miss Frances, Mrs. Fields, Herbert, and Joseph, 1910.**
Photo by White Studio © Billy Rose Theatre Division, The New York Public Library for the Performing Arts.

It makes sense that Fields wanted his children to avoid the highs and lows of the profession. He was all too well acquainted with them, having made and lost several fortunes both on stage and at the races. Lew's insistence on both the finest talent and "brilliant stage effects" for his shows was a double-edged sword. It earned him reviews like the one for 1911's *The Hen-Pecks*, which was called "another of those elaborate and skillfully mounted musical comedies for which Lew Fields is distinguished."[33] But this lust for the lavish had also, previously, contributed to the demise of his partnership with Weber and, in 1911, to demands from Lee and J. J. Shubert, owners of the country's largest theater-owning organization, to cut down on expenses.

Ironically, Lew Fields chose this moment in time to do something which was, for him, highly unusual. He took a vacation. In the middle of *The Hen-Pecks'* successful New York run, Lew, Rose, and the children boarded the *Lusitania* and sailed for a five-week tour of Europe. The show, without its star, went on a two-month hiatus. It was Lew's first extended break in four years, but it was by no means a work-free trip. Lee Shubert went along. As often as they could, the pair of producers observed European entertainment in search of fresh ideas for American audiences. When not engaged with Shubert, the Fields family visited London, where they observed the coronation ceremonies of King George V. They spent two weeks in Paris and toured parts of Austria and Germany. In Berlin, young Dorothy celebrated her seventh birthday with a stay at the palatial Hotel Adlon. Steps away from the Brandenburg Gate, the hotel was considered the social center of the city. It must have felt like something out of a fairy tale for the much-adored baby girl of the Fields family. The family returned from Europe on August 4, 1911. Within an hour, Lew was back at the Broadway Theatre, rehearsing to resume his role in *The Hen-Pecks*.

He remained in the role through the production's September 23 closing. With the pressure from the Shuberts still weighing on his mind, Fields took *The Hen-Pecks* on tour. The show stopped at several Shubert-owned theaters as it made its way across the country. While stopped in Chicago, Fields was also working to launch a production called *Hanky Panky* at the Lew Fields American Music Hall. At the same time, he had seven different companies performing various productions on stages across the country. A journalist named Mae Tinee spoke with Fields after a Chicago performance of *The Hen-Pecks*. Fields asked her, "I wonder if you know what I'm trying to do at the Music Hall." The reporter answered, "Make money, I suppose. Isn't that it?" "That's it—to a certain extent," Fields smiled, adding that he was also driven to offer Chicagoans an outlet where "tired businessmen and weary women can go there and forget their troubles in one long laugh."[34]

The laughter stopped, however, during one particular Chicago performance. During the run of the show, Fields received word that his father was gravely ill. Lew raced home to New York. By the time he reached his parents' apartment at 600 West 150th Street, Solomon Fields was dead at the age of seventy-one. The years between his arrival in the United States and his death in November of 1911 had been kind to Solomon Fields. He and Sarah had added three more children to their family, and his tailoring business had been remarkably successful. Among those who attended his funeral was his famous son's former partner. Afterward, Joe Weber and Lew Fields shared a carriage. Their drive back home took them past the Bowery, which sparked a conversation about their early days and the boyhood antics of two immigrants made good. They talked, they laughed, they realized how much they missed each other, and they decided the time was right. Within one month, it was official: Weber and Fields were back in business. The children Lew and Rose had fought so hard to shelter from the theater would soon be exposed to it in ways that would change their lives forever.

# Chapter 2
## "Growing Pains"

Almost since Weber and Fields had split, American audiences had been aching for a reunion of the country's "two most heartily-loved comedians." One writer made the case that their reunion was "very near a life and death necessity." Ripley D. Saunders wrote in the *St. Louis Post-Dispatch*:

> The playgoing public was tired to the bone of the problem play, the "triangle" play, the political corruption play, the crooked-finance play, the religious discussion play. Little old New York was fairly famishing for good, wholesome, genuine stage fun, for honest laughter, for a tickling of its ribs that should cause such an explosion of mirthfulness as cyclonically to dispel the all-enveloping atmosphere of gloom, which had settled down over the metropolis like a sable pall.[1]

After more than seven years apart, Joe Weber and Lew Fields were ready to give the public what it wanted. The Broadway Theatre—a 1,700-seat house where *The Hen-Pecks* had played in 1911 and where Lew Fields kept an office— was booked. The plan was to assemble an all-star lineup of the old company and present an evening reprising its best bits. In addition to Weber and Fields, Lillian Russell, Fay Templeton, Willie Collier, and others took the stage. The show was *Hokey Pokey*, more commonly referred to as the "Weber and Fields Jubilee." It was described as "a Pot-Pourri of Reminiscences in Two Acts." Once the reunion was announced in December of 1911, anticipation quickly reached fever pitch. Its opening date had not yet been set when a banker named Chester Dale mailed Lew a five-dollar check. He wanted to be sure a seat was reserved for him. Buyers at the auction for opening night tickets were just as eager. With single seats ranging from five to thirty-five dollars, the auction netted more than any other similar event in the previous ten years. Publishing magnate William Randolph Hearst bought a box for an astonishing $900. Judging by reviews, it was a worthy investment. "Broadway hasn't had such a laugh for eight years," wrote one critic. "The reception that the favorite players got . . . has never been equaled in the memory of the oldest first-nighter."[2]

Dorothy Fields was among those first-nighters. Sitting in a box with her family, the shy, dark-eyed seven-year-old got her first taste of big-time entertainment around the same age that her father had entered the business. It had to be spectacular, hearing the man she'd known only as "Pop" receive an ovation that had "never been equaled." The impact of this initial encounter with the theater can't ever be known, but it's easy to imagine that it was a night she never forgot.

In a run that lasted from February 8 to May 11, 1912, the Weber and Fields Jubilee performance was seen by nearly 200,000 people and grossed more than $300,000.[3] The New York production was successful enough that a national tour was a foregone conclusion. Eighty members strong, the Jubilee company would travel in its own special train. There were "three palace cars, three sleeper cars, a dining car, an observation car, and two baggage cars" to carry not only the cast and crew but also the stars' families and a number of journalists embedded with the tour.[4] The cast would perform thirty-seven times in thirty-two cities, and by the end of the month-long trip, the company would cross five thousand miles.

Perhaps hoping to re-create the time the family had enjoyed together on their tour of Europe the previous summer (or maybe the children, so excited by their opening-night experience, insisted), Lew and Rose Fields made a surprising decision. Laying aside their history of keeping the children away from the theater, they decided to bring them along. By now, Frances was eighteen, Joseph was seventeen, and Herbert and Dorothy would turn fifteen and eight in the course of the summer. Dorothy always remembered the trip vividly, calling it "a wonderful experience."[5] To the cast and crew, the boss's shy baby girl was "the company pet." To Willie Collier's son, Buster, she was the perfect playmate. The two had their run of the many trains and, curious to see the sites of new-to-them cities, often jumped off when the caravan was stopped. Twice, the precocious pair was left behind, prompting the train to return for its youngest passengers. Always inquisitive about her surroundings—not unlike her father who'd made his living by listening to what was going on around him—Dorothy and her buddy Buster were fascinated by the paraphernalia of putting on a show. The sets, the props, the costumes, and—in the case of Lillian Russell—the wigs were too tempting to stay away from.

Lillian Russell's wigs, in fact, provided Dorothy with one of her most vivid memories of the trip. Dorothy and Buster were sneaking through the train cars when they passed Russell's suite. She had two staterooms—one for Russell herself and one for Russell's many wigs. When Dorothy and Buster passed Russell's room, the door was open just enough for the children to peek in and see one of Weber and Fields's leading ladies without "a spear of hair on her head! We screamed," Dorothy said. "Of course, we were sworn to silence—not that we would have talked to anybody but maybe the conductor or the porter. Nobody was interested in what we had to say."[6]

Russell's embarrassment aside, the tour continued until it reached Pittsburgh in mid-June. Before putting in her two-show day on June 12, 1912, Russell married Alexander P. Moore. Moore was the publisher of the *Pittsburgh Leader* and, later, a United States ambassador to Spain and Peru. Likely owing to the anti-actor prejudice of the deacons who declined their request (Joseph Fields once told an interviewer, "Back in Pop's day, I guess actors were looked upon as second-class citizens and loose characters"[7]), the couple wasn't allowed to marry in the First Methodist Episcopal Church, as they'd planned to do. Instead, the ceremony was held at Pittsburgh's grandest hotel, the recently redecorated Hotel Schenley. Russell was attended by her sister and a little girl with a big secret named Dorothy Fields; Buster Collier served as the page. After the ceremony and a wedding breakfast, Russell returned to the Grand Opera House just in time to make her matinee performance.

The visit to Pittsburgh marked the end of the Weber and Fields Jubilee of 1912. With its closing, stock was taken of the tour's success. In less than four weeks, the company had grossed $500,000, breaking theatrical records for both attendance and box office receipts. It was the most successful tour ever undertaken by Weber and Fields. True to Lew Fields's form, it was also their most expensive. For all of its financial success, however, Fields might have considered the Jubilee a familial failure. His children had lived for a month fully immersed in their father's world; both new to them and completely thrilling, the world of the theater was no longer an unknown. The three youngest Fields children would have a hard time ignoring the irresistible beckon of what their parents had for so long considered a forbidden fruit.

Once they had returned from the Jubilee, though, the Fields children were allowed to see more and more of their father's work. Direct participation in the theater was still discouraged. The Fields's daughters were expected to (eventually) marry well; their sons, Lew and Rose insisted, would become lawyers, doctors, or something equally distinguished. They were, presumably, unaware that Joseph had been sneaking in to watch his father's rehearsals since before Dorothy was born. Let in by the theater's manager, Joseph would sit in a second balcony to watch with awe as his father pieced together show after show. After the Jubilee, access was easier. Probably hoping it'd help Lew to recoup some of the money they'd invested in his shows, the Shuberts leased Weber and Fields their new theater at Forty-Fourth Street. They named it Weber and Fields 44th Street Theatre. Dorothy remembered spending every Saturday sitting in a box at a different show. These outings through the 1910s gave the inquisitive young lady a bird's-eye view of the American musical as it looked in those early iterations:

There was a formula musical comedy in the days when [Pop] did them . . . block comedy scenes, comedy scenes about, for instance, a soda fountain, where Pop would have twelve minutes of hilarious stuff that had nothing to do with the story. He would find maybe four or five such scenes and have a score written. There would be just a thread of a love story, and they were rousing hits.[8]

It was around this time that Lew Fields dubbed Dorothy the keeper of his scrapbooks. Enormously proud of her father, this was a mission she relished with great pleasure. Not only was she allowed to attend a performance of many of Lew's productions, but afterward, she'd scour newspapers and magazines in search of each show's reviews or write-ups. Lew Fields probably assumed that this was a relatively innocuous assignment; however, just as exposing the children to the Jubilee environment had whet their appetites for more theater, Dorothy's scrapbook duty was a tutorial in show-building that would serve as a firm foundation for her eventual career as a lyricist and librettist. Initially, she kept only the raves. As she matured, however, Dorothy paid closer attention to the criticism:

> I began to be impressed by what made a good book—how, even if you had a great comic star, like my father, you need to have a sensible story, a plot that developed, with a beginning, a middle, and an end that would tie everything together . . . if you don't have a story that will hold the audience, you won't have a successful show.[9]

These were the ideas taking shape in Dorothy's head when she was not yet ten years old. Conversely, sister Frances did as her parents had hoped she would. In August of 1914, Lew and Rose stood proudly by as their twenty-year-old firstborn married Charles Lionel Marcus. A 1909 graduate of Columbia Law School, Marcus was impressively employed as the vice president of the Bank of the United States. His father, Joseph, was the bank's founder and president. The couple married in first-class style in the hydrangea-draped Gold Room at Delmonico's Restaurant. Located at Fifth Avenue and Forty-Fourth Street, Delmonico's was just a four-block walk from Weber and Fields's current Broadway house. It was the first fine-dining establishment in the country, as well as the first American eatery to be called a restaurant. Known for its "unheard of luxury," its private dining rooms, and its thousand-bottle wine cellar, Delmonico's offered precisely the sort of circumstances under which Lew Fields wanted to send his "princess" into polite society. Not even such an impressive display of Lew Fields's wealth could make the Marcus family happy with Charles's choice, though. For all of his money, Lew Fields still represented a segment of society with which much of the upper crust preferred to not personally associate. This was precisely why Lew and Rose were resolved that their children would not work in the theater. What the Fieldses saw as a step up for Frances, the Marcuses viewed as a step down for Charles.

A decade younger than Frances, Dorothy could not have been aware of the social politics at play on the day her sister became a bride. She attended Frances as she had Lillian Russell, wearing a white organdy dress with a blue satin sash and carrying a basket of roses and sweat peas. It was a beautiful evening with dinner and dancing for each of the 150 guests present to witness what Joseph and Herbert Fields jokingly referred to as "the merger."[10] When the outbreak of World War I preempted the couple's plan to honeymoon in Europe, Charles and Frances went West instead; they visited Yellowstone Park before settling into an apartment at 219 West Eighty-First Street.

Their selection of a home just eleven blocks away from where the Fields family lived is indicative of how emotionally close the six Fieldses were. Lew, Rose, and the children had moved in at 307 West Ninetieth Street sometime around 1910. Their five-story home ("the tallest house on the block," Dorothy remembered)[11] would be a touchstone for the family, until it was sold in September of 1922 and altered into apartments. The Fieldses regularly ate meals together and, even as the children entered adulthood, they lived together at different points in each one's life. Lew Fields entrusted his son-in-law with the care of his fortune, which fluctuated wildly depending on his success at the box office or his gambling failures. One writer noticed the family's "interlocking, water-tight devotion" and stated, "There never was such a cliquey clan so crazy about one another."[12]

The younger Fieldses were also increasingly crazy about theater. No longer forced to sneak into his father's rehearsals, Joseph started producing amateur shows with his DeWitt Clinton High School classmates at the age of fourteen. Later, he did as Lew wanted him to and enrolled at Columbia Law School; however, when the United States entered World War I, Joseph dropped out of Columbia to enlist in the Navy. While training at the Pelham Bay Naval Training Station in the Bronx, Joseph helped write a Navy show called *Biff! Bang!* It played Broadway's Century Theatre in May and June of 1918 and raised more than $60,000 for Navy Relief. Always a proud father, Lew attended the opening night performance. Afterward, he shook a finger in Joe's face, warning him, "Don't think you're not going to be a lawyer!"[13] Dutifully, Joseph remained in the Navy until the end of the war, concluding his service as a gunnery officer on the USS *Finland*. He never returned to Columbia; he decided instead to settle in Paris after the Treaty of Versailles was signed in June of 1919. While there, Joseph sent his siblings some French perfume. His brother and sisters liked it so much that Joseph decided to set up a Paris-based perfume business. In its first year, the company made more than $800,000.

Back at home in New York, Lew Fields continued his attempts at stifling Herbert's and Dorothy's natural flairs for the dramatic. This was proving to be a bigger problem than he had expected. "Their noses were always in the theater," Joseph Kaye wrote in the *Cincinnati Enquirer*.[14] Lew even told one reporter that Herbert "shows symptoms of being funny, but I am in hopes that he will outgrow it."[15] Lew's biggest attempt at keeping Herbert out of show business was an ironic one: hoping his younger son would be an abysmal failure on stage, Lew had him cast in the companies of 1916's *Step This Way* and 1917's *Miss 1917*. Lew starred in both shows; he also produced *Step This Way*. Convincing his show business buddies to include Herbert in the company of *Miss 1917* was not a hard sell. With a book by Guy Bolton and P. G. Wodehouse and music by, among others, Victor Herbert and Jerome Kern, *Miss 1917* was the same sort of frothy fare that audiences of the era loved. A reviewer for the *New York Sun* asked a first-nighter what he thought of the show. When the attendee started to answer, "Well, the plot's about . . . ," the writer cut him off. "Cut out the plot. You know that nobody cares anything about the plot anyhow in a musical show. Who are the girls? How are the girls? How are the comedians?"[16]

The girls were great, as were the comedians. Herbert Fields held his own, as well, and convinced his father to cast him again in 1919's *A Lonely Romeo.* Produced by Lew Fields and the Shubert Brothers, *A Lonely Romeo* opened in June of 1919. Notices for the show were jubilant, which was typical for a Lew Fields vehicle. Herbert even completed a bit "which brought him applause."[17] In spite of its positive reviews, though, the show stumbled at the hands of an ongoing actor's strike. When other shows were forced to shutter, *A Lonely Romeo* remained open ("and with the Entire Original Cast").[18] Still, Lew knew freshening up the score may steal some of the headlines away from the Equity strike. The master marketer found his answer as the family summered, this time on Franklin Avenue in Far Rockaway. In a meeting arranged by the family's summer neighbor, Lew Fields met a Columbia freshman named Richard Rodgers.

Born two years—almost to the day—before Dorothy Fields, Richard Rodgers was the son of a prominent New York doctor and his theater-loving wife. He'd taken to writing music as a boy; by the time he was fifteen, he was scoring shows for the Akron Club, a men's-only social and athletic club to which his older brother, Mortimer, belonged (Rodgers himself was too young). The shows were performed at places like the Plaza Hotel or the Waldorf Astoria (in its original location at Fifth Avenue and Thirty-Third Street) and presented by club members and their friends (both male and female) as fundraisers for churches, synagogues, private schools, and the like. Rodgers's first Akron Club piece was called *One Minute, Please.* According to a review, it was "presented by amateurs in a manner that met the approval and admiration of professional people who were present."[19] Rodgers was writing as many of these so-called "amateur shows" as he could. He was also attempting to write popular songs with his new partner, Lorenz Hart. By the summer of 1919, Rodgers and Hart had a number of songs that they felt were worthy of auditioning with industry insiders. Their friend Phil Leavitt, another Akron Club alum, gave them the opportunity. Leavitt's family had leased a vacation home in the Queens neighborhood of Far Rockaway. The Franklin Avenue home was next door to the Fields family's rental. Leavitt, who was sweet on Lew Fields's fifteen-year-old daughter, Dorothy, asked if she would arrange for her father to hear some of Rodgers and Hart's music. Dorothy agreed. On what Rodgers remembered to be a "sweltering Sunday afternoon,"[20] he arrived in Queens right on time. Hart had begged off due to a headache (this would become his standard operating procedure when it came to "selling" the pair's work).

Lew Fields met Rodgers at the front door. The entire Fields family was waiting inside. Among them, of course, was Dorothy, whom Rodgers described as having "the most dazzling eyes I had ever seen." The ever-gracious Fields family did all that it could to make Rodgers feel at home. He settled onto the piano bench and started playing piece after piece of the Rodgers and Hart repertoire. Lew was certainly the decision-maker in the room, yet Rodgers found himself "trying harder to impress young Dorothy than her father."[21] In the end, he accomplished both. Lew purchased a song called "Any Old Place with You" and promised to interpolate it, mid-run, into *A Lonely Romeo* at the Casino Theatre. The song was added to the show on August 26, 1919, launching the professional careers of Rodgers and Hart, who would go on to immeasurable success as writers of both musical comedies and popular songs. "This was the first leg up," Rodgers said.[22]

At summer's end, the Fields family found itself back on West Ninetieth Street. To Dorothy's delight, the home of her new friend Richard Rodgers was just blocks away on West Eighty-Sixth. The pair became close—Rodgers had "romantic leanings"[23] for Dorothy, and she referred to him as "my first boyfriend."[24] When school resumed that fall, he returned to Columbia in Morningside Heights and she to the Benjamin School for Girls at 144 Riverside Drive; nevertheless, Rodgers and Hart were often at the Fields's brownstone, where Rodgers taught Dorothy to play piano. He also collaborated with Herbert on ideas for shows. Herbert, having tested the waters of performance in his three-show Broadway run, was increasingly interested in writing for the theater rather than performing in it. Dorothy, on the other hand, was anxious to take the stage. Rodgers saw to it that she had several chances. Together with the lyrics of Lorenz Hart and, in some cases, the librettos and/or direction of her brother Herbert, Dorothy began to perform in amateur shows—Akron Club and otherwise—which featured music by Richard Rodgers.

The first of these was *You'd Be Surprised* in March of 1920. Presented by the Akron Club at the Plaza Hotel, the show had as its tongue-in-cheek subtitle "an Atrocious Musical Comedy." With settings that spanned from Spain to China to "long ago, BC" to "the Grill of the Hotel Plaza," the subtitle was probably warranted; nevertheless, Dorothy was beside herself to be performing with her new circle of creative friends. In *You'd Be Surprised*, Dorothy played the role of a florist named Carmen. With several songs by Rodgers and Hart, Herbert supplied the lyric for a number called "Mary, Queen of Scots." The musical also featured a single number with lyrics by Oscar Hammerstein II, he whose grandfather had worked so closely with Weber and Fields. Several years older than the show's other creators, Hammerstein would become an esteemed colleague in the decades ahead. The show's review in *Theatre World* magazine was particularly warm toward second-generation performers, like Dorothy: "Blood will tell, and it did, as it was noticeable that the children whose parents are and were stars of Stageland or otherwise interested in theatricals stood out in their lines and songs."[25]

The following year, Dorothy was back for more. Increasingly at home on the stage, she performed in the Akron Club's production of *Say Mama!*—which was directed by Herbert. There was a cheeky note in the program for the 1921 show, as well. This one reminded audiences that what they were watching was anything but professional: "An amateur is a person who acts for his own amusement to the sorrow of other people," read the note, expressing the not-too-serious way in which the lighthearted company members approached their work.[26] Regardless, the *New York Evening Mail* called the show "at the top of the season's amateur theatrical productions." Dorothy herself was said to have "genuine comedy ability" for her performance of Billie Krandall. Her two solo numbers as "a chorus girl vamp"[27] gave her ample opportunity to stretch her dramatic, comedic, and vocal muscles.

There is reason to believe that Herbert and Dorothy initially kept news of these shows a secret from their father. In a September 1920 interview with the *New York Tribune*, Lew alludes to Herbert's acting very mysteriously before finally "[making] a clean breast of it. He had been mixing up in amateur theatricals."[28] The interview refers specifically to the Columbia Varsity Show, which Herbert had developed that winter with Rodgers and Hart; however, it's reasonable to assume that, given Lew's opinions on the matter, Herbert and Dorothy had kept news of their new hobby under wraps for as long as they could.

If he knew about them, reviews like the one Dorothy received for *Say Mama!* likely made her father very nervous. Regardless of her parents' desire that Dorothy should follow sister Frances's path into marriage and home life, Dorothy's sights were set increasingly on the stage. Perhaps each ovation reminded her of the rush of the Weber and Fields Jubilee when she listened to crowd after crowd roar for more of her father. Whatever the reason, Dorothy continued to accept almost any role she was offered. Her Akron Club productions were followed by several shows in which she performed as a student and, later, teacher at the Benjamin School for Girls. Richard Rodgers came along. Rodgers—who completed his Akron Club run with *Say Mama!*—continued to write prolifically. Some of these shows were professional, such as when Lew Fields again purchased music by Rodgers and Hart and included it in his score for 1920's *Poor Little Ritz Girl*. Others were amateur, like a trio of shows he wrote for Dorothy and the other young ladies of the Benjamin School.

With only women in the Benjamin School casting pool, several students performed in male roles. Dorothy was among them. In 1922, she played Tikipu ("Bottle Washer and General Drudge") in a musicalization of Laurence Housman's *The Chinese Lantern*. The following year, she was Francois Villon in Rodgers's four-act adaption of Justin Huntly McCarthy's *If I Were King*, and in 1923, Dorothy took on the role of Rudolph Rassendyll, "a young Englishman," in *The Prisoner of Zenda*. Herbert directed all three outings. As she neared the end of high school, Dorothy made her post-graduation plans. They most certainly did not include a wealthy, professional husband. She also knew that college was out of the question—later in life, she'd often comment that her poor math skills took higher education off the table ("I couldn't pass algebra," she said);[29] nevertheless, determined that her future would be self-determined, Dorothy excitedly applied to join a summer stock company in Tarrytown, New York. She was accepted. A representative of the company informed her via mail that the opportunity of a lifetime lay just twenty-five miles from her Upper West Side home. For Dorothy, this was it—a launching pad for the life the warm, witty, wonderful young woman had imagined for herself.

But she never got the letter.

**Dorothy Fields as Francois Villon in the 1923 production of *If I Were King* at the Benjamin School for Girls.** Music Division, The New York Public Library for the Performing Arts.

# Chapter 3
## "I Feel a Song Coming On"

With his 1920 purchase of seven Rodgers and Hart songs for the score of *Poor Little Ritz Girl*, Lew Fields became known as a champion for youth in the theater. He told a reporter,

> Experience is important, but it isn't the whole show . . . Young people take chances and get away with them, because they haven't sense enough to know the risks. Youth rushes in where booking agents fear to tread . . . give me youth dressed up in nothing but overalls in preference to old age, bejeweled with experience, but afraid to spit on its hands and put them to the plow.[1]

Ironically, Lew had come to this conclusion while watching the Columbia Varsity Show whose creation Herbert had kept a secret from his father. Upon seeing the show, Lew was, once again, impressed with Rodgers's tunes—"[He] has real talent," Lew told a reporter for the *Columbia Spectator*. "I think that within a few years, he will be in a class by himself."[2] In many ways, Lew set out to bring his prophecy to fruition. Not only did he add those seven songs to another nine written by Sigmund Romberg (music) and Alex Gerber (lyrics) for *Poor Little Ritz Girl*, but he also produced several other Rodgers and Hart musical comedies. A number of these—*The Girl Friend* (1926), *Peggy Ann* (1926), and *A Connecticut Yankee* (1927), for instance—had librettos by Herbert Fields, who was now working regularly on Broadway, generally as the book writer for Rodgers and Hart.

Clearly, Lew's embargo on Herbert's working in the theater had been lifted as soon as he saw his son's trajectory for success as a librettist. Unfortunately, Lew's enthusiasm for youth did not transcend to the work of his youngest child. When Dorothy's letter of acceptance arrived from that Tarrytown summer stock company, Rose destroyed it before Dorothy even knew it existed. "Three years later," Dorothy said, "Mother confessed."[3] In the absence of the letter, Dorothy assumed she'd been rejected. She floundered, desperate to find something to do. It was the mid-1920s. In small doses, women were beginning to be a part of the workforce. Dorothy wanted to be among them—whether it was on the stage or not. Lew and Rose Fields could not understand Dorothy's resistance to the more conventional life they'd mapped out for her. "I was a girl," Dorothy explained. "A girl gets married and lives happily ever after. Except that I didn't want it that way. I wanted to work and be an individual on my own, and from the very beginning, I did work."[4]

Specifically, Dorothy taught drama at the Benjamin School. Following Herbert's lead into the literary world, she also started writing—though not yet to the extent that he did. She was fond of writing what she called "smarty verses." These were pithy little poems full of witty zingers from the mind of Dorothy's razor-sharp intellect. "Almost a snob about erudition,"[5] Dorothy was very quickly noticed for her writing. Several of her poems were published in Franklin P. Adams's "The Conning Tower" column in the *Morning World* newspaper. Her selection for a column of such renown illustrates how exceptional these early works were. A member of the famed Algonquin Round Table, Adams started his career as a sports writer and humor columnist. By the mid-1920s, he was known as "the nation's premier columnist," and "The Conning Tower" was "the best [column] in the world."[6] With affirmation like this, Dorothy began to think that writing, in some form or fashion, may be the career for her. She even considered writing, in verse, a book about famous women in history.

Dorothy's ambition scared Lew and Rose. Her continued successes—both on stage and on the page—made them proud, as it would any parents. Still, they had many misgivings about her unquenchable thirst for professional experiences. A 1925 newspaper article put it this way: "Dorothy was their choicest treasure, someone to be shielded from all rough contacts with life, something to idolize and dote on in secret—not in the thick of a thronged opera house or smoky music hall."[7] Hoping some time away from working would cause her to reconsider her goals—and maybe even meet an eligible young bachelor, Lew and Rose arranged for Dorothy to spend a month in the Adirondack Mountains. Not long after, she checked in to Lake Placid's Grand View Hotel. The 250-room hotel was situated high on a hill in a hundred-acre private park that overlooked breathtaking Mirror Lake. Its location, three hundred miles north of New York City, was not only beautiful but also full of summertime activities—particularly for a woman as athletic as Dorothy. In addition to watersports, the area boasted golf courses, tennis courts, fishing, camping, and a handful of other enticing diversions. "Nowhere else is there anything like it," boasted one advertisement. "The fields are greener, the air purer, the sunlight brighter, the sports more varied."[8]

Not long after she arrived, Dorothy crossed paths with Dr. Jacob Jesse Wiener. "Jack," as she always called him, was ten years Dorothy's senior and already an accomplished physician at the Montefiore Hospital for Chronic Diseases in the Bronx. Wiener was one of a rotation of doctors who took a turn serving as the hotel's physician. The couple was said to have bonded over a love of sports, which seems feasible, given Dorothy's natural athleticism. "The attraction was instant and mutual," said an article in the *Tampa Bay Times*. "In what must have seemed . . . no time at all, they became engaged."[9]

The engagement may have been quick—it was announced in October of 1924—but twenty-year-old Dorothy was in no rush for the ceremony itself. Why she accepted Wiener's proposal in the first place is a mystery. Discouragement may have set in to her generally optimistic frame of mind. Perhaps the reality of her father's resistance was wearing on her. Maybe, though this seems unlikely, Dorothy had a change of heart and decided that marriage *was* the only answer to life after high school. It's also possible that she legitimately did fall in love. The reality can never be known, but with the perspective of time, it was almost as if she agreed to the engagement in hopes that it would appease her parents and, perhaps, get her father to stop halting her professional prospects.

Regardless, Lew and Rose were thrilled with the engagement. After all, Wiener was a doctor from a well-to-do Belle Harbor (New York) family. His parents owned one of the largest bakeries in the Rockaways, and one of his brothers was a municipal court judge. Like Charles Marcus, Jack Wiener appeared to be a perfect fit for the life the Fieldses had imagined for their baby girl. That life couldn't have looked less like the one Dorothy had imagined for herself, though. Not surprisingly, she repeatedly put off setting a date for the wedding until her fiancé finally pressed her on the issue. They agreed they would marry sometime after May of 1925; this would come at the end of her father's nationwide tour. No doubt, Lew and Rose imagined a gala event similar to the one in which Frances had been married a decade earlier. Instead, for reasons that are, again, unknown, Dorothy and Wiener changed their course; they married instead in March of 1925[10] in a secret ceremony at the home of a rabbi on the Upper West Side.

For one as close to her family as Dorothy was, it is highly unusual that she'd choose to marry without any other member of the Fields clan present. Some have suggested that she did this in order to save her father the expense of a wedding as elaborate as sister Frances's had been. Lew, whose bent towards both betting and theatrical extravagance continued to bedevil his bottom line, was just a few years removed from a bankruptcy declaration, which included selling the brownstone on West Ninetieth to rent an apartment at 562 West End Avenue. Times were still tight. Another possibility is that she didn't want to draw attention to the union. There was no write-up in the *New York Times* or other area newspapers, as there had been when Frances married. Whatever the reason, the privacy in which she shrouded her nuptials definitely underscored Dorothy's apparent feelings toward them. She and Wiener shared the news with her parents by meeting them at the Denver hotel where Lew and Rose were staying on tour. When they finally honeymooned, Dorothy and Wiener returned to the Adirondacks, this time renting a cabin. Dorothy, it's said, spent most of their first night there pacing on the front porch, pondering, presumably, the enormity of her mistake. Within very short order, she moved back in with her parents at the apartment on West End Avenue. She and Wiener remained legally married for the next fourteen years, though they almost always maintained separate residences. In her life, he was not much more than an afterthought.

In the months following her wedding, Dorothy continued to try her hand at different jobs. After teaching at the Benjamin School, she and a friend started a dance school for children—Dorothy accompanying on the piano as her friend taught. She was also a doctor's assistant and, for a time, a laboratory technician for brother Joseph's wildly successful perfume business. Joseph had returned from Paris in 1923. Afterwards, Dorothy and Herbert worked in his employ, alongside Rose's brother, Herbert Harris, and Harris's wife, Bobbie. Dorothy was even said to have developed a fragrance of her own:

> By way of amusing herself one afternoon, she wandered into the laboratory [and] began to mix together a bit of this and a bit of that. Suddenly, she realized that the concoction was giving off an unusual and delightful odor. Hastily filling a vial, she hurried to Harris' office [and] sprinkled the mixture around it. He liked it; so did Mrs. Harris . . . so did brothers Joe and Herbert. Since a hundred percent approval is necessary for production, Dorothy's discovery went into manufacture![11]

While continuing to run the perfume business, Joseph also wrote unproduced scripts on the side. Dorothy, when she wasn't working, continued to attend theater. She also continued to improve her tennis game. That's what took her to her aunt and uncle's Long Island home in the early spring of 1927. Dorothy went to play tennis but came back with a new friend and a new direction for her career.

Leo and Rae Fields Teller lived at 15 Wyckoff Place in Woodmere, Long Island. Dorothy's uncle Leo was, like her father, a theater manager. At the time, he owned the Teller's Shubert Theatre in Brooklyn; however, he'd previously managed theaters both in Manhattan and Chicago; prior to that, he'd had a founding interest in the same department store (A.I. Namm) where Rose Fields had worked before marrying Lew. Dorothy was in her early twenties, the apple of her father's eye, and just as capable as he of holding court whenever an audience was around. That particular day, she'd played tennis with family and friends at the Woodmere Club. Afterward, everyone congregated less than a mile from the club at the comfortable house on Wyckoff. Very proud of her relationships with Broadway's hottest up-and-comers, Dorothy was playing a medley of Rodgers and Hart tunes on the Teller family's piano. That's when a Teller family friend walked in from playing golf with Dorothy's cousin. His name was J. Fred Coots. Only seven years older than Dorothy, Coots was a songwriter on his way up. His first hit, a number called "Mr. Ford, You've Got the Right Idea," was published in 1916. After its success, Coots was commissioned to compose the songs for several Broadway musicals, including 1922's *Sally, Irene, and Mary*. Produced by the Shubert brothers, the show ran for 313 performances, wildly impressive by the standard of the day, before being revived a few years later. A few years after that, Coots would become a holiday legend when, in 1934, he wrote the perennial Christmas hit "Santa Claus Is Comin' to Town." On that day in the mid-1920s, however, he was visiting the Teller family in Woodmere, New Jersey.

"I got to the house, and the conversation seemed to be revolving around this young lady, who was supposedly a wonderful lyricist," Coots said. "I met her, and as we got to know each other, we decided we'd write some songs together."[12] Full of hope and not lacking in self-confidence, Dorothy was more than willing to expand her writing repertoire to include lyrics. That Coots was a proven composer with Broadway experience made the opportunity all the more appealing. Dorothy jumped at the chance. Together, they wrote a handful of songs—"Music good, lyrics terrible," she later described them; nevertheless, the pair pounded the pavement around Tin Pan Alley, attempting to sell one of the five or so songs they'd written together. They never did. Dorothy recounted, "When Mr. Coots insisted I had talent, the publishers answered, 'If she's so damn talented, why doesn't her father do something for her?'"[13]

In fact, her father was "doing something." Though Lew seemed to have warmed to Herbert's involvement in theater, he still considered Dorothy's forbidden. As she and Coots made their rounds at the Tin Pan Alley publishing houses, Lew called up his friends in the music business and insisted that they turn the duo away. "Tin Pan Alley" was a phrase both literal and figurative. Literally, there was a geographical area of New York where the majority of these music publishers conducted their business. After its beginnings in the late nineteenth century, the Alley was located at several different New York addresses. Each of these mirrored popular theater's moves from the vaudeville houses around the Bowery to legitimate theaters farther uptown. The Alley's first address—though, at this point, the phrase "Tin Pan Alley" had not yet been coined—was near Union Square. From there, it moved about fifteen blocks north to the area most often thought of when Tin Pan Alley is discussed—a stretch of West Twenty-Eighth Street between Broadway and Sixth Avenue. There, brownstones all in a row housed a myriad of different publishers, each seeking to discover its next big hit. It is of this constant cacophony of melodic activity that one writer observed:

> Tin Pan Alley is a street of many noises. As one walks along it, from a window across the street the voices of a male quartet roar out a comic song, while opposite a woman's soprano cuts in . . . just as the soprano reached the most pathetic part, a tinkling piano accompanied by a near-tenor recited . . . a lilting "coon song."[14]

Songwriters would routinely visit the publishers, peddling their latest ditties. If one publisher wasn't interested, perhaps the next one would be. Down the street they'd go. By the same token, singers would drop in looking for something new to sing. The area was a hotbed of harmonies, a living, breathing neighborhood of the new sound of the twentieth century. By the time Dorothy and Coots were making their rounds in the mid-1920s, most of Tin Pan Alley had moved again.

This time, it was centered on a bigger stretch of the city, spanning Broadway between Forty-Second and Fiftieth Streets, in the heart of the theater district as it is now.

Figuratively, though, "Tin Pan Alley" was—and continues to be—synonymous with a type of song that is uniquely American. With the coming of mass production, pianos suddenly became affordable—and a foregone conclusion in most American parlors. As an article from 1903 noted, "What home is so humble that it hath not a piano?"[15] Pianists, however, needed something to play on their new keyboards. Enter sheet music. By providing this music, Tin Pan Alley—and the music publishing industry that the name came to represent—disseminated a new kind of song from sea to shining sea, a product that came to be as symbolic of the American experience as Uncle Sam and apple pie. It was on this hallowed ground that Dorothy Fields and J. Fred Coots sought their collective fortune.

Though the pair found no hits on Tin Pan Alley, Coots found some interest elsewhere. A Broadway producer named Sam H. Harris considered adding a couple of the Coots/Fields collaborations to the score for a planned revival of *The Cocoanuts*, which starred the Marx Brothers. Due to some rights issues related to Coots's relationship with the Shuberts, the interpolation never happened. Instead, Irving Berlin wrote the show's entire score. The next day, as Coots explained it, Coots visited Tin Pan Alley, stopping by the offices of Mills Music. Coots chatted first with Jack Mills, founder and president of the publishing house, and then with his professional manager, a charismatic Bostonian named Jimmy McHugh. McHugh was born to a plumber and his pianist wife. Though his father had hoped McHugh would follow him into the family business, McHugh was far more interested in the music he'd learned from his mother. He worked for a time as an $8-a-week office boy for the manager of the Boston Opera Company. He'd attend the evening performance and find himself, the day after, picking out the tunes he'd heard on one of the company's many rehearsal pianos. Realizing he'd inherited his mother's propensity for piano, McHugh eventually left the opera company to become a Boston-based "song-plugger." He peddled tunes for Irving Berlin's wildly successful publishing house. In 1921, McHugh left Boston for New York City. He quickly found himself selling songs of his own—like 1924's "When My Sugar Walks Down the Street" (lyrics by Gene Austin) and "I Can't Believe That You're in Love with Me" (lyrics by Clarence Gaskell) in 1926. He also worked as the professional manager for the Mills Music Publishing Company. That's how he'd met Coots. When Coots visited Mills Music, McHugh excitedly told him about his new assignment writing at a Harlem hot spot called the Cotton Club. Coots immediately had an idea:

> I said to him, "Who's going to do your lyrics?" and he said he didn't have anyone. I sat down and played Dorothy's five songs for him, and McHugh said, "My Lord, she's a genius!" I called Dorothy, and she came into the City to meet Jimmy. She walked in, and I said, "Dorothy, this is Jimmy McHugh." She nodded, smiled, and

extended her hand. "Jimmy, this is Dorothy Fields." He stepped forward, shook her hand, and said, "The pleasure is all mine," and then I said, "I now pronounce you words and music."[16]

Coots called connecting Dorothy Fields and Jimmy McHugh "one of my greatest pleasures."[17] His recollection of that first meeting is somewhat over-simplified, however. McHugh was definitely impressed with Dorothy. In a 1967 manuscript for an unpublished autobiography, he described her as "a vivacious, charming creature with a beautiful face and big eyes."[18] Her writing, however, left something to be desired. McHugh gave the self-professed "saucy little girl" who used "all sorts of fancy, snobby language"[19] some advice. He later recounted it like this: "[She] was trying to write up to the people, and I told [her] to write down, give them that which they understood, something that should not tax their intelligence."[20] Irving Mills, vice president of the firm and Jack Mills's younger brother, took things a step further. He told Dorothy, "Hop on a current thing. Timing. That's what counts with a pop song. Timeliness."[21] It was sound advice, which Dorothy heeded. Years later, her massive body of work would have as one of its hallmarks her masterful use of colloquial language.

Not long after that first conversation, McHugh set sail for England. He left on the SS *Leviathan* on June 11, 1927. Dorothy was vacationing that summer, as well. She and Wiener were again at the Grand View Hotel when Dorothy received a postcard from McHugh in which he asked if she'd like to collaborate on some songs. This time, her mother didn't intercept the letter.

# Chapter 4
## "I'm Doin' That Thing"

"I practically leaped at the opportunity," Dorothy Fields said of Jimmy McHugh's suggestion that they should write songs together.[1] That she would find Mills Music as her first professional home was somehow fitting. The publishing house was started nearly ten years before when Jack Mills decided there was more to life than selling neckties. Born in Russia in 1891, Mills emigrated to the United States five years later with his parents and younger brother. Hyman and Sophia Minsky raised their boys—prior to the Americanization of their names, Jack and Irving were Jacob and Isadore—on the Lower East Side of Manhattan. Jack had gotten an eighth-grade education before going to work at a department store. Between customers, he'd write songs with titles like, "I Don't Need a Doctor; I Just Need a Beautiful Girl" and "I'll Buy the Ring and Change Your Name to Mine." When he attempted to peddle his wares along Tin Pan Alley, neither song sold. Mills decided that if no one else would publish his songs, he'd do it himself. Borrowing $4,500 and a broken-down piano, he launched Mills Music in 1919. His brother soon joined him in the business. After Jack's early rejections in the publishing industry, he decided that his firm would be one that was known for taking risks on new songwriters. His door would always be open to talent that just needed someone to take a chance on it. That policy paid off. Thirty years after opening its doors, Mills Music owned a catalog of more than 45,000 songs and was considered the biggest independent music publisher in the world. When Mills retired in 1965, he sold the company for a whopping $5 million. Mills Music was credited with the discoveries of talents like Duke Ellington, and much of Mills's early success was owed to a twenty-three-year-old lyricist named Dorothy Fields, who was given her first assignment in October of 1927.

That's when she visited the so-called "House That Jack Built" at 148–50 West Forty-Sixth Street. The building, constructed in 1923, was a sight to behold. Of the hundreds of theater celebrities who attended its gala opening, most considered it "without doubt the last word in modern construction." Mills Music occupied the first two of the building's six floors. There were offices for the company professionals, as well as a number of piano rooms, an arranging department, and the orchestration counter. Mills Music, as one of Tin Pan Alley's premier publishing houses, was always abuzz with activity. The October day on which Dorothy Fields met with Jimmy McHugh was no different. Meeting in McHugh's office—which had been described by a reporter as "the most handsome and beautifully furnished professional room in the country"[2]—Dorothy remembered the occasion like this:

> There were at least twenty people in Jimmy's quarters. They were singers, musicians, authors, and composers. Outside was a buzzing of voices, playing of pianos, and the practicing of new numbers on the professional floor. Swell chance for a potential songwriter to meet with any success here, but I reasoned that I might as well dally round until McHugh would dispose of my efforts.[3]

Determined to succeed, Dorothy was energized by the electricity in the air of the office. The cacophony of collaboration probably reminded her of the rush of performing in all of those amateur theatricals. She was thrilled when she was offered her first official writing assignment from Mills. In later years, Mills would build its catalog of songs by buying up the inventories of smaller companies, but early on, its *modus operandi* included capitalizing on current events. Just as Irving Mills had recommended to Dorothy that her lyrics capture the zeitgeist of an era, Mills Music was known for releasing songs relevant to the headlines of the day. For instance, when Italian opera singer Enrico Caruso died in August of 1921, Mills Music released "They Needed a Songbird in Heaven, So God Took Caruso Away." Thirty-one-year-old Rudolph Valentino, an Italian actor known as Hollywood's original Latin lover and made popular by his work in silent films, like *The Four Horsemen of the Apocalypse*, died unexpectedly in 1926. Almost immediately, Mills Music printed "There's a New Star in Heaven." Most of these songs didn't stand the test of time, yet they were helpful in turning a quick buck, and they certainly represented the cultural milieu of the time in which they were written.

Dorothy's first big chance came in the form of one of these "current events" kinds of songs. Irving Mills offered Dorothy fifty dollars and twenty-four hours to write a lyric about "the Miss America of Aviation," Ruth Elder. With her fellow Floridian George Haldeman to co-pilot the plane, Elder took off from New York's Roosevelt Field on October 11, 1927. She was attempting to be the first woman to ever make a transatlantic flight. The bright orange and yellow Stinson Detroiter—*The American Girl*, it was christened—was capable of flying a hundred miles per hour, making the journey a thirty-six-hour endeavor. Needless to say, executives at Mills Music saw this as an opportunity for another hit. Dorothy was more than willing to take on the job. Irving Mills gave her a head start on her work, offering her the first two lines of the song: "You took a notion to fly 'cross the ocean." Dorothy balked at her new boss. "I said timidly but with great conviction, 'Mr. Mills, you don't "take a notion" to "fly" 'cross the ocean'"[4]; nevertheless, she took the assignment and the fifty dollars.

Unfortunately, Dorothy was never able to realize the fruits of those first lyrical labors. Elder and Haldeman encountered engine problems about 360 miles from land and were forced to ditch the flight into the ocean before being rescued by a Dutch tanker near the Azores islands. Dorothy's work was successful enough, though, that the team at Mills Music kept her around. She was exactly what McHugh had been looking for. He'd written most recently with lyricist Al Dubin. Together, they'd turned out songs that McHugh referred to as "knock-down-and-drag-out ballads." He was ready for a change of pace. "I wanted to write pretty songs," he said. "I was looking at all times for somebody who had the flair, the charming lyrics, sort of a Larry Hart technique, and a good vocabulary."[5] Dorothy Fields was the perfect person for the job. She and McHugh first collaborated on "Collegiana," capitalizing on the dance craze of the Roaring Twenties. Written in the style of songs like DeSylva, Brown, and Henderson's "Varsity Drag," "Collegiana" proved to both Dorothy and McHugh that, perhaps, theirs was a collaboration worth continuing. With a melody that moved—jumped—along, the song basically begs to be danced to. Its lyric, written by a twenty-three-year-old Dorothy Fields, demonstrates several qualities that would become hallmarks of her later work, and in Dorothy, McHugh got just what he wanted. That "Larry Hart technique" he was looking for is clear in Dorothy's use of the interior rhymes. She would later call this a "mistake,"[6] her early inclination to be easily influenced by other writers. Still, her own masterful use of the vernacular—one, no doubt, passed down to her from her doting, if initially disapproving, father—is already present. Colloquial phrases like "easy as pie" evoke the image of a college co-ed, while "Miss Pollyanna" is a contemporary character from the literature and film worlds of the day. An eleven-year-old orphan girl, Pollyanna Whittier had entered the public consciousness in a 1913 novel by Eleanor H. Porter and again in a 1915 stage play by Catherine Chisholm Cushing. There was also a 1920 silent film starring Mary Pickford. Here, Dorothy co-opts a familiar character, suggesting that her defining characteristic was a direct result of dancing the "Collegiana." References like these made the song relatable to a broad audience and anchored it in its own idiom; they are also a clear indication that she'd taken to heart both Irving Mills and McHugh's suggestions that she write more informally.

After the success of "Collegiana," Dorothy and McHugh tried their luck again. This time, they went to work writing songs for the floor show of Harlem's Cotton Club. In addition to his work at Mills Music, McHugh had been writing songs for the Cotton Club almost since its 1923 opening. He'd used a number of different lyricists for the job and, eventually, invited Dorothy to take a turn. "McHugh said, 'Would you like to do some songs for the Cotton Club in Harlem?' And I said, 'I would write for the Westchester Kennel Club! I don't care what it is!'"[7] To hear McHugh tell it, Dorothy said she'd first have to ask her parents. Though she'd been married to Jack Wiener for nearly four years at this point, she still lived, most of the time, with Lew and Rose. McHugh remembered the Fieldses had "somewhat dubiously" agreed to the assignment for which McHugh said he paid her $100 a week. In a 1966 interview with Martin Gershen, Dorothy recalled being paid $60 a week.[8] Which number is accurate is likely lost to history. It's sufficient to say, however, that Dorothy was thrilled with the new opportunity, and Lew was devastated by it. He had insisted "Ladies don't write lyrics." Dorothy countered back, "I'm not a lady; I'm your daughter,"[9] riffing on an old Weber and Fields routine in which one asked, "Who was that lady I saw you with last night?" and the other responded, "That was no lady, that was my wife!"[10] For Lew Fields, this couldn't have been a more horrifying scenario. Not only was his daughter tipping her toes in the shallow end of show business, but she was doing it at a nightclub run by Chicago's finest mobsters. Regardless of Lew's thoughts on the matter, Dorothy and McHugh readied themselves for her Cotton Club premiere on December 4, 1927.

Located at the intersection of 142nd Street and Lenox Avenue, the Cotton Club had begun its life in 1920 when a former heavyweight champion named Jack Johnson turned the one-time banquet space into a supper club called the Club Deluxe. In 1923, British gangster Owney Madden discovered the space. It was the height of Prohibition, and Johnson's club seemed like the perfect spot from which to peddle Madden's self-labeled beer. Madden and company proceeded to make two major changes to the club when they took it over: first, they redecorated. Seating capacity was stretched from about four hundred people to around seven hundred. Second, they changed the club's name to the Cotton Club, possibly owing to the establishment's majority-white clientele. Though assumed by many to be a completely segregated establishment, the Cotton Club did, in fact, allow black patrons, but its proprietors discouraged these guests by offering blacks "scant courtesy and poorer service. And the air is surcharged with the suggestion that they are not wanted." Neither were black patrons allowed "under any circumstance"[11] to sit with white customers. These despicable and archaic policies aside, the Cotton Club quickly became a place to see and be seen by whites and the handful of blacks who were willing to adhere to the club's degrading policies.

The Cotton Club's calling card was its spectacular floor show. Initially produced by a man named Lew Leslie, the shows featured a full orchestra and a collection of "high-yaller" (a slang for the black dancers' light skin tone) chorus girls, who were required to be tall (at least 5'6"), young (under twenty-one), talented, and titillating. These shows premiered with the club's 1923 grand opening and were wildly entertaining. High-quality amusements combined with the sale of alcohol was Owney Madden's recipe for success. Owing to these and the Cotton Club's expansive dinner menu, patrons were willing to overlook monthly police raids and club management's tight connection to organized crime.

The floor shows were refreshed twice a year. The December 1927 show for which Dorothy and McHugh wrote some of the music was called *Dan Healy's*

*New Winter Revue*; it was named for the producer who'd taken Lew Leslie's place. This particular show was unique, because it marked the debut of a new bandleader. Andy Preer, who'd previously played the club with his group the Missourians, had died. As his replacement, McHugh had suggested Duke Ellington, a bandleader whose work Mills Music managed. Ellington was a native of Washington, DC; he'd been in New York since the early 1920s when he and his band started to play the Kentucky Club at Broadway and West Forty-Ninth Street. Irving Mills had been Ellington's manager for most of his time in New York. For Ellington's move uptown, McHugh composed several new songs. Dorothy, who was given credit for her work orally but not listed in the evening's program, added lyrics to two of them: "Doin' the Frog" and "Harlem River Quiver." Though she'd later say she wasn't proud of songs like these—"Who today remembers my 'Harlem River Quiver'?" she asked in 1973[12]—reviews of her work were positive. "Even in a night club revue," *Variety* reported, "her words to music are impressive."[13]

The night was more memorable, however, for the songs that she didn't write than for the ones that she did. Though they remained opposed to Dorothy's involvement in show business, Lew and Rose were, nonetheless, in attendance to support their daughter's latest endeavor. Also at the table were Dorothy's siblings, brother Joseph's wife, and a friend of Lew Fields named Walter Winchell. Winchell would later become one of the country's premier gossip mongers with both a syndicated newspaper column ("On Broadway") and a radio program ("Saks on Broadway"). In 1927, however, he was a writer for New York's sensational rag the *Evening Graphic*; he was also, according to Dorothy, "a great booster of the Cotton Club."[14] There they all sat, excited to hear the first major public performance of Dorothy's work.

> My family was very proud for a quick minute. Then Ms. What's-Her-Name came on for her specialty. Did she sing the songs Jimmy McHugh and I wrote for her? She did not. . . . She belted out three of the most shocking, ribald, bawdy, dirtiest songs anyone had ever heard in the 1920s. . . . My father said, "You didn't learn those words home!" I said, "I didn't write those words!"

It took some convincing, but finally Lew Fields believed his daughter. He pleaded with Dorothy, "Will you, for God's sake, get out of showbusiness?"[15] and made his way to the gangster in charge. Mortified by what he'd heard—this was the man who'd cleaned up vaudeville acts, so that women could attend the theater without fear of impropriety—Lew used the full weight of his show business stature to demand that an announcement be made, clarifying that his daughter had not written those songs. The gangster agreed. While Dorothy never publicly called the name of the singer in question—"I won't tell you her name; she might still be alive," she would say when asked[16] or, sometimes, "She shall be nameless"[17]—McHugh had no qualms about outing the guilty party. Her name was Lethia Hill. One of the songs she sang was called "Flat Tire Papa, Don't

You Try to Retread Me" (a review of a later Cotton Club extravaganza described
Hill's "Kitchen Man" number as having "more innuendoes than a John S. Sumner
lecture"[18]). Dorothy would later refer to the experience as the "worst moment in
all my forty years in showbusiness." It didn't, however, keep her from writing
for the Cotton Club. She and McHugh continued providing songs for the uptown
revues until 1930 when composer Harold Arlen and lyricist Ted Koehler took
their place. Dorothy would often talk about how well she was treated by the mob-
connected management at the club. "In the afternoons when we had rehearsals,
they'd go into the kitchen and bring out the cookies and tea,"[19] she said, always
contending that they treated her like a little sister and were very careful not to
say anything inappropriate to her. They may have been afraid to, lest they get
anymore pushback from her famous father. Still, Dorothy often felt uncomfortable with the language of some of the songs she and McHugh were called upon
to write for the Cotton Club. Though Dorothy was never forced to write lyrics
as crass as those Hill had sung on that 1927 opening night, there were times
when she would refuse to have her name attached to certain songs. Later, Fields
would be known for lyrics that abounded with double entendre. Discretion and
propriety, particularly at the outset of her career, were of the utmost importance
to the well-bred Miss Fields. The pair's time at the Cotton Club was significant.
Ever the salesman, McHugh was able to leverage the experience to convince two
producers to hire the new team of "Fields and McHugh." Before long, Lew Fields
would never again resist his daughter's ambition.

# Chapter 5
## "Here Comes My Blackbird"

The song came to them as they walked along Fifth Avenue. Stopping to peek in the window at Tiffany's, Dorothy Fields and Jimmy McHugh observed a young couple gazing in at the baubles behind the glass. As McHugh remembered it, the young man said to the young lady, "Gee, I wish I could give you everything, Baby, but I'm afraid all I can give you is plenty of love."[1] Though they hadn't intended to eavesdrop, the songwriters knew there was something to what they'd just heard. They raced back to the Mills Music offices on West Forty-Sixth Street and got to work. Before a bar of music had been written, Dorothy rephrased what they'd heard and suggested the title of "I Can't Give You Anything but Love, Baby." That very day, McHugh wrote the first draft of the melody, finishing it the next night. Soon thereafter, he cited their Cotton Club success in order to convince a producer named Harry Delmar to interpolate their new song into his *Delmar's Revels*.

Harry Delmar was a former vaudevillian, who'd made some waves as part of the performing duo Hackett and Delmar. He'd previously produced brief, variety-style revues, but *Delmar's Revels* was his first attempt at a longer-form entertainment. It was also his Broadway debut. For the production, he amassed a vast collection of talent. In addition to headliners like Bert Lahr, Frank Fay, Patsy Kelly, and Blossom Seeley (a Lew Fields discovery whose Broadway debut was *The Hen-Pecks*), the company included forty-eight showgirls and twenty-seven principal performers. Most of the music in the show, which included the perennial hit "Me and My Shadow," was written by Jimmy Monaco, Jesse Greer, and Lester Lee with Billy Rose and Ballard MacDonald providing lyrics. When it opened at the Shubert Theatre in November of 1927, the show received mixed notices. Some heralded the piece as "one of the finest shows of its type produced in years."[2] Others suggested that the $5.50 ticket price was too high for the quality of the entertainment. Regardless, *Delmar's Revels* was solidly of the ilk of many shows being created for Broadway around that time. As it was described in the *Brooklyn Times Union*, "Of course, there is no book or connected story with the *Revels*, just an admixture of adroitly combined high class vaudeville acts, freely spiced with beautiful girls and ravishing scenes and costumes, all of which made for one of the most entertaining evenings any confirmed theatergoer could hope."[3] *Delmar's Revels* ran for 112 performances, ending its run in March of 1928.

Exactly when "I Can't Give You Anything but Love, Baby" was interpolated into the show is not known; however, the song isn't mentioned in any of the opening night reviews, nor are Dorothy and McHugh credited with writing a song for the show. Regardless of when it was added, however, it didn't stay in the show for long. The song was set up as a number for Bert Lahr and Patsy Kelly. In the scene, the two played down-on-their-luck kids, sitting on a cellar step. Lahr opened with the verse:

> Gee, but it's tough to be broke, Kid.
> It's not a joke, Kid. It's a curse.
> My luck is changing; it's gotten
> From simply rotten to something worse.
>
> Who knows, some day I will win, too.
> I'll begin to reach my prime.
> Now, though I see what our end is,
> All I can spend is just my time.

At the end of the verse, the curtains parted, revealing those forty-eight dancing girls, all dressed as different gemstones—emeralds, sapphires, garnets, diamonds, and others. Lahr continued with the now-legendary chorus:

> I can't give you anything but love, Baby.
> That's the only thing I've plenty of, Baby.
> Dream awhile, scheme awhile,
> We're sure to find
> Happiness, and, I guess,
> All those things you've always pined for.
> Gee, I'd like to see you looking swell, Baby.
> Diamond bracelets Woolworth doesn't sell, Baby.
> Till that lucky day, you know darned well, Baby.
> I can't give you anything but love.

For whatever reason, Delmar hated the number. Critic Gilbert Gabriel did too. He famously referred to it as "a sickly, puerile song." Dorothy and McHugh were told to take their song and get out of the theater, which they did. Down but not out, McHugh was already working his connections to secure the pair's next job. He found it in a producer friend named Lew Leslie. Leslie had been the original producer of the Cotton Club floor shows. Though Leslie was later replaced by

Dan Healy, Leslie and McHugh remained in touch. Leslie's ambition was to be an impresario along the lines of Florenz Ziegfeld. He studied Ziegfeld's work and saw every iteration of his spectacular *Follies*. Having started producing his own revues in 1916, Leslie quickly discovered a niche that would set him apart from his hero: he would champion black talent on and around Broadway. Among others, he'd eventually help to launch the careers of superstars like Lena Horne, Ethel Waters, and Bill "Bojangles" Robinson. His first great success was guiding the work of Florence Mills.

Mills had gotten her Broadway start in 1921's *Shuffle Along* (music by Eubie Blake, lyrics by Noble Sissle). The show was a watershed moment for a number of reasons: first, it was completely created—written, produced, and performed—by black artists. It wasn't the first such show. There had been others, like 1898's *A Trip to Coontown*. That same year brought *Clorindy, or the Origin of the Cakewalk*; 1903 offered *In Dahomey*. There were others as well, but *Shuffle Along* was the first all-black musical in more than a decade. Second, it sparked the slow process of integrating Broadway audiences. For the first time, black theatergoers were allowed to purchase tickets in the rear of the orchestra instead of being relegated to seating in the upper balconies. Finally, the exuberance surrounding the record-breaking *Shuffle Along* reignited white audience's interest in black entertainment. This is probably what piqued Leslie's interest in the genre—opportunism. Leslie saw a new audience appetite, one distinct from what was being served by his hero Ziegfeld, and set out to fill it.

Upon seeing Florence Mills's work in the show, Leslie was convinced that she could be a superstar. In the aftermath of *Shuffle Along*'s success, he developed several shows around his multitalented headliner. *Plantation Revue* (1922) and *Dixie to Broadway* (1924) played Broadway to notices like "one of the best of the colored entertainments that has ever been staged for the benefit of metropolitan theatregoers"[4] and "the most exciting of all musical comedies now current in New York."[5] Leslie, having achieved his dream in relatively short order, became known as "the Ziegfeld of the colored producers," while Mills became "the sensation of two continents"[6] when Leslie's production *Blackbirds of 1926* toured Europe's major cities and played London for an incredible nine months. Her performance was so captivating that it was reported that the Prince of Wales (Edward VIII) returned to see the show more than a dozen times. Leslie hoped *Blackbirds* would become his *Follies*. He envisioned Ziegfeld-like annual revues, all of them starring his own "blackbird," Florence Mills. She'd been the one to suggest the name as they walked through Hyde Park in London. A little bird had nestled at her feet before eventually flying away when Mills and Leslie approached it. Mills told Leslie she was just like that blackbird, afraid of the world. The idea stuck.

Mills, Leslie, and company returned to the United States in September of 1927. By that fall, Leslie was making plans for the next iteration of his enormously successful *Blackbirds* franchise. Tragically, however, Mills fell suddenly ill. She died on November 1, 1927.[7] Across the globe, her legions of fans were shocked and heartbroken. Her body lay in state in the chapel of Harlem's H.A. Howell funeral parlor for four days, as nearly 60,000 people filed through to pay their last respects. Among the mourners was Jimmy McHugh; he'd been invited there by Lew Leslie. As the two discussed the colossal loss of a star like Mills, Leslie suggested that, perhaps, McHugh should write the next iteration of *Blackbirds*. McHugh was thrilled at the opportunity though surprised at the timing of Leslie's suggestion. On Sunday, November 6, more than 150,000 jammed the Harlem streets to mourn the death of the thirty-one-year-old chanteuse. Her copper casket processed from Seventh Avenue to 125th Street through to Lenox Avenue and up to 137th Street before stopping for the funeral at the Mother Zion African Methodist Episcopal Church, which was legendary for its role in the Underground Railroad. In the aftermath of Mills's death, the incredible impact of her life became the topic of much discussion on editorial pages across the country. One writer summarized her accomplishments like this:

> Florence Mills, as an artist and as a genuine person, did a real service to her race. Her career has advanced the whole cause of the Negro. She did not have to apologize for her color; she did not have to smirk and flatter to get recognition for her talents; she did not have to "show off for white folks." She simply, in the language of Broadway, did her stuff—and it was good stuff . . . the thing to be remembered is that Negro actors, writers, artists, and even ordinary Negro citizens can find their long and often tragic path eased by the solid ability of Miss Mills.[8]

Though Leslie was devastated to lose his star, he had to feel some sort of gratification at having given her the outlet in which to showcase her spectacular gifts. In the months after the funeral, Leslie was ready to try again. He contacted McHugh, suggesting the two should get a new show together and promising to visit the Cotton Club to hear the work of McHugh's new lyricist, Dorothy Fields. Upon visiting the Harlem hotspot in the weeks after Mills's funeral, Leslie liked what he heard. Now that the producer had settled on a songwriting team, he just needed to secure a location to stage the new show. McHugh had an idea. He knew of a club at 146 West Fifty-Seventh Street that was about to close. Leslie could take over the club and use it as a showcase for his new *Blackbirds*, thereby offering audiences all the entertainment of the Cotton Club without the long trip to Harlem. Leslie was intrigued; he began investigating Le Perroquet ("Little Parrot") de Paris as a possible spot for staging his planned *Blackbirds of 1928*.

Le Perroquet de Paris had opened in November of 1926. It was the pet project of Roger Wolfe Kahn, the then eighteen-year-old son of investment banker and philanthropist Otto Kahn. An up-and-coming bandleader, Roger Kahn saw the club as an opportunity to promote his music and launch his vision of eventually overseeing orchestras in Statler-branded hotels nationwide. No expense was spared in the 7,000-square-foot ballroom or in the auxiliary rooms attached to it. The dance floor was mirrored; tables had glass tops under which goldfish swam. Overhead, six parrots—"le perroquet"—had the run of the club. With its five dollar cover charge, the club aspired to be the premier place for after-theater drinks and dancing. The younger Kahn's youthful inexperience quickly showed itself, however. In a year's time, he'd lost a massive amount of his father's money and realized he was better off focusing on music alone. The timing was perfect for Lew Leslie. In late December 1927, he leased the space from Kahn and remodeled it. By January of 1928, the space had been opened again under the name Les Ambassadeurs. Dorothy and McHugh were working quickly to fill Leslie's need of music for his floor show. McHugh would work in the Mills Music offices every night from midnight to three or four a.m. Dorothy would arrive around seven in the morning to hear McHugh's overnight output and write the lyrics. "She'd often have the lyric finished in one or two hours," McHugh recalled. "She was a brilliant, fast writer. By noon, we often had the song finished."[9]

Things were falling into place for Leslie. He had songwriters for his new show, a performance space, and even a star to replace Florence Mills. After seeing them perform when he'd previewed Dorothy's work at the Cotton Club, Leslie had poached Adelaide Hall, Aida Ward, and several other performers from the company, a fact which drew understandable ire from the Cotton Club brass. In spite of a threat that Owney Madden and company planned to sabotage the opening of Leslie's new club in retaliation, the show opened uneventfully. At the time, only half of its score was written. Songs like "Diga Diga Do," full of thinly veiled sexual innuendos, made the floor show at instant success. Still, Leslie felt like something was missing. He asked Dorothy and McHugh to write "a crooning ballad that could also be used as a dance number." Dorothy spoke up, suggesting that maybe "I Can't Give You Anything but Love, Baby" would fit the bill. The pair played the song for Leslie; he loved it. Though McHugh warned him that the song had already been kicked out of *Delmar's Revels*, Leslie was undeterred, saying, "Listen, Brother. I don't care what happened to this song in the past. I'm going to make it the biggest hit in the country."[10]

Leslie would eventually make good on his promise. For reasons that aren't completely clear, he suggested they change the title and lyric to "I Can't Give You Anything but Love, Lindy," an obvious homage to Charles Lindbergh. The legendary American aviator had completed the first solo, nonstop transatlantic flight in June of 1927. Perhaps the suggested change was an attempt to capitalize on Lindbergh's continued notoriety in the same way that Mills Music would publish songs surrounding current events. Regardless of his rationale, that's the way the song was sung for the early part of its life (according to McHugh, the change back to "Baby" was made when the show opened in New York). When the score for *Blackbirds of 1928* was completed, the team decided it should transfer to Broadway's Liberty Theatre. They made their way downtown by way of an early May tryout at Nixon's Apollo Theatre on the boardwalk in Atlantic City.

By this point, the *Blackbirds* score was complete. In addition to "Diga Diga Do" and "I Can't Give You Anything but Love, Baby," the show had specialty numbers, like "Doing the New Lowdown" for Bill "Bojangles" Robinson and "I

Must Have That Man" for Adelaide Hall. There was also a song called "Porgy" that was inspired by a trip that Dorothy and McHugh made to see Dorothy and DuBose Heyward's play of the same name. The play had opened at the Guild Theatre in October of 1927. Though it'd later be the foundation for George and Ira Gershwin's 1935 folk opera *Porgy and Bess*, *Porgy* was first musicalized by Dorothy Fields and Jimmy McHugh. After seeing the play, they decided to satirize it for a number in *Blackbirds*. Obviously harkening back to the burlesques she'd seen her father produce, the "Porgy" sketch "started in legitimate 'spiritual' form, went into the 'St. Louis Blues,' and ended with a shrieking frenzy silhouetted against the background to the tune of Gershwin's 'Rhapsody.'"

The show opened at Broadway's Liberty Theatre on May 9, 1928.

As is customary for Broadway, the *Blackbirds* opening was a gala affair. First-nighters ranged from Fred and Adele Astaire to the entire casts of *A Connecticut Yankee* and *Present Arms*, which were both currently running shows written by Rodgers, Hart, and Herbert Fields and produced by Lew Fields. Of particular note about the opening was the integrated seating of the orchestra. Though they were by no means there in equal number, some black showgoers were permitted to join the whites in the lower bowl of the theater, following the precedent set by *Shuffle Along*. In general, the audience was excited to see what the so-called "Ziegfeld of Harlem" would offer as his follow-up to the inimitable Florence Mills. There was also a fair amount of curiosity about the Broadway debut of the daughter of another great impresario, Lew Fields. According to one review, Lew was "very beaming" and "conspicuously present."[11] Presumably, he was beginning to realize the error in his previous insistence that his talented children apply their gifts to non-theatrical endeavors—Dorothy would later say, "My father became reconciled to our going into show business when it seemed as though we would be successful."[12]

Notices of the *Blackbirds* opening were mixed. Critic Burns Mantle described the show as "a large, swiftly-moving, panoramic entertainment dotted with talent and never permitted to sink into sluggish attempts at wit in imitation of the whites." He went on, "It excels as few of the colored revues manage to do in those departments of entertainment to which the colored performers are peculiarly fitted."[13] Another writer benignly suggested the revue would "accomplish a fairly successful engagement,"[14] while a third called the show "one of the best of its kind ever presented."[15]

"Of its kind" is an important distinction to make. At this point in Broadway history, the slow wheels of change were beginning to turn. While the majority of musical fare on Broadway consisted of revues, like *Blackbirds*, or musical comedies, like the frothy fare Herbert Fields had been successfully generating with Rodgers and Hart, the concept of an "integrated" musical—one in which all of the artistic elements combine to advance a single, compelling narrative—was beginning to take shape. Nowhere was this on more prominent display than in Jerome Kern (music) and Oscar Hammerstein's (lyrics) groundbreaking *Show*

*Boat*. An adaptation of Edna Ferber's 1926 novel of the same name, *Show Boat* had opened just weeks after Dorothy and McHugh debuted at the Cotton Club in December of 1927. Dorothy would later call it "absolute Heaven," writing for "book" shows of the ilk that *Show Boat* would spawn.[16] She would eventually get her turn at those types of musicals. For the time being, however, the up-and-coming almost twenty-four-year-old was reveling in her newfound success and cherishing the pride with which her father was finally beginning to view her career. She received his resounding endorsement when he offered her and McHugh their first post-*Blackbirds* assignment. They would write the music and lyrics for a musical comedy called *Hello, Daddy*, starring none other than the show's producer, Lew Fields.

# Chapter 6
## "Raisin' the Roof"

*Blackbirds of 1928* was not an instant hit at the box office. With a number of ho-hum reviews, audiences weren't sure if the $1.10 to $3.30 ticket prices were worth the cost of admission. Lew Leslie refused to give up on the show. In what proved to be a genius marketing play, he announced *Blackbirds* would play an additional performance each week on Thursdays at midnight. He'd done this before with both 1922's *Plantation Revue* and 1924's *Dixie to Broadway*. "I started the fad, because I thought there were any number of Broadway actors who could not see my show at regular performances, since they were working themselves," Leslie explained. Over time, midnight entertainments like these became the glamourous thing for Jazz Age theatergoers to do. "Just why this should be is hard to fathom," said Leslie. "Perhaps it offers the one place to go instead of home."[1]

Between these additional performances and word of mouth advertisements, *Blackbirds* became the hottest ticket in town within three months of its opening. Also hot was the ballad Leslie had suggested Dorothy and McHugh add to the score. When Walter Winchell heard "I Can't Give You Anything but Love, Baby" on opening night, he told McHugh, "Jimmy, you've got the biggest hit you ever had,"[2] and he was right. Though McHugh had had some success writing popular songs before beginning his collaboration with Dorothy Fields, it wasn't until he worked with her that McHugh had either a show running on Broadway or a hit of the enormous popularity that "I Can't Give You Anything but Love, Baby" attained. The song sold more than two million copies; in addition, there were—and continue to be—multiple recordings, including many made in 1928 by the likes of Louis Armstrong, Duke Ellington, Gene Austin, and Ukulele Ike (Cliff Edwards). More than seventy years after the premiere of *Blackbirds*, the American Society of Composers, Authors, and Publishers (ASCAP) announced its list of songs that defined the music of the twentieth century. Dorothy and McHugh were one of only three songwriters or songwriting duos to be represented in three different decades—"I Can't Give You Anything but Love, Baby" was the pair's first entry on the list.[3]

Suddenly, the young lady who was supposed to get married and live a quiet life as a doctor's wife was in high demand as a songwriter. She and McHugh were still refreshing the music for the Cotton Club floor shows twice a year, they were working on the songs for Lew Fields's next big theatrical outing, and *Blackbirds of 1928* was one of the biggest hits Broadway had seen in a decade, banking nearly $20,000 a week. It ultimately ran longer than any show that Lew Fields had ever performed in or produced and, at one point, had three companies running at once. Dorothy was in the thick of things and loving every minute of it. She and McHugh spent most of their time together. Though both married to other people—she to Wiener and he to Bess McHugh, who was back in Boston with their son, Jimmy Jr.—they generally attended professional dinners and show openings with each other. By nature of Broadway in the 1920s, these were frequent occurrences. Broadway openings happened far more often than they do now. In the season that *Blackbirds* opened (1927–1928), there were 282 openings. The 2018–2019 season saw thirty-eight openings. In a 1959 interview, Oscar Hammerstein II explained some of the reasons for this disparity:

> In those days, it was more of a free-for-all, slapdash kind of thing, the musical comedy. Someone would find a theater unbooked, and someone else would try to whip up a book and music and lyrics and get a star and fill the theater, if they could. In those days, most of the managers gambled their own money. They didn't go around getting money from the public . . . so the producers in those days lost his own money in a flop . . . whatever he had, he put in, and if he had a success, he rode very high and spent a lot of his money freely. . . . I would say in those days, the theater was less legitimate but more adventurous and certainly more financially courageous than it is today . . . today, more money is being risked, but it's being risked by more people, and the more shrewd producer today lets someone else put up the money, and he gambles his time and his skill and hopes to get 50% of the profits instead of 100%.[4]

Hammerstein's explanation certainly seems to mirror Lew Fields's experience as a producer. Throughout his professional life, his financial situation would rise and fall depending on the success of whatever show (or, sometimes, shows) he was with at the time. As time went by, the cost of producing a show greatly outpaced the rate of inflation. This led to producers having to rely on longer runs to recoup their more significant investments. Longer runs meant fewer available theaters, and fewer available theaters meant fewer openings. This is just another way in which Broadway has changed since its early days when high turnover and quick turnaround was the norm.

After working through the fall on *Hello, Daddy*, the show was ready to open in December of 1928. The musical comedy was based on a play called *The High Cost of Loving*, a German farce in which Lew Fields had performed in 1914. Herbert provided the libretto, Dorothy and McHugh the music. The story is about three men, who, as they're discussing their youthful indiscretions, discover that they've each been supporting the same illegitimate "son" and his retired dancer of a mother for some number of years. Something like a reverse take on the plot of 2001's *Mamma Mia, Hello, Daddy,* with its exquisite choreography by future film legend Busby Berkeley, survived well into the next summer; it played a healthy 198 performances. In his first stage outing in two seasons, Lew Fields shone with his customary hilarity. The story, though, "was mainly used to fill in the chinks between the musical numbers."[5] Dorothy and McHugh's score was the highlight of the show. Wrote Burns Mantle, "It is probably the songs that will do the most for *Hello, Daddy,*" adding the show is "more melodious than any of the recent contributions."[6] Perhaps part of this was owing to the play of a young clarinetist named Benny Goodman in the show's orchestra pit. The bulk of the music's success was due to a songwriting duo whose partnership was beginning to fire on all eight cylinders. Dorothy was "making rapid strides as a lyricist"[7]; her lyrics were "good, chatty, sufficiently sentimental, and well-tailored." McHugh's music could "be whistled without struggle."[8] Though none of the songs from the show became lasting standards, tunes like "In a Great Big Way," "I Want Plenty of You," and "Futuristic Rhythm" were excellent practice for the team's next assignment, which had already been offered.

The idea behind Florenz Ziegfeld's *Midnight Frolic* was not a new one. Producers like Lew Leslie had implemented late-night shows for each of his Broadway outings, and many suggest that some of the appeal of the Cotton Club was that its later start time allowed for theater-folk to perform in their own shows before going to see another one uptown. This was a trend of which Ziegfeld had been a part since 1915. That's when he opened what was essentially a nightclub on the rooftop of his breathtaking New Amsterdam Theatre at 214 West Forty-Second Street (a space restored by Disney Theatrical Productions for the 1997 opening of *The Lion King*). Having produced his signature *Follies* each year since 1907, Ziegfeld grew tired of watching audiences leave his show to go spend money at someone else's nightclub; he decided he'd build his own. A luxury experience awaited the patrons willing to pay the five dollar cover charge (nearly $130 now) and ride the elevator to the roof of the glamorous New Amsterdam.

*Midnight Frolic* shows were similar to the *Follies* in that they featured beautiful dancing girls in exquisite art deco dress; however, there were also several differences between the two. First, while Ziegfeld insisted on a certain level of modesty for the *Follies*, he relaxed his standards somewhat when it came to costuming his *Frolic*. This led to young ladies who were often scantily or even scandalously clad. Second, every night, each audience member was asked to vote on which girl they thought was the most beautiful. At the end of the season, Ziegfeld doubled the salary of the girl with the most votes. Third, Ziegfeld provided each guest with a little wooden hammer. A brilliant marketing technique, Ziegfeld justified the distribution by claiming his audiences would be tired from clapping so much. The hammer enabled them to bang on the tables instead of their sore hands. Finally, the *Frolic* was akin to the later Cotton Club revues in that it was structured more like a cabaret presentation than a legitimate Broadway entertainment. The floor show even featured a twenty-five-minute intermission during which audiences could dance to a live orchestra.[9]

When it opened on January 8, 1915, the *Frolic* fast became a favorite of the smart set. It was particularly popular when a performer named Will Rogers took the stage. Rogers, who'd go on to be one of America's highest-paid performers (and would later be immortalized on Broadway in 1991's *Will Rogers Follies*), got his start on the rooftop of the New Amsterdam Theatre. Many of the same patrons attended the *Frolic* night after night. This required that Rogers be able to improvise in order to keep his audience amused. In preparation, he'd study current events and comment on the news of the day, often interacting with members of his adoring crowd. Much of Rogers's subsequent success would come while he was still under exclusive contract to Ziegfeld. In spite of its popularity with audiences, though, the original incarnation of the *Midnight Frolic* ceased operations in 1921. The closing had nothing to do with a decline in demand; instead, the nation's new Prohibition law, implemented in January of 1920, was the cause. Said Ziegfeld,

> The best class of people from all over the world have been in the habit of coming up on the roof, and when they are subjected to the humiliation of having policemen stand by their tables and watch what they are drinking, then I do not care to keep open any longer.[10]

Though Prohibition had not yet been repealed—it remained the law of the land until 1933—Ziegfeld nevertheless decided to reopen the *Frolic* in February of 1929. Why he chose to do this is unknown. It certainly wasn't for lack of other projects. At the time the *Frolic* reopened, Ziegfeld had five shows running, including *Rosalie*, *Whoopee!*, and the landmark *Show Boat*. Perhaps he saw the success of the Cotton Club and was, once again, resolved that he, too, should have a piece of the nightclub pie. That certainly isn't a big leap to make, as Ziegfeld could have hired any songwriting team he desired, yet he chose to retain the Cotton Club's in-demand musical tandem of Dorothy Fields and Jimmy McHugh. An associate of Lew Fields, Ziegfeld had produced *Miss 1917*, in which Lew starred. He'd also given Herbert Fields one of his first opportunities to act on Broadway in that same show. That a producer of his renown would hire a lyricist just over a year into her career is an indication of how highly he valued Dorothy's talent. For that first iteration of the *Midnight Frolic*, she and McHugh wrote numbers like "Looking for Love" and "Raisin' the Roof" as the songs to which the famed Ziegfeld girls took the *Midnight Frolic* stage.

The new rooftop venue was as glamorous as the old one had been. It was designed by architect and scenic designer Joseph Urban. Credited by many with having originated the American Art Deco style, Urban was prolific. He'd worked as scenic designer for both the Boston and Metropolitan Opera Companies before beginning his work designing multiple productions of Ziegfeld's *Follies*. Urban came to the *Frolic* project not long after completing work on the interior design and exterior decorations of Mar-a-Lago. The Palm Beach, Florida, home built by Post Cereal heiress Marjorie Merriweather Post had been completed in 1927, the same year work was done on the lavish Ziegfeld Theatre, which Urban also designed and which now stands as a movie house at Sixth Avenue and West Fifty-Fourth Street. The result of Urban's work on the New Amsterdam's rooftop was "an after-theater meeting place with distinction, elegance, and charm" featuring "the most beautiful dance room on this side of the ocean."[11] To experience Ziegfeld's brand of sophistication, audience members paid a new cover charge of $6.60. That price purchased showgoers a seat and the opportunity to see not only Ziegfeld's girls but also headlining acts, like Frenchman Maurice Chevalier, who played the club just a few weeks after its reopening.

By all accounts, Dorothy Fields had made it. Fifteen months after commencing her professional debut at the Cotton Club, she had two shows running on Broadway, two nightclubs for which she was providing music, and one bestselling song that the world couldn't get enough of. By June of 1929, Mills Music ran an ad in *Variety* calling Dorothy and McHugh "America's Foremost Songwriters." She was not yet twenty-five years old and already netting about $60,000 a year for her lyric-writing, the modern equivalent of nearly one million dollars. Her next assignment would lead to some of the biggest adventures of her life.

**Dorothy Fields, Jimmy McHugh, and other songwriters in a 1929 drawing by Al Hirschfeld, "MGM Composers and Songwriters."** © The Al Hirschfeld Foundation. www.AlHirschfeldFoundation.org.

# Chapter 7
## "I'm Livin' in a Great Big Way"

The year 1927 was a watershed one on both Broadway and in Hollywood. Just as *Show Boat*'s December opening indicated that change was (eventually) coming to the Great White Way, so did the October premiere of *The Jazz Singer* harken to new horizons in Hollywood. After the film's first Los Angeles showing, Frances Goldwyn, wife of MGM studio executive Samuel Goldwyn, said to her husband, "[this is] the most important event in cultural history, since Martin Luther nailed his Theses on the church door."[1] She wasn't wrong. In the wake of *The Jazz Singer* and the subsequent mainstreaming of the film industry, there weren't many aspects of American life that would remain unchanged. *The Jazz Singer* starred the so-called "World's Greatest Entertainer," Al Jolson, "who disguises a Hebrew soul under blackface make-up."[2] The movie was Vitaphone's adaption of Samson Raphaelson's 1925 play about "a boy who ran away from home, because he rebelled against strict traditions and desired to become a performer on the stage."[3] With its release, the era of silent movies essentially ended. It would take some time for all films to be fully integrated with sound, but suddenly, the technology existed to synchronize a recorded track—be it singing, speech, or musical underscoring—with film. Moviegoers were captivated by the result. Broadway historian Miles Kreuger aptly summarized the phenomenon like this:

> Within weeks [of the advent of talkies], audiences throughout the nation had the common experience of witnessing the same star introduce a song in precisely the same mounting and performed in a movie palace of unrestrained opulence and comfort.[4]

This changed everything. Though, prior to film, the majority of popular songs started their lives on the stage, the Broadway audience represented a very narrow segment of the American population. More than sixty percent of modern Broadway showgoers are tourists; in the 1920s, this wasn't the case. The difficulty and

51

expense of travel made the New York theater audience a very local community. Songs introduced on the stage were disseminated via the sale of sheet music and phonograph records. As the private use of radios became normalized in the early to mid-1920s, increasingly standardized programming meant that listeners nationwide were finally able to experience the songs in some manner of uniformity, but, as with phonographs, there was still a variety of performers singing a variety of arrangements. Irving Berlin, arguably the greatest contributor to the American popular songbook, saw the changes brought about by the popularity of *The Jazz Singer* as a boon to songwriters:

> If a songwriter is fortunate enough to have a good song of his sung or themed well in a good picture, that song remains that way, because it is recorded and so presented to the public in thousands of theaters at the same time. Heretofore, if a musical production developed one or two song hits, it took several months to popularize them, for the very obvious reason that the production generally opened and played in New York for six months or a year, and the songs were heard nowhere outside except by orchestras that played them.[5]

For all of the ground it broke, though, *The Jazz Singer* was by no means the first film with music. Music and movies had been linked since long before the coming of the so-called "talkies." In the early years of the silent era, it was common practice for directors to commission the composition of background music for their films. Some would even promote theme songs inspired by the title of the film. These were considered solid marketing tactics for either the movie or its stars. By the release of *The Jazz Singer*, the interpolation of some kind of music into a film was much more the rule rather than the exception. After *The Jazz Singer*, though, synchronization—where the action and, later, dialogue is synced with the soundtrack—became expected. In response, movie studios flooded the market with musicals; there were more than sixty released in 1929 alone. In short order, movie musicals were the Hollywood norm.

Needless to say, this required a great deal more manpower than had been necessary in California before. In response, songwriters moved to the West Coast in droves, each seeking his or her own share of the so-called "Gold Rush." Dorothy Fields was among them. She and McHugh signed a contract with Metro-Goldwyn-Mayer (MGM). In addition to the royalties from their new and existing work running on multiple stages in New York and, in the case of *Blackbirds of 1928*, on the road, they were each paid $1,000 a week for their earliest work on film. The contract allowed them to continue working on projects in New York (which they did), provided they spend several weeks at a time on the MGM lot and return to the West Coast whenever they were needed. Hollywood's gain was Tin Pan Alley's loss. Almost all of the major songwriting talent, at some point, left for the West Coast—Irving Berlin, George and Ira Gershwin, Oscar Hammerstein II, Jerome Kern, and a legion more. It was estimated that about seventy-five percent of songwriters went west. And who could blame them? With eternal sunshine and guaranteed incomes, Hollywood's offer seemed too good to be true.

Many, though not all, of the songwriters were smitten with their new digs. "It's great out here," said writer Sammy Clare, who signed with the Radio-Keith-Orpheum (RKO) studio. "I like it. Of course, I might be lonesome if there weren't so many of the boys out here. You walk through the lobby at the Roosevelt Hotel, and it's just like being at Lindy's or the other hangouts on Broadway."[6] Most of the songwriters were like Clare; next to the paychecks, they most enjoyed the camaraderie. The city itself was beautiful, but in 1929 it was far from the sprawling metropolis it would soon become as a result of the movie boom. Willie Collier, who worked for years as part of the Weber and Fields company and was with the family in Allenhurst the day that Dorothy was born, described those early days in Los Angeles like this:

> You get to bed early here—there's nothing to stay up for!—the National Guard could use Hollywood Boulevard as a rifle range anytime after nine o'clock at night and never harm a soul. Broadway's midnight rose is Hollywood's early morning glory. All the transplanted Gigglewater Canyon boys and girls get up with the birdies, eat breakfast, and finish a half a day's work before their brothers and sisters back home have gotten up.[7]

Though written with Collier's customary comedic flair, his description still serves to paint a relatively vivid picture of the burgeoning city just before it began its period of massive growth. Living in Hollywood was different than it had been in New York. Working was too. While most of the songwriters embraced the California way of life, they were not as enamored with the studio's system of songwriting. Each studio had a different method of working, but MGM's involved having each of their songwriting teams contribute songs for the same films. These songs could be used as opening or closing numbers, title songs, background music, or, as time went on, numbers sung by characters in the film, like Jolson had done in *The Jazz Singer*. The songs submitted would then be judged by the studio executives. The favorites would be used in the film. The others would be put in the songwriters' metaphorical "trunks" to pull out and use, reworking as necessary, for future projects. Minus the competition with their fellow songwriters, this was exactly what Dorothy and McHugh had done when "I Can't Give You Anything but Love, Baby," had been cut from *Delmar's Revels*. They saved the song to pull out when Lew Leslie asked them to insert an up-tempo ballad into *Blackbirds of 1928*.

Though songwriters at MGM kicked against this process, they learned to live with it. Guaranteed incomes that ranged from $12,500 to $35,000 a year were more than enough to quiet their complaints. That these earnings were paid up front—rather than those that were paid after a show was up and running (and in amounts that depended upon the success of the show) in New York—made the film industry even more appealing. *Love in the Rough* was among the first films for which Dorothy and McHugh provided music in Hollywood. Starring Robert Montgomery, Dorothy Jordan, and Benny Rubin, the film was an adaptation of Vincent Lawrence's 1925 play, *Spring Fever*. Montgomery played a shipping clerk named Jack Kelly, who earns a two-week golf vacation and joins his boss at an exclusive resort. While he's there, Kelly falls in love and elopes with the daughter (played by Jordan) of a millionaire. Fortunately, the girl's father likes golf too, so he's not too put off by his daughter's spontaneous wedding. Dorothy and McHugh provided five songs for the score, including "Go Home and Tell Your Mother," "I'm Learning a Lot from You," and "Like Kelly Can."

The movie was thoroughly forgettable. It nevertheless allows an opportunity to make an interesting point about the conventions of music in early films. As Dorothy explained it, "There was a theory that every time you did a song in a picture, it had to be excused by either having a guitar or a banjo on the set. They refused . . . [to] have the music come from nowhere." The way that played out in *Love in the Rough* was with musicians dressed as caddies. "Every time we did a song, the caddies would accompany this love song, behind the bushes, and then the music would creep in,"[8] Dorothy said. Within a couple of years, audiences would adapt to the spontaneous play of music. In the early going, though, musicians were always present. It was Hollywood's way of helping its audience—the vast majority of which had never attended the playing of a musical comedy in New York—understand what Broadway goers had always accepted.

For Hollywood's boom, Broadway was about to go bust. When the stock market crashed in October of 1929, the economy of Broadway was hit hard. In the 1929–1930 season, there were 233 openings. The next year, there were only 187. As Broadway struggled, Hollywood soared. Tickets to the legitimate theater may have been beyond the reach of many New Yorkers, but at just thirty-five or forty cents, movies were accessible for most Americans, and they provided a necessary escape to the reality of life during the Great Depression. The studios worked furiously to feed the public's new appetite for film. In the 1929–1930 season, more than $165,000,000 was spent on moviemaking. There were 30,000 people employed by twenty-six different studios. The songwriters who made the move to California got out of New York just in time. The flexibility in Dorothy and McHugh's contract with MGM allowed the duo to continue working on both coasts, and they did it at an almost frenetic pace. This was particularly beneficial to the pair, both of whom had, like most of the country, suffered financial losses in the aftermath of the stock market crash. Days after the crash, Dorothy and McHugh were walking on West Fifty-Seventh Street when she remembered she had an appointment to have her hair done. McHugh suggested they catch a cab to the salon. She refused: "No, Jimmy. No cabs. We'll walk." Even the mighty had fallen in what was arguably the greatest financial disaster in American history. While Dorothy was with the hairdresser, McHugh found a $100 bill on the ground outside of a bank. He broke the hundred and distributed it among his newly needy friends, including giving some to Dorothy, who used the gift to pay for her cut.[9]

In response to situations like these, successful songwriters, who'd grown accustomed to being flush with cash, were driven to work not only by a desire to produce more music but also by a drive to restock their personal coffers. Many of them saw the big money of film work as the quickest way to achieve this end. Being able to simultaneously write for shows in New York was the icing on the cake. In 1930, Dorothy and McHugh wrote music for four films (*Kelly's Vacation*, *Love in the Rough*, *March of Time*, and *Social Success*), while still managing to mount two new revues on Broadway. The first of these was Lew Leslie's *International Revue*. The "international" came from the fact that Leslie had spent months in Europe, searching for material and performers to give his new show an exotic appeal. The resulting production was two acts that consisted of thirty scenes. In conducting auditions for the show, Dorothy came across someone who would not only become one of her closest friends but who would also become one of Broadway's biggest stars. Dorothy and McHugh were auditioning singers at the Mills Music offices when an unknown stenographer named Ethel Merman walked in. The songwriters were impressed with her voice; the producer, however, wanted to go a different route. He cast Gertrude Lawrence instead, owing, according to Dorothy, to the "passionate crush" Leslie had for Lawrence. Less than a year later, Dorothy sat in the audience on opening night of George and Ira Gershwin's *Girl Crazy*. She watched as that same Ethel Merman made her Broadway debut, singing "I Got Rhythm" with an orchestra that included Benny Goodman, Glenn Miller, and both of the Dorsey Brothers. "I've never seen anything like it on the stage, except Mary Martin when she did 'My Heart Belongs [to Daddy],'" said Dorothy. "It . . . was an ovation like you just can't believe."[10] Within the decade, the two powerhouse women would get the chance to work together multiple times, and their personal lives would become as congenial as their professional ones.

After a tryout in Philadelphia, Lew Leslie's *International Revue*—with its star, as Leslie had insisted, Gertrude Lawrence—opened at the Majestic Theatre on February 25, 1930. Dorothy and McHugh were unable to attend the New York opening, as they were back at work for MGM on the show's first night. Touted as having "the greatest cast ever assembled on stage," it starred Lawrence, Harry Richman, Jack Pearl, Argentinita (whom Leslie had imported from Spain), and others; in spite of its star power, however, critics were not kind:

> How anyone who sponsored so amusing and expert a musical show as *Blackbirds* could have allowed his name and money to be associated with a production so tedious and uninspired as the *International Revue* is beyond belief. Here is an ornate extravaganza that is top heavy with its mass of dull material and even its unusual number of stars fails to lift it above the mediocre.[11]

In its New York premiere, the painfully long second act was still in full swing at midnight. Writers and audiences alike expected that Leslie would continue shaping the show until it became a success, just as he'd done with the slow-starting *Blackbirds*. As it turned out, however, lightning did not strike twice. Lew Leslie's *International Revue* closed on May 17, having played just ninety-five lackluster performances. Though the show itself was a flop, its score produced a handful of hits for Dorothy and McHugh. Among these were "Exactly Like You," which would later be popularized by the Benny Goodman Trio, and "On the Sunny Side of the Street." The number before "Sunny Side" was written for Jack Pearl and called "The Margineers." Completely forgettable—Dorothy herself said she "didn't remember any of it"[12]—the song was a comic look at the terrible effects of the stock market crash. As a foil to that cynicism, Harry Richman next offered optimism by singing "On the Sunny Side of the Street." The number was precisely what audiences of the post-Depression era needed to hear. By now, Dorothy had perfected Irving Mills's advice to "hop on a current thing"; in spite of the *International Revue*'s less-than-stellar showing, the timely song became an anthem for a country down on its luck.

> If I never have a cent,
> I'll be rich as Rockefeller.
> Gold dust at my feet
> On the sunny side of the street.

By this point, three years into her career as a professional songwriter, Dorothy's voice was fully developed. No longer tempted to write in the style of her friend Lorenz Hart or any other of her peers, Dorothy knew what she wanted to say, and she was adept at saying it quickly. Often, she and McHugh would have only a night to churn out a song. Working, as they did, side by side on the piano bench, this was no problem for the prolific duo. Generally speaking, both she and McHugh preferred to start with the song title. He'd then write the melody and play it for Dorothy, who'd write the lyrics. That was the way they worked for most of their very successful eight-year partnership.

After *International Revue*, the pair's next Broadway outing was one produced by Lew Fields and Lyle D. Andrews. *The Vanderbilt Revue* was even less of a success than the *International Revue* had been. Essentially a massive cast of a hundred entertainers performing a slate of vaudeville acts and comedy scenes, the show was marketed by its producers as "the smartest and most colorful musical of all time."[13] *The Vanderbilt Revue* would eventually open at New York's Vanderbilt Theatre. It featured music by a number of songwriting teams, including Dorothy and McHugh. To some extent, this intermingling of songwriters—using a variety of tunesmiths to provide music for a revue instead of a single team—had always been done. It became more the norm, however, after the Gold Rush. With so many writers living out West, producers back East had to make some changes in order to accommodate the writers' new bicoastal schedules. One way they did this was by employing the tactic of using a variety of talent to create a Broadway revue. With regards to Dorothy and McHugh, this would be the case for each of their future stage collaborations, including 1931's *Rhapsody in Black* and *Shoot the Works* (they also wrote a pair of songs for that year's *Singin' the Blues*, a "play with music").

Dorothy and McHugh added four songs to the score of the *Vanderbilt Revue*. Of them, "Blue Again" is the only number with significant staying power. A *Variety* review of the show's Wilmington, Delaware, tryout called it "the outstanding tune of the show."[14] Possessed of an uncharacteristically tricky lyric, "Blue Again" stands out as one of several anomalies in Dorothy's catalog:

> I'm blue again, blue again
> And you know darn well that it's you again.
> 'Cause you said last night that we were through again,
> And now I'm blue again.
>
> I'm alone again, alone again,
> And I'm out around on my own again,
> Because my mockingbird has flown again,
> And I'm alone again.
>
> Though I say I hate you,
> I love you more every day.
> Though I aggravate you,
> Darlin', I'm longing to say
>
> That it's you again, you again,
> And we'll meet at half past two again,
> But tonight, we'll fight and be through again,
> And I'll be blue again.

The charm of "Blue Again" could not offset a slew of mediocre reviews for the *Vanderbilt Revue*. Wrote Rowland Field in the *Brooklyn Times Union*, "Last night's revue had its bright moments, but it, on the whole, does not shape up particularly well as a musical entertainment in these times when competition is so keen in this town."[15] The *Variety* reviewer was more damning in his assessment of the show. "Strong comedy is a great necessity for musical revues, and that's what *Vanderbilt Revue* lacks mainly. It misses elsewhere, too, and fails to warrant elevation over the flop class."[16] Lew Fields, who, with partner Joe Weber, had been called one of "New York's Favorite Comedians,"[17] was embarrassed. Convinced he had lost touch with what audiences wanted, he closed the show after an agonizingly short thirteen performances; it was the shortest run of his five-decade career. He never worked on Broadway again.

Another blow to the Fields family was dealt just weeks later. Each member of the family had invested heavily in the bank operated by the family of Frances's husband, Charles Marcus. They'd encouraged many of their friends—among them, McHugh—to do the same. On December 11, 1930, that bank, The Bank of the United States, went belly-up in one of the biggest banking busts in American history. After months of whispers that the bank was not sound, some of its roughly 400,000 depositors began to withdraw their funds in panic. The run resulted in total deposits dropping from $225,000,000 to $160,000,000 in two months' time. When the bank suspended its business on December 11, customers, many of them lower-wage earners from New York's garment industry, were forced to settle for as little as 50 cents on the dollar.[18] Their devastation was made all the worse, coming, as it did, just over a year after Black Tuesday (October 29, 1929) rocked the stock market, ushering in the ongoing Great Depression. Though the bank had been run since 1926 by Charles's younger brother, Bernard, the fallout for both Charles and the Fields family was enormous. Frances and Charles were forced to leave Manhattan to settle in the suburbs; eventually, their marriage, which had produced twin sons, would end in divorce. Lew Fields found himself, as he had in the early 1920s, on the verge of financial ruin. Fortunately, his three younger children had defied his orders that they should stay out of show business. When Lew Fields was down, it was the success of Joseph, Herbert, and, especially, Dorothy that would pick him back up.

# Chapter 8
## "Every Night at Eight"

As it turned out, Dorothy and Jimmy McHugh's decision to continue working in New York as they got settled in Hollywood was a good one. The studio's first musical-making boom was short-lived. By the end of 1930, most studios had either done away with or significantly downsized their songwriting operations. MGM retained Dorothy and McHugh but deferred the duo's two-year contract for several months. This gave the pair time to write for shorts in California. It also made them available to write a score for what would be their final collaboration with Lew Leslie. Though they didn't know it at the time, *Clowns in Clover* would be one of the last stage shows they would write as a duo.

Having focused on so-called "colored revues" for the better part of a decade, Leslie decided to flip his own script: he created an all-*white* show. His plan was that the show would tryout in Detroit and Chicago in the summer of 1932 before landing on Broadway later that year. The show—typical in its structure of nearly three dozen sketches threaded together by Dorothy and McHugh's music—starred Walter Woolf and Kay Strozzi. There were ten original songs (including "Don't Blame Me," which had the longest life span) as well as "The Margineers," which was borrowed from 1930's *International Revue*. A reviewer at Chicago's Apollo Theatre production of *Clowns in Clover* was bullish on the music, writing "The lyrics of Dorothy Fields are bright and belong where they are placed, and Jimmie [*sic*] McHugh has turned in some tunes that should be whistled before the week is old." Still, the overall production was panned as "fair entertainment for hot weather."[1] About the Detroit tryout, Len G. Shaw said the show features an "all-white company that fairly bristles with talent, which, unfortunately, finds itself with little to do."[2] With so little excitement stemming from the show's early goings, *Clowns in Clover* never made it to Broadway.

Leslie reeled from the sting of another failed attempt at matching the success he'd found with shows like the *Plantation Revue* and *Blackbirds of 1928*. He suggested that "vulgarity and the persistent use of formula"[3] were to blame for the demise of the revue and that an ever-increasing number of movie houses were stealing the legitimate theater's audience. There may have been something to his accusations. Certainly, the advent of talking pictures had made film a formidable alternative to stage shows. In addition, tastes, like the country, were changing. A post–*Show Boat*, Depression-era Broadway had recently been infused with the hyper-realistic naturalism of companies like the Group Theatre. Modeled after Constantin Stanislavsky's Moscow Art Theatre, the Group was an ensemble of nearly three dozen actors and actresses committed to producing cutting-edge, world-changing theater characterized by psychological realism and political activism. The Group produced its first show on Broadway in September of 1932. Though it disbanded after just a decade of existence, the impact of the Group Theatre and the artists who embraced its ideology—among them Lee Strasberg, Stella Adler, Marc Blitzstein, Elia Kazan, Sanford Meisner, and Clifford Odets—was significant. Having survived the one-two punch of World War I and the Great Depression, Americans were sadder but wiser. It stands to reason that at least some of the art they consumed would begin to reflect that new cynicism. Each of these components played a role in the shifting shape of the American musical and the way it would change before Dorothy Fields returned to New York for good.

In the meantime, she and McHugh continued to work almost anytime they were given the chance. One of their most exciting gigs came when the pair was asked to write music for the grand opening of the new Radio City Music Hall at Sixth Avenue and Fiftieth Street in New York. Part of Rockefeller Center, that "modern dream of magic in the midst of the world's most stupendous city,"[4] Radio City Music Hall was downright opulent. Its gala opening was one befitting its spectacular Art Deco design. Billed as "the supreme stage entertainment of all time,"[5] the opening went on as planned on the dark and stormy night of December 27, 1932 (almost two years to the day after the Bank of the United States disaster). Dorothy and McHugh were the only songwriters on the extensive bill. They'd been added by producer S. L. Rothafel—the eponymous "Roxy"—just two days before the event, simply because "Roxy liked the way she sang her songs."[6] Other entertainers who performed that evening included the Flying Wallendas aerialists, the Tuskegee Choir, Ray Bolger, Weber and Fields, and the Roxyettes, who'd later be called the Rockettes, dancing for the first time on the stage they would make famous. Their routine was set to a tune called "With a Feather in Your Cap"; it had been written just for the occasion by Dorothy and McHugh. At the end of the first act, the writers took to the stage themselves. It was the first time since her days at the Benjamin School that Dorothy herself had been in the spotlight and not her songs. Excited for a chance to return to her first love, performing, the wildly successful and self-assured woman stepped to a microphone in the center of one of the world's most prestigious stages. Behind her, McHugh accompanied on the piano as she sang "Hey, Young Fella (Close Your Old Umbrella)."

(VERSE)
You had nothing to sing about.
The days were dreary and wet.
Had no sunshine to cling about
And lots of rain to forget.
You wore your flannels and stayed indoors
Like a birdie might do.
How you shivered and prayed indoors,
'til one day, I said to you.

(CHORUS)
Hey, Young Fella,
Better close your old umbrella.
Have a glorious day; throw your rubbers away,
'cause it ain't gonna rain no more.

Say, Young Fella,
Put your rain coat in the cellar.
While you're tying your tie, take a peek at that sky.
Well, it ain't gonna rain no more.

(BRIDGE)
Look at that brave little rainbow,
Fighting those clouds up above.
I'm in the rain, Mr. Rainbow,
With a horseshoe in my glove.

Hey, Young Fella,
Better close your old umbrella.
Let's go out in the sun, start havin' fun,
'cause it ain't gonna rain no more.

Originally written for the failed *Clowns in Clover*, "Hey, Young Fella" could not have been a more appropriate choice for the auspicious occasion. As she'd done with 1930's "On the Sunny Side of the Street," Dorothy Fields once again expressed in her lyrics the hopeful optimism of a nation that had been brought to its knees and was beginning to bounce back. Nowhere was that recovery more evident than in the grandeur of the new Radio City Music Hall. "Hey, Young Fella," which was reprised for the 1933 film *Dancing Lady*, is a quintessentially "Fields-ian" lyric. There are no tricky turns of phrase. In it, she uses everyday words, like "wore your flannels" to represent a nation that had been, metaphorically, shut in. "Close your old umbrella" is Dorothy's way of saying "things are looking up." Lyricist Sheldon Harnick (*Fiorello*, *She Loves Me*, and *Fiddler on the Roof*) would later refer to these as "'kitchen sink' words." He called Dorothy's masterful use of them one of her "special gifts," noting her "magical ability to mix sophisticated and imaginative ideas with utterly prosaic . . . words and images, resulting in lyrics of a remarkably appealing freshness."[7]

"Appealing" is an appropriate word not only for Dorothy's lyrics but also for her performance that night in 1932. In the *Variety* review of the four-hour long production, Dorothy and McHugh were said to "Manage a lot better than others on this bill who do nothing else but appear on stages."[8] Dorothy's work was so appealing that Roxy asked her to stay with the show as it continued to run at Radio City for the next several weeks. She was elated to accept his invitation. Not only was he paying her the incredible sum of $1,500 a week (which would be the modern equivalent of about $30,000 a week), but she was also able to, finally, have a taste of the stage career that had, up to now, eluded her. During the run of the show, she was interviewed by a reporter for *Variety*. Asked if performing made her nervous, Dorothy responded with characteristic confidence, "You're not nervous when you know nothing. It's when you're wise that you worry." That same writer made the point that it made sense for Dorothy to be comfortable on stage. After years of demonstrating her songs to music publishers, she'd been performing all along. "All she had to do was see to it that she was introduced as a writer and not as a performer," he wrote. "That way, nobody could expect anything. If they liked her, it was to the good. They did."[9]

They liked her so much, in fact, that Dorothy and McHugh were subsequently signed to a short-term radio contract with the WJZ network. At the time, WJZ

**Dorothy Fields and Jimmy McHugh at the NBC Radio Studios, ca. 1933.** Photofest.

was the flagship station for the NBC Blue Network, as opposed to WEAF, which operated on NBC's Red Network. These short-term contracts were not at all un-common. Will Rogers had one, as did George Gershwin and many more. With the implosion of the sheet music industry, plugging songs on the radio—directly to the folks who might buy their recordings—was an excellent means of marketing music to the masses. If a songwriter had a voice as appealing as Dorothy's, so much the better. Most of these programs were presented in fifteen-minute incre-ments; "Fields and McHugh," as it was called in radio listings of the day, was no exception. On six Fridays in the early spring of 1933, Dorothy and McHugh could be heard plugging their songs (and, sometimes, the songs of others) in a program that was described in *Variety* as "an inviting quarter hour."

Though the program had Ford Bond as its announcer, Dorothy was front and center, assisting him as its emcee and acting as the show's primary performer. McHugh was her able accompanist. Each week, they would open and close with what was still the team's signature song, "I Can't Give You Anything but Love, Baby." What stands out from the scripts of the broadcasts, however, is how warm and engaging Dorothy was. It's easy to see why audiences were so easily won over by her Radio City performances and why reviewers were completely charmed each week that she took to the airwaves. A writer for *Variety* described her "cigarette contralto, which is backed by a fine sense of delivery and is pleasant to the ear."[10] Mark Barron wrote in his column that "Dorothy Fields's tuneful lyrics sound even better when she croons them herself."[11] For five years, the world had been under the spell of Fields's lyrics. Now, it was equally as enchanted by the woman herself. Dorothy was thrilled. She relished the oppor-tunity to perform again, whether it was on her own program or in a guest spot on programs, like Rudy Vallee's Fleischmann Yeast Hour.[12] "It revitalizes you when you do radio and tv," Dorothy told Dave Garroway in a 1955 interview for his *Friday with Garroway* radio program. "You feel as though you're alert, and you're alive. Can't just sit home writing song after song after song after song."[13]

By the conclusion of their radio contract, Dorothy and McHugh were ready to return to Hollywood. The timing was right, from an industry standpoint. On the coattails of films like *42nd Street*, which Warner Bros. released in March of 1933, as well as *Golddiggers of 1933* and *Footlight Parade*, both of which would be released by year's end, the musical film was enjoying a renaissance that would continue for decades. Dorothy and McHugh headed back to MGM—or "Metro," as trade papers often called it. One of their first assignments was a picture called *Meet the Baron*. The film starred Jack Pearl, who'd debuted their "The Margi-neers" in Lew Leslie's 1930 *International Revue*. In addition to writing songs for the film, Dorothy also got to try her hand at dialogue. This was an exciting development for the little girl who'd grown up scouring her father's reviews for instructions in book-building. The budding dramatist in Dorothy savored op-portunities like these. Though they didn't come along often, each assignment sharpened a skill she'd put to regular use in the decades ahead.

Hollywood, at this point, was more sophisticated than Collier's hayseed description of it during the Gold Rush. It was still not the sprawling metropolis that it would eventually become. Dorothy compared Hollywood in the 1930s to the idyllic community of Ridgefield, Connecticut. She loved it there. "The money was very attractive, and 'the living was easy,'" she said, quoting a lyric by her friends George and Ira Gershwin.[14] Part of this was owing to the amount of free time the writers had. A major distinction between working in New York and working in Los Angeles was the amount of time required to be with a project. In New York, the creators—composer, lyricist, librettist, director, and so on—worked collaboratively to generate a show. They were with it at every point, from conception to opening night. This was rewarding but also time-intensive. In Hollywood, the writers wrote their songs—generally very quickly—and handed them off to the film's director, whose job it was to stage and shoot the numbers. Often, Dorothy once remarked, they'd forget what they'd written until they saw it on the silver screen. "You become completely disassociated with it," she said. "That happened to me a couple of times. I was amazed at the songs we had written!"[15]

While most songwriters would admit that they missed the collaborative process that they'd known in New York, they also enjoyed the copious amounts of free time with which they found themselves in Los Angeles. They made the most of it. *Wizard of Oz* composer Harold Arlen, who, with lyricist Ted Koehler, had taken over songwriting duties after Dorothy and McHugh left the Cotton Club, called it "a great life. Most of us played golf or tennis or swam and did our writing at the same time. I wrote at home. I could write at midnight or at five in the afternoon, at nine, it made no difference, as long as I came in with something the so-called producers liked."[16] While Dorothy's habit had always been to work first thing in the morning, she definitely made the most of her free afternoons and evenings. She bought a sprawling house on Arden Drive in Beverly Hills. It became the base of operations for the entire Fields family. By then, brothers Joseph and Herbert were both in Los Angeles, writing screenplays. Even Lew and Rose had migrated west to avail themselves of their daughter's legendary hospitality. One writer referred to Dorothy as "one of those rare hostesses who can make a stranger feel he is paying a return visit at the home of friends."[17] It is impossible to find a record of anyone who knew Dorothy who did not agree with the writer's generous assessment. The door to the Fields's home was always open, and a steady stream of the nation's most talented tunesmiths were her frequent and welcomed guests.

In spite of the fun that they had, there was still work to be done; Dorothy and McHugh found themselves with plenty of it. Their other film endeavors included *Hooray for Love*, which featured Fields's old friend Bill "Bojangles" Robinson and Fats Waller, and an Alice Faye vehicle called *Every Night at Eight*. Writing for *Every Night at Eight* was an endeavor to which Dorothy, after her experience at WJZ, could particularly relate. The plot centered on amateur radio performers who rise through the ranks to become big stars. Several of the songs written for the film became standards—"I Feel a Song Comin' On," "Speaking Confidentially," and the second best-selling song of 1935, "I'm in the Mood for Love." At the expiration of her contract with MGM, Dorothy began to receive assignments from other studios. It was the first time since 1927 that she'd written with anyone other than Jimmy McHugh. As always, Dorothy thrived. She wrote Columbia Picture's *The King Steps Out*, with composer Fritz Kreisler (whom she never met). She also wrote *In Person* with Oscar Levant, but it was an assignment from the RKO studio that would change the course of Dorothy's career.

**Dorothy Fields, 1934 portrait.** Bettman/Getty Images.

She was asked by producer Pandro Berman to write a lyric for a melody that had been written by Jerome Kern. Kern was considered to be "the Dean" of American songwriters. Not only had his 1927 *Show Boat* heralded a new era for the American stage musical, but earlier his "Princess Musicals" (so named because they played New York's Princess Theatre) were among the nation's earliest examples of integrated storytelling. These were a teenaged Dorothy's first introduction to what she called "the respectable musical comedy."[18] Though Kern had written music for a number of shows that Lew Fields had either produced or starred in (he'd also written the score for *Miss 1917*, in which Herbert played), Dorothy had never met him, nor was Kern aware that Dorothy had been offered the assignment. He was a notorious curmudgeon who was respected by all and feared by most. Knowing this stern reputation, Dorothy was understandably nervous about taking the assignment, but never one to shy away from a challenge, she accepted it. Berman gave her one night to write a lyric to a tune Kern had written for a movie called *Roberta*.

While all of the other music had already been written for the film and the scenes shot, this particular number was originally planned as no more than underscoring for the moment that star Irene Dunne descends a staircase in an exquisite $8,000 costume. When Berman saw the costume, he thought, "She really should sing something in anything as expensive as that." The song needed to be one that could accomplish the double duty of both showing off the costume and expressing affection for Dunne's love interest, played by Randolph Scott. Ever the professional, Dorothy submitted the song "Lovely to Look At" right on time. Berman loved it. He was so confident that Kern would feel the same way that he had the number shot without Kern's approval. Everybody on the lot was nervous, anguishing through the two or three nights before Kern saw the scene for himself. They needn't have worried. "The Dean" was delighted with Dorothy's work. So was the Academy of Motion Picture Arts and Sciences. "Lovely to Look At" was nominated for an Oscar in 1935 and became the tenth best-selling song of the year.

> Lovely to look at,
> Delightful to know and Heaven to kiss.
> A combination like this
> Is quite my most impossible scheme come true.
> Imagine finding a dream like you!
> You're lovely to look at,
> It's thrilling to hold you terribly tight.
> For we're together, the moon is new,
> And oh, it's lovely to look at you tonight.

A few weeks later, Kern returned to California. He was anxious to meet his secret collaborator. When Dorothy walked into the room where he was sitting at the piano, Kern rose from the piano bench, walked over to Dorothy, and kissed her cheek in appreciation for her spectacular work. His next project was a picture called *I Dream Too Much* starring Lily Pons. He requested that Dorothy Fields do the lyrics. By June 5, she'd signed on to the assignment. She would be paid her customary $1,000 a week to write lyrics; Kern would be paid five times that as composer.

This was the beginning of the end for Dorothy's collaboration with McHugh. The pair would work together on another film or two, but the more she worked with Kern, the harder it became for her to continue writing with Jimmy McHugh. The pair's official split was announced in the August 21, 1935, issue of *Variety*. According to the article, they split because McHugh refused to accept a $1,000-a-week assignment from Twentieth Century Fox to write the music for Shirley Temple's *The Littlest Rebel*. He contended that the Robbins Music Corporation—the publishing house affiliated with MGM—didn't get the rights to publish the music. Instead, the Sam Fox Movietone Company would get them. McHugh resisted this, saying he wanted to prove his loyalty to Robbins, even though Robbins himself told McHugh to take the job.

This bizarre and abrupt conclusion to such a long-standing and successful partnership seems wildly suspicious. Perhaps McHugh was jealous of Dorothy's growing partnership with one of the greatest composers in the industry. McHugh longed to be considered of the same ilk as Kern, George Gershwin, or Irving Berlin. Maybe he couldn't handle that Dorothy seemed to be replacing him with one of his heroes. Maybe there was more to their relationship. Opinions on whether their collaboration reached beyond the professional are mixed. In her book *On the Sunny Side of the Street: The Life and Lyrics of Dorothy Fields*, Deborah Grace Winer suggests "their personal chemistry never clicked the way their songs did."[19] McHugh biographer Alyn Shipton implies the opposite, saying that after they went to Hollywood, the pair was "effectively a couple."[20] McHugh himself called the relationship "very friendly." When asked about the end of their collaboration, he responded,

> I don't think I should [say], because this is something of a personal nature. A lot of people have wanted to do life stories and wanted to make of Dorothy Fields and Jimmy McHugh all kinds of stories, but I don't think that I would ever permit it to be done, and I know Dorothy wouldn't want it, unless it was done in a very wholesome fashion. Dorothy was married to a very wonderful doctor . . . he was a dear friend of mine, and naturally, Dorothy is, and I will always love her forever, I think, because she was just one of the greatest.[21]

He added that, at the time of the interview (1959), they remained "very delightful friends." This may very well have been the case, but Dorothy was not nearly as exuberant when she was asked about McHugh in the early 1970s. Writer Max Wilk asked, "What was McHugh like as a collaborator?" Her terse response was "Very facile. Taught me a lot. I sat beside him at the piano and wrote as he composed."[22] This seems like a guarded answer, given the enormity of the success they shared. Dorothy could be downright effusive when talking about her later collaborations with Kern, Cy Coleman, and others. That she almost dismisses Wilk's question is a curious thing. It's certainly not evidence of impropriety, but it seems that there was more to the conclusion of their collaboration than meets the eye. The answer is one that is, most likely, lost to history. Whatever the rift may have been, it doesn't negate the incredible success of their eight-year partnership. Dorothy's continued collaboration with Kern wouldn't last as long as the one with McHugh, but it would be just as successful. She'd enter 1936 having written lyrics for two of the top ten songs of 1935. She was buoyed by the hope of a new partnership (the one that produced #10, "Lovely to Look At") and bolstered by the success of an old one (which produced #2, "I'm in the Mood for Love").

# Chapter 9
## "You Couldn't Be Cuter"

**Dorothy Fields and Jerome Kern, ca. 1936.** Photofest.

Jerome Kern, "the Dean" of American songwriters, had worked with lyricists from Ira Gershwin to Otto Harbach, P. G. Wodehouse to Anne Caldwell. In his work with Oscar Hammerstein II, Kern had helped to overhaul the shape of the modern musical. He could have had his pick of whichever collaborator he desired, yet, when given the opportunity to select a lyricist for his first endeavor after *Roberta*, Kern chose thirty-one-year-old Dorothy Fields. From the start, Dorothy and Kern were as thick as thieves. If the personal component of her partnership with McHugh was as cold as Winer suggests, then working with Kern was equally as warm. She had a habit of assigning nicknames to her friends and colleagues; Kern's was "Junior," because, at 5'5", slender Dorothy towered over his significantly shorter stature. Anyone who knew Kern was surprised that the persnickety perfectionist let her get away with the tease. His reputation with other writers was not good. "He didn't get along [with anyone]," Dorothy said. "He didn't have to get along. He'd walk into the studio and do what he had to do and go home."[1] With Dorothy, that was not the case. For all of his quirks and stern perfectionism, Kern allowed himself to be downright playful with his new partner. Years later, Dorothy would list Kern as her favorite collaborator; theirs was a "very wonderful association"[2] and "the most fun."[3]

It wasn't just Jerome Kern with whom Dorothy became close. She referred to his wife, Eva, and teenaged daughter, Betty, as family. They were constantly together. Almost every day, Dorothy would travel the fewer than two miles from her home on Arden to the Kern place at 917 Whittier Drive in Beverly Hills. Dorothy and Kern would do their work for the day. They always started relatively early. This had been a lifelong habit of Dorothy's, and it's one that she insisted was essential to good songwriting:

> The human being works best when he is freshest—and when is he freshest if not after his night's rest? It is poor creativity, which is fatigued creativity. Why wait until you are worn out by the day's activities before you start your serious work? That work, in my opinion, should come first.[4]

On this, she and Kern agreed. She would actually credit Kern with teaching her this discipline, yet there is evidence that she possessed the same ethic during her time with McHugh. Part of this, particularly later in her life, was practical. After her 1939 divorce from Wiener, Dorothy quickly remarried. The new couple's first child was born the following year, leaving Dorothy with a busy household to manage in addition to her flourishing career. She had to be sure both aspects of her life—work and home—were well attended to. First thing in the morning, she'd plan her menus and arrange the day for her husband and children. Then, she'd work until midday, taking a break for lunch and to watch a soap opera. Dorothy was well-known for writing on lined legal pads using blue pencils. She'd start each day with blank pages and an oversized wastebasket. "When the basket is filled, that's when I quit, no matter what time it is," she told a reporter.[5] "After that," she told another, "I'm a housewife."[6] Son David Lahm would later corroborate this, saying he rarely saw his mother work. "If there was a collaborator involved, there might be an afternoon session," he said. "I was at school. It all took place out of sight of my knowledge."[7] That she'd worked in this pattern from the outset of her career made the eventual transition into marriage and homelife easier for Dorothy, but it frustrated some of her later collaborators. Cy Coleman, at the time a confirmed bachelor who preferred to work way into the night, was particularly bothered by her 8 a.m. phone calls. Dorothy would later remark that "getting them up early"[8] was the only trouble she ever had in any of her collaborations. With Kern, her system agreed with his.

When the time came to visit the studio—the two of them worked most often, though not always, with RKO—she did the driving; Jerome Kern did not drive. In fact, Dorothy remembered Kern being cross with her only once, and the situation was brought about because of her car. She had recently been in Palm Springs with George Gershwin, who was helping her with her golf game. Gershwin had just purchased a beautiful new Cord car. Spectacularly stretched and shiny, with lots of chrome and giant white walls, it was one of the most beautiful automobiles Dorothy had ever seen. She bought herself one in the same bright blue as the pencils that she always used to write her lyrics. A few days later, she arrived on Whittier Drive, full of pride and excited to show off her new purchase. Kern was disgusted. He refused to ride in her "vulgar, repulsive car."[9] In response, she kept the car but had it painted black.

After *Roberta*, the pair's first assignment was *I Dream Too Much*. The picture, originally called *Love Song*, starred French coloratura Lily Pons in her film debut and featured a young Lucille Ball in the secondary role of Gwendolyn Dilley. Though reviews called it a "pleasant if somewhat minor operatic comedy," which "suffers from inaction and a limited sense of humor,"[10] Dorothy and Kern added four songs to the score, including "I Got Love" and a number that Pandro Berman liked so much he changed the film's title to match it, "I Dream Too Much." They also wrote music for *When You're in Love* (1937), *Joy of Living* (1938), and *One Night in the Tropics* (1940). Without a doubt, their most successful collaboration was the 1936 movie musical *Swing Time*, an RKO vehicle for Fred Astaire and Ginger Rogers who'd been voted the country's box office champions. Originally called *I Won't Dance*, the film's title was changed because studio executives were afraid audiences would hear the name and assume there was no dancing in the film. Instead, the newly monikered *Swing Time* hit cinemas that September. *Swing Time* is the story of Lucky Garnett (Astaire), a dancer and gambler, who misses his own wedding. The father of the bride insists that, before Lucky can try again to marry his daughter, he must earn $25,000 as proof of his good intentions. Lucky goes to New York in search of his fortune, but instead, he finds dance instructor Penny Carroll (Rogers). One reviewer called it the "thinnest story Astaire and Rogers have had to work with," but added that the film "is gay, smart entertainment built around one of the few perfect things in motion pictures—the dancing of Fred Astaire."[11]

Dorothy and Kern were hired to write the score. This was new. Typically, writers were called upon to write three or four songs for a film. That Dorothy and Kern were charged with scoring the whole thing was a departure from the norm, but they were certainly up to the assignment. They wrote most of what would become *Swing Time* in a suite at the Beverly-Wilshire Hotel (this was prior to the completion of Kern's home on Whittier Drive). While some numbers came easily to Kern, others did not. The syncopation of "Bojangles of Harlem" was particularly difficult for him. Astaire joined Dorothy and Kern for several days, as they worked on the song. As Kern continued to struggle, Astaire was frustrated with some of what he'd heard. Kern stepped out for a moment, and Astaire pulled Dorothy aside asking, "Can we ever get a tune that I can dance to?" When Kern returned, Astaire hoofed all over the room in an attempt to inspire Kern. It worked. Eventually, the Dean composed "Bojangles of Harlem," an energetic dance number performed to his usual perfection by a very relieved Fred Astaire.

Other songs written for the film include "Never Gonna Dance" and the only two numbers for which Dorothy penned the lyrics prior to Kern's writing the music. One of these is "Pick Yourself Up." This timeless number about tireless persistence was quoted by President Barack Obama in his 2009 inaugural address. The other is "A Fine Romance." Kern called this one "a sarcastic love ballad." It brilliantly showcases Dorothy's verbal acuity, that she was capable of expressing love both directly and indirectly. Taking inspiration from the fact that, in each of their six films together, Astaire had refused to kiss Rogers—he said their on-screen romance should be evident in their dancing instead—Dorothy captured the exasperation of Rogers's character with phrases, like "A fine romance with no kisses" and "I've never mussed the crease in your blue serge pants / I never get the chance." The song goes on in this same manner and is a textbook example of Dorothy's use of ordinary phrases ("yesterday's mashed potatoes," "I'll take Jell-O") to express extraordinary feelings. It's also an example of something highly unusual in the music of the period—a female character willingly expressing her own sexuality, frustrated though it may have been:

A fine romance, with no kisses
A fine romance, my friend, this is!
We should be like a couple of hot tomatoes,
But you're as cold as yesterday's mashed potatoes.
A fine romance, you won't nestle,
A fine romance, you won't wrestle
I might as well play bridge with my old maid aunt.
I haven't got a chance.
This is a fine romance!

A fine romance, my good fellow
You take romance, I'll take Jell-O
You're calmer than the seals in the Arctic Ocean
At least, they flap their fins to express emotion.
A fine romance with no quarrels
With no insults and all morals
I've never mussed the crease in your blue-serge pants
I never get the chance.
This is a fine romance!

The most successful song in the score was almost dropped from it. For all of his accolades, Kern was somewhat insecure. Dorothy told the story of them being together at one of the many parties attended by the tight-knit group of songwriters in Hollywood—Sigmund Romberg, Harry Ruby, Harold Arlen, Harry Warren, and others. As typically happened, the convivial crowd asked George Gershwin to sit down and play the piano. As Dorothy drove him home from the party, Kern asked, "Why doesn't anyone ever ask me to play? Don't they like my songs?" The truth was, his songs weren't the problem at all. Gershwin was just a much better piano player than Kern. The insecurity showed up as he composed too. Kern used a bust of Wagner—Kern was a huge fan of opera; Dorothy was too—as a litmus test for how the new work would be received. Kern kept the bust on his piano. Whenever Kern played a new number for someone, he'd gage their interest in the piece by the response they gave to the song. If the response wasn't energetic enough for his liking, Kern would turn the bust around and say, "Wagner isn't smiling; he doesn't like it." The song would then fall onto the cutting room floor. On the day that Dorothy first heard the melody to "The Way You Look Tonight," she walked to the piano, which was covered, as she recalled, in "baskets of pencils and erasers and all the junk in the world." Kern began to play; Dorothy listened, blank-faced. "Honestly, there was something so poignantly beautiful about the release of that song," she said. Seeing her dazed response, Kern assumed the worst. "He turned the bust of Wagner around and said, 'Well, alright; we won't use it.'" As soon as she'd collected herself, Dorothy informed Kern that "Wagner" was way off. Not only did she like the song, she loved it. She set out to work on the lyric that would win them both an Academy Award.

> Someday, when I'm awf'ly low,
> When the world is cold
> I will feel a glow just thinking of you,
> And the way you look tonight.
>
> Lovely, with your smile so warm
> And your cheeks so soft
> There is nothing for me but to love you
> And the way you look tonight.
>
> (RELEASE)
> With each word, your tenderness grows,
> Tearing my fears apart!
> And that laugh that wrinkles your nose
> Touches my foolish heart
>
> Lovely, never, ever change.
> Keep that breathless charm,
> Won't you please arrange it, 'cause I love you.
> Just the way you look tonight.

The Academy Awards were nine years old when Dorothy earned her statue. On March 4, 1937, more than 1,200 people packed the ballroom in the Los Angeles

**Dorothy Fields and Walt Disney, both of whom won an Oscar at the 1937 Academy Awards.** Copyright © Academy of Motion Picture Arts and Sciences.

Biltmore Hotel for the ceremony that was hosted by actor/producer George Jessel. "The Way You Look Tonight" was chosen from among a slate of nominees that included "Did I Remember?" (Walter Donaldson, music; Harold Adamson, lyrics), "I've Got You under My Skin" (Cole Porter, words and music), "A Melody from the Sky" (Louis Alter, music; Sidney Mitchell, lyrics), "Pennies from Heaven" (Arthur Johnston, music; Johnny Burke, lyrics), and "When Did You Leave Heaven?" (Richard A. Whiting, music; Walter Bullock, lyrics). Dorothy was, understandably, thrilled to be recognized for her work. She was the first woman to win an Oscar in the songwriting category. Remarkably, she was the only woman to hold the distinction for more than thirty years. The next woman to win an Oscar for Best Original Song was Marilyn Bergman. She and her husband Alan co-wrote the lyrics to the 1968 winner, "The Windmills of Your Mind" from *The Thomas Crown Affair*. At the time of this book's writing, the Oscars have been awarded for nine decades. Fewer than fifteen women have taken home the statue for songwriting. Dorothy was always self-assured, confident of her ability;

nevertheless, years later, her Oscar still sat, dead center, toward the rear of her desk. The recognition meant a great deal to her.

After *Swing Time*, Dorothy and Kern wrote music for several more films. During that time, Dorothy was also connected to other composers, including one of the songwriters she'd competed against for the Academy Award. A September 1937 notice in *Variety* indicated that Dorothy had signed on to write lyrics for the music of Arthur Johnston ("Pennies from Heaven"). The notice attributes this to "Kern's general indisposition, which necessitates creative inactivity for a year or so."[12] Though there's no indication that the Fields/Johnston project ever got off the ground, the information about Kern in the notice suggests a reason why Dorothy's output in the late 1930s slows to a handful of songs for a single film a year. It also explains why she would jump at the invitation to return to New York in 1939 in order to write a Broadway musical with her friend Arthur Schwartz.

# Chapter 10
## "A Lady Needs Change"

The more Hollywood continued to grow, the less Dorothy liked it. After five consecutive "Golden Years,"[1] as she called them, on the West Coast, she was ready to spend more of her time back East where she and composer Arthur Schwartz immediately went to work on a show he'd come up with called *Swing to the Left*. With a libretto by novelist and essayist J. P. McEvoy, the musical was a biting satire of Hollywood with enough politically charged themes to thrill the activist members of the Group Theatre. Labor unions were particularly on the skewer in the show. Dorothy and Schwartz wrote a hilariously satirical song called "My New Kentucky Home" in which even the sun works an eight-hour shift, having given in to union pressure. From there, the writers set up a scenario involving a movie studio that hires a left-leaning screenwriter intent on elevating the industry with his heady brand of filmmaking. He runs into trouble with his leading lady, a hot-headed vamp who's more Mae West than Eleanor Roosevelt. Director Josh Logan, who'd later direct *Annie Get Your Gun* (1945) and co-write *South Pacific* (1949), would have none of it. According to Schwartz, Logan warned his fellow creators:

> Leftist themes are fine for a revue . . . since it's a revue's right to criticize, but why clutter up a gay musical narrative with weighty commentary? . . . why fret Ethel Merman with problems of "unearned increment," "self-determinism," and "ideology" when she performs a kinder service to mankind vibrating the rafters with a rhythm song.[2]

When it opened at the Majestic Theatre on February 9, 1939, Logan had won. The musical had been significantly depoliticized; "My New Kentucky Home" had been removed, because, without the context of the story as originally written, it was no longer funny. The show's name was changed to *Stars in Your*

*Eyes*. The cast included Jimmy Durante and a chorus boy named Jerome Robbins in one of his first Broadway shows. It was most notable, however, as the first of several professional collaborations of Dorothy and the friend she called "Mermsy," known to audiences as Ethel Merman. Merman played Jeanette Adair, the Hollywood star with a violent temper, who's filming on Sound Stage Seven of the Monotone Picture Corporation. Brooks Atkinson's review of the show, as reimagined by Logan, was ecstatic. He borrowed Jimmy Durante's word "exubilant" to describe the "musical jamboree," which featured the "gustiest performance[s]" of both Merman's and Durante's careers.[3] This is significant. Merman had made her Broadway debut, belting the iconic "I Got Rhythm" in the original company of George and Ira Gershwin's 1930 *Girl Crazy*. In 1934, she introduced the inimitable character of Reno Sweeney in Cole Porter's *Anything Goes*. Durante was, according to Atkinson's review of 1936's *Red, Hot, and Blue* (another Cole Porter vehicle, which starred both Merman and Durante), "one of the most likable influences in showbusiness." That Atkinson thought so highly of their performances in *Stars in Your Eyes* speaks volumes about his opinion of the show.[4] Though the original intent of Dorothy, Schwartz, and McEvoy had been drastically altered by Logan, it stands as proof that Dorothy had grander visions for the potential of the American musical to be a form with something to say instead of just something to sing about. The situation is instructive about Dorothy as a collaborator too. She was certainly willing to stand her ground when called upon to do so, yet, for all of her success, she was reasonable enough to make concessions when called upon for the good of the show. Whether Logan's changes truly were for the good of the show will never be known. *Stars in Your Eyes* ran for a disappointing 127 performances (Merman remembered it as "an undervalued gem"[5]); it is impossible to know if *Swing to the Left* would have been a bigger hit.

Happy to be working again on Broadway, Dorothy was also ready to try again at marriage. Though she and Jack Wiener had remained together, their relationship had been purely a legal one for more than a decade. Citing their several years of separation, Dorothy was granted a divorce in June of 1939. Afterward, as one paper put it, she "went back to her Beverly Hills home and continued lyric writing."[6] It was almost as if the whole thing had never happened. At some point during the long separation, Dorothy had been introduced to a man named Eli Lahm. Like Wiener, Lahm was older than Dorothy. Thirteen years her senior and an executive with a blouse manufacturer, Lahm immediately captured Dorothy's attention. She was smitten with him. They'd been introduced by a mutual friend named Herbert Sondheim, who was, like Lahm, in the clothing industry. Sondheim was a dressmaker, specializing in affordable versions of Parisian fashion. His wife, Janet, better known as "Foxy," was one of his chief designers. Together, the Sondheims threw magnificent parties. The smartest set was frequently found at their apartment in the tony San Remo building on Central Park West. Both Dorothy and Lahm were often on the guest lists. On July 14, 1939, the day before

Dorothy's thirty-fifth birthday, the two married. Not much is known about the ceremony; as with her wedding with Wiener, there was no fanfare in the newspapers. She probably preferred it that way; nevertheless, Dorothy and Lahm settled very quickly into a happy routine of domestic life. Lahm was said to be "nuts about her,"[7] and she relished her new role as wife. It's likely that she was more ready to assume the role as a monumentally successful thirty-something woman than she'd been as a twenty-year-old girl who felt forced by her parents to marry yet still wasn't sure exactly what shape she wanted her life to take. Though not many specifics are known about their relationship—there are few pictures and even less anecdotal information—Dorothy and Lahm seemed to be happy together in ways that she and Wiener never were.

Ironically, the Sondheims' marriage didn't play out the same way. They were divorced the year after Dorothy and Eli were married. In the aftermath of her 1940 split from Herbert, Foxy and their son Stephen moved to a country house in Bucks County, Pennsylvania. There, the ten-year-old boy soon befriended a neighbor named Jimmy Hammerstein, who was the younger of Oscar Hammerstein II's two boys. Eventually, Stephen Sondheim himself would become a lyricist and composer and a great fan of the work of the woman he called "Aunt Dorothy." In fact, songs written for his 1971 musical *Follies* were each a pastiche of different songwriters from the 1920s and 1930s. The lyrics for the number called "Losing My Mind" were written in the style of Dorothy Fields, whose work Sondheim loved.[8]

Dorothy was ready for some new endeavors. She'd risen to the top of the songwriting ranks and had the Academy Award to prove it. Financially, she was independent and secure in ways that most people have never experienced. Personally, she was in a romantic relationship that was fulfilling and rewarding to her, but professionally, she needed a new challenge; brother Herbert had an idea. After his success as a Broadway librettist in the 1920s and early 1930s, Herbert had joined the rest of the Fields family in Hollywood. He'd applied his writing ability to screenplays and amassed a handful of credits in the film industry. While helping Dorothy and Jerome Kern to develop the story idea for *The Joy of Living* (though they contributed to the story, they did not write its screenplay), Herbert was impressed with his sister's storytelling. In the "chip-off-the-old-block" way the Fields children often related to one another, Herbert said, "Nobody told me that Dorothy could turn a phrase as expertly as she could rhyme 'June' and 'moon.' I had to find out for myself. When I did, I said to her, 'Quick. Let's get on this!'"[9] Clever Dorothy, who could match her brother joke for joke, said about the proposition, "Herbert gets lonesome when he writes."[10] Kidding aside, she jumped at his suggestion and set out to add "Screenwriter" to her long list of accomplishments.

Their first assignment was for a film called *Father Takes a Wife*. Four days after completing her work on the script, thirty-six-year-old Dorothy delivered her first child. David Fields Lahm was born in December of 1940. Dorothy could not have been happier to, finally, become a mother. Though busy attending to her infant son, she still found time to continue collaborating with her older brother. While awaiting the September 1941 premiere of the film, the new mother co-wrote the first of eight Broadway librettos with Herbert. *Let's Face It!*—with music and lyrics by Cole Porter—premiered in October of 1941; it was the first of three times Herbert and Dorothy would work with Cole Porter (Herbert had worked with Porter several times prior to joining forces with his sister). Dorothy was as busy as she'd ever been, and she'd hardly written a song all year. The dramatist in her, which had first shown itself as she pored through her father's reviews when keeping his scrapbooks as a little girl, was coming into its own. She was thrilled; Lew was too. The basis of *Let's Face It!* was a 1925 play called *Cradle Snatchers*. Lew had wanted to make a musical out of the piece by Norma Mitchell and Russell Medcraft for years, but he never got around to it. When Herbert and Dorothy remembered the story, no one was more excited to see the project revisited than their father. The man who had told his children, "What book? In a musical? . . . Give them laughs, gags, blackouts, belly laughs . . . They don't come to a musical comedy for a story!"[11] had changed his tune. As she and Herbert pounded out the pages for *Let's Face It!*, Lew constantly looked over their shoulders, asking, "The book! The book! Where's the book? What's the storyline?"

**Dorothy Fields with her brothers, Herbert Fields and Joseph Fields, ca. 1939.** Photofest.

Unfortunately, he didn't live to judge the quality of their efforts. Lew Fields died on July 21, 1941. The seventy-four-year-old comedian, whose final performance had been playing himself (opposite Weber) in a 1940 biopic of Lillian Russell, succumbed to complications of pneumonia. Joseph and Herbert were working in New York when their father died, but Lew was surrounded by his daughters, his wife, and his partner, Joe Weber, as he passed (Weber, who was born less than a year after Lew, would also die less than a year after his long-time stage partner). Dorothy would mourn the loss of her father for the rest of her life. Though he'd battled against her desire to work in the theater, Lew had long since laid down his arms. He was, Dorothy said, "inordinately proud"[12] of his magnificently successful children; they, too, were inordinately proud of their remarkably uncommon father. The season after Lew Fields passed, three of his children would account for four different shows on Broadway, prompting Dorothy to wistfully comment, "How I wish Pop were here now."[13]

Just a few months after their father's death, Dorothy and Herbert celebrated two major openings. The first of these was their one and only film collaboration, *Father Takes a Wife*. Produced by RKO and directed by Jack Hively, the movie was something of a real-life *Sunset Boulevard* for its leading lady, Gloria Swanson. Swanson, superstar of silent film, had been absent from the silver screen for the better part of a decade. *Father Takes a Wife* was to be her triumphant return. If the film's reviews were any indication, Dorothy's decision to try her hand at screenwriting was a wise one. In the *New York Times*:

> It is doubtful if Gloria Swanson could have hit upon a more complimentary vehicle to end [her] absence from the screen . . . Dorothy and Herbert Fields have provided the silent film queen with an amusing comedy which permits her to run the familiar gamut without ever taxing her capabilities as an actress.[14]

*The Chicago Tribune* called it "ver-ree [*sic*] funny," adding "the dialog [*sic*] is so snappy . . . that you never get a moment's let down."[15] Lew would have been pleased. He also would have been happy with the way Dorothy and Herbert handled their adaptation of *Cradle Snatchers*. The new show—now called *Let's Face It!*—opened at Broadway's Imperial Theatre on October 29, 1941. It starred song and dance man Danny Kaye and featured Nanette Fabray, Vivian Vance, and Eve Arden, who was understudied by a then-unknown Carol Channing. When they'd settled on the source material, Dorothy and Herbert thought they'd make easy work of updating the fifteen-year-old story. As they got going, they realized how antiquated it was. They were able to maintain the original premise—three married women who attempt to make their philandering husbands jealous—but were otherwise forced to develop totally new situations. The outcome of their work, coupled with Porter's music and Danny Kaye's comedic talent, was a recipe for stage magic. The show played a whopping 547 performances, closing in March of 1943. Some of its success may have been owed to the timing of its opening. Premiering on Broadway a mere six weeks before the attack on Pearl Harbor, the show offered audiences a welcome reprieve from the tensions that were mounting in the world outside the theater walls. The comic relief quickly reached around the globe: there were also companies at the Hippodrome Theatre in London (where the show ran for 348 performances) and at His Majesty's Theatre in Melbourne, Australia. Rights for a movie adaptation were sold for $225,000, the 2020 equivalent of nearly $3,500,000. The film, which opened in 1943, starred Bob Hope in the role originated by Danny Kaye. With scriptwriting, Dorothy Fields had found something else at which she excelled. Needless to say, she and Herbert decided to continue their collaboration.

After the difficulty they'd had updating *Cradle Snatchers* to make *Let's Face It!*, the pair tried to write only original stories from that point on. That wasn't always possible, but for their next project, again with Porter, they were able to start from the ground up. They called on one of the earliest lessons Dorothy learned in her days at Mills Music: she took her inspiration from what was happening in the world around her. In the case of *Something for the Boys*, which was written in the thick of World War II, their central character was a war worker from Newark, New Jersey. Her name was Blossom Hart. Ethel Merman played the role, reuniting Dorothy and her friend in their first show together, since *Stars in Your Eyes*. Blossom finds out she and two new-to-her cousins—Chiquita, a burlesque dancer, and Harry, a carnival barker—inherit equal shares in a Texas ranch that backs up to an airfield. Because the ranch brings in no revenue, the cousins decide to operate it as a boarding house for soldiers' wives. The lieutenant colonel in charge of the field gets the wrong idea about the ranch; he orders it closed but not before the daughter of a prominent senator is seen there, which invites an investigation by the US government. Backed by Twentieth Century Fox, the show cost nearly $140,000 to produce. It previewed in both Philadelphia and Boston, where a reviewer for the *Daily Boston Globe* noted, "Herbert and Dorothy Fields have a nice collective wit for musical show books . . . *Something for the Boys* is gay and lively and with enough of a military motif to make it topical."[16]

With positive notices and strong word of mouth from its tryout performances, the show returned to Broadway with a nearly record-breaking $120,000 in advance sales. Reception to its January 7, 1943, opening was as warm in New York as it had been out of town. In the *Wall Street Journal*, Richard P. Cooke called *Something for the Boys* "something for everybody." He also admitted that the Fields siblings had "composed a book, which is absurd to the analytical mind but eminently suitable to the circumstances."[17] It ran for exactly one year at the Alvin Theatre and was Herbert and Dorothy's first time to work with producing wunderkind Michael Todd. Todd had made his Broadway debut with 1937's *Call Me, Ziggy*. That show was short-lived, as was the one that followed after it, 1938's *The Man from Cairo*, but he started to get the attention of the theatrical establishment with his 1939 production of *The Hot Mikado*. Adapted from Gilbert and Sullivan's operetta *The Mikado* and inspired by the Federal Theatre Project's Chicago production of *Swing Mikado*, *The Hot Mikado* featured an

**Dorothy and Herbert Fields at a 1943 rehearsal.** Walter Sanders/Getty Images.

all-black cast led by Bill "Bojangles" Robinson. It was universally loved. Burns Mantle wrote in the *New York Daily News* that the show was staged "with such perfect timing and in such excellent taste that it stands absolutely unrivaled so far as my playgoing experience is concerned."[18] Other luminaries took note. As legend goes, Lee Shubert was so excited by the show that he came backstage at intermission on opening night and offered to buy a fifty percent stake in what he was sure would be a megahit; Todd declined the offer, later telling one reporter he'd made the decision by the flip of a coin. Cole Porter saw *Hot Mikado* seven times during its two and a half month run on Broadway. The two would later work together on a pair of shows, an arrangement likely inspired by Porter's love of Todd's *Mikado*. In spite of Broadway's excitement about the show, Todd did what no one expected him to. He closed it. He then announced it'd reopen at the New York World's Fair. Between its two New York engagements, *Hot Mikado* played more than six hundred performances and was seen by more than one million people before taking off on its nationwide tour. Todd's gamble had paid off. His P. T. Barnum–like flamboyance quickly earned him the reputation of being a producer who liked to

> dream up new ways of doing old things. The secret of his success is not that he manages to do the impossible but that he always seems to find a novel approach to something which others have been content to do the same way year in and year out. Where tradition is concerned, he is nothing more or less than a vandal.[19]

Further evidence of Todd's "novel approach" to both life and business is found in the story of his joining the Navy at age thirty-six. The fact that the impresario had one show running on Broadway, another on the road, and two more in the works didn't stop the Minneapolis native from submitting to his civic duty. He patriotically signed on, assuming, as Dorothy Kilgallen reported in her "Voice of Broadway" column, "no matter where he goes, there'll be a telephone, so he'll carry on via Alex G. Bell."[20] Though there are several mentions in various newspapers of Todd being assessed for the Navy, one has to wonder if the whole induction was another publicity stunt. The idea was first mentioned in March of 1944. He was to report that month. There is no indication, however, that he ever actually did. On the contrary, the historical record shows him renting a West Fifty-Sixth Street office space in May of 1944, arranging a Paris company of his show *Stars and Garters* in September of 1944, and auditioning players for his new musical in November of 1944, but nowhere is there a mention of him serving overseas. Perhaps the whole charade was intended to draw attention to the military themes of *Something for the Boys*. Regardless, the Navy's loss was Herbert and Dorothy's gain. The show's New York production ran concurrently with Todd's 1942 opener, a burlesque revue called *Stars and Garters*. Together, the shows grossed $60,000 a week. That same year, *Something for the Boys* was made into a film. Vivian Blaine played the role originated by Ethel Merman. Carmen Miranda and Phil Silvers played her cousins, Chiquita and Harry. The Fieldses' new producer, unconventional as could be, was at the top of his game.

Herbert and Dorothy's third collaboration with Cole Porter would be their second with Michael Todd. *Mexican Hayride* opened at the Winter Garden Theatre on January 28, 1944. Just three weeks earlier, Dorothy had delivered her second child—a daughter named Eliza—at Doctor's Hospital. There is a noticeable slowdown in Dorothy's workload when her children were small. This was her intentional choice. That her quantity of work dipped does not mean that the quality of it did. Though she continued to co-produce a libretto every year or two, she was no longer crisscrossing the country, as she had done throughout the 1930s. She wanted to be as available as possible for David and Eliza, while still maintaining a vibrant career that she absolutely loved. "My first interest, of course, is my home and my children," she said. "Then, of course, my profession and my friends."[21] *Mexican Hayride* was Herbert and Dorothy's final collaboration with

**The Fields family in 1943 (clockwise from right) Frances Fields Marcus Friedlander, Dorothy Fields, Rose Fields, Joseph Fields, Herbert Fields.** Walter Sanders/Getty Images.

Cole Porter. Dorothy loved working with Porter but recalled that he was not very concerned about the book—or attending rehearsals (Dorothy preferred to attend most, if not all, of rehearsals). He'd come to some. Mostly, though, he'd just write the songs and hand them over to the Fieldses to set in the show.

Elsewhere on Broadway, lyricists and librettists alike were beginning to think of the story as equal in importance to the songs. Certainly, this is how Dorothy and Herbert felt. Dorothy resisted the label of "popular songwriter." Though she'd written songs that became popular, a distinction she'd often make, she was a dramatist at her core. She saw the story of a show as "all-important" and insisted that "no musical can be successful unless the story will hold the audience."[22] Son David Lahm rightly suggested that her understanding of this made her an even stronger songwriter. "By writing book, I think she began to understand how a song could help the audience understand a character or how a song could move the story along," he said.[23] Perhaps she'd learned this from Jerome Kern, one of the earliest dramatists to adapt this way of looking at things, or maybe their agreement on the matter is what made them such successful collaborators. After the premiere of *Swing Time*, Kern said that the story is the pace setter for the music. "If a song stands out like a sore thumb, there is something radically wrong," he said.[24]

Increasingly in the 1940s, this was becoming the hallmark of a new kind of musical. Dorothy rightly suggested that her friends Richard Rodgers and Oscar Hammerstein II led the charge on the change. Their *Oklahoma*, which was a 1943 adaptation of Lynn Riggs's play *Green Grow the Lilacs* and the first of Rodgers and Hammerstein's eleven collaborations, started where Kern and Hammerstein had left off with 1927's *Show Boat*. Both Dorothy and reviewers like Lewis Nichols of the *New York Times* suggested that, for its emphasis on compelling storytelling, this new kind of musical ought to be called a "musical play" rather than a "musical comedy." There were several reasons for this change. First, audience tastes changed. As they matured, dramatists had to keep pace. The Group Theatre and others like it had helped to introduce psychological realism to the legitimate theater. This began to spill over into the world of musicals. Each element— singing, dancing, acting—had to keep pace. A second reason for the change was a more pragmatic one. Most early musical comedies had been built around the star power of a singularly sensational leading man or lady—Fred Astaire, for instance, or Al Jolson. As these personalities left the stages of the East Coast to make movies out West, the talent pool on Broadway was just as deep but not as well known. Theater makers, deprived of the strength of their stars, suddenly had to find strength in something else: most often, this was the story. Dorothy Fields was proud to be a part of this change. The next phase of her career would find her mastering her new skills as a librettist while renewing her experience as a lyricist.

# Chapter 11
## "Close as Pages in a Book"

The idea for what would become *Up in Central Park* started in the mind of its producer Michael Todd. After their highly successful collaborations on *Something for the Boys* and *Mexican Hayride*, Todd suggested that his next endeavor with Dorothy and Herbert Fields be a musical inspired by the look and feel of a Currier and Ives painting. These images would certainly have been very familiar to American audiences. Nathaniel Currier and James Ives were the Norman Rockwells of the nineteenth century. Active between the years of 1835 and 1907 (Ives joined Currier Press in 1852 and, by 1857, the company bore both men's names), the artists and those who worked with them were known for low-cost lithographs depicting American life. A *New York Times* writer described the prints as "marvelous scenes full of the beauty of an unspoiled America, landscapes reflecting idyllic and ideal aspirations." These "predecessors of photojournalism"[1] had become popular when the *New York Sun* commissioned Currier to do a print of the 1840 sinking of the steamship *Lexington*. In the years that followed, the firm would generate more than 7,000 images, many of them now iconic depictions of life in the ever-expanding United States. Some of these were sold via street vendors; others were disseminated as marketing materials by corporations who'd use the prints to fill calendars or decorate candy tins and liquor labels. For a small amount of money—depending on size, prints sold for between twenty-five cents and four dollars each—Americans could decorate their homes with Currier and Ives' pastoral vision of life as they knew it.

Popularity of the prints never dipped. The firm dissolved in 1907, having been run by heirs of Nathaniel Currier and James Ives, since the men died in 1888 and 1895 respectively, but their massive body of work lived on. Prints continued to be highly collectible with many selling for several hundred dollars apiece in the 1930s. In the hyper-nationalistic aftermath of World War II, Currier and Ives' depictions of Americana were even more the rage. Perhaps this is what drew Todd to the idea. Composer Leroy Anderson wasn't far behind him. He started writing the song that would become "Sleigh Ride" in 1946. Four years later, Mitchell Parish would immortalize Currier and Ives by mentioning their "picture prints" in the lyric he'd set to Anderson's beloved tune. Herbert and Dorothy Fields were intrigued with Todd's suggestion of a Currier and Ives–inspired musical; they immediately thought that Central Park would make the perfect setting for Todd's concept and went in search of the all-important story to go along with it. One of their first stops was the morgue of the *New York Times*. There, the pair pored through stacks and stacks of decades-old newspapers, looking for a suitable scenario. When they came across the so-called "Boss Tweed scandal," they knew they were onto something. William Magear "Boss" Tweed was the leader of New York City's Tammany Hall political organization in the 1860s and '70s. Tweed and his associates would stop at nothing to maintain control of the city's Democratic machine—buying votes, embezzling city funds, fixing contract competitions, none of these were beyond the scope of what Tweed and company were willing to do in order to have their way. A series of investigative articles in the *New York Times* exposed Tweed and the corruption of his team. Together with the efforts of *Harper's Weekly* cartoonist Thomas Nast, the *Times* articles led to the dismantling of the Tweed Ring—and to the perfect setup for Dorothy and Herbert's new show. They'd tell the tale from the perspective of a fictional *Times* reporter named John Matthews, who'd broken the story about the fraud related to the construction of Central Park. In the doing of it, he'd fallen in love with Rosie Moore, who, as fate would have it, was the daughter of one of Tweed's men.

With their story in place, they just needed a composer. Dorothy recommended Sigmund Romberg. "Rommie," as she called him, had a long history with the Fields family. He'd written nine songs for Lew's *Poor Little Ritz Girl* (Rodgers and Hart had provided the other seven). Best known for operettas like 1924's *The Student Prince*, Romberg was the perfect person to take on a score for a show set in the late nineteenth century. He'd been on a three-year hiatus from Broadway and hadn't written a new musical in twelve years. When the call came from Dorothy, "Rommie" was ready to get back to work. Together, the two contributed songs like "It Doesn't Cost You Anything to Dream," "When She Walks in the Room," and "Close as Pages in a Book." Dorothy's lyrics for the show were "worthy of her own high standard." Romberg's music was "ingenious, tuneful, and charming." The show was a hit. After its opening on January 27, 1945, Todd hosted a spectacular party held, appropriately, at Central Park's Tavern on the Green. He hired hansom cabs to transport his more than five hundred guests from the Century Theatre to the park. With food "reminiscent of the pre-war days," drinks, and dancing, one writer said of the party, "If you didn't have a good time, it was your own fault."[2]

Dorothy Fields was thriving. Happy at both work and home, she was, once again, a vital part of the New York theater community; it felt good to be back home. In addition to her lives both personal and professional, Dorothy was well known for her significant involvements with different charities. Among other things, she, at different times, served as Chairman of the Manhattan Business and Professional Women's Campaign Committee for the Girl Scouts; she was the chairman of the Theatrical Women's Division of the Federation of Jewish Philanthropic Societies of New York; and, with composer Burton Lane, she wrote songs to benefit the American Heart Association. Though incredibly busy, Dorothy made time throughout her long career to support those causes in which she so deeply believed. One of those causes was the Stage Door Canteen.

**Dorothy Fields at the Stage Door Canteen, ca. 1943.** Photo by Carl Van Vechten, used with permission, © Van Vechten Trust.

During World War II, the Canteen was operated by the American Theatre Wing. The wing itself was the second coming of an organization founded during World War I by prolific playwright and director Rachel Crothers, whose nearly thirty Broadway outings included *The Three of Us* (1906), *Nice People* (1921), and *As Husbands Go* (1933). In 1917, she'd assembled a group of six other women to form what was called the Stage Women's War Relief. Together, these theater artists—and the others who joined them—raised money and provided entertainment for the US troops. The group disbanded a few years after the war ended, but at the outset of World War II, the federal government asked Crothers and company to revive their efforts. The American Theatre Wing was born. In its new iteration, the Wing was placed under the able direction of Jane Cowl, a playwright, actor, and director, and actor Selena Royle. Among the other ways in which the Wing contributed to the war effort was its support of the Stage Door Canteen. Housed in the basement of the 44th Street Theatre—which, at its 1912 opening, had been the Weber and Fields Music Hall—the Stage Door Canteen was a place where servicemen of any ilk could go to be fed and entertained by Broadway's brightest lights. Similar venues sprang up in Boston, Cleveland, Los Angeles, Newark, Philadelphia, San Francisco, and Washington, DC. Overseas, there were canteens in Paris and London. Seven nights a week, two thousand uniformed servicemen were fed, served, and entertained by artists, all of whom donated their time and talents to the cause—among them was Dorothy Fields. Dorothy was the "captain of the kitchen"; Alfred Lunt, the famed actor and director, was a dishwasher in her "employ." As she worked her shift one night, Dorothy was chatting with a lady[3] from the Traveler's Aid organization. Traveler's Aid, which had been in operation since 1851, was designated by President Franklin Roosevelt as one of six social service entities that comprised the United Service Organizations (USO). In that capacity, representatives from Traveler's Aid assisted troops in transit. The Traveler's Aid volunteer told Dorothy about a young sergeant she'd met; he'd just returned from Coney Island and came in with a row of sharpshooter's medals stretched across his shirt. Inspiration dropped "from God's hands into" hers when Dorothy heard the word "sharpshooter." She thought, "Gosh, wouldn't it be marvelous to have Ethel Merman as Annie Oakley?"[4]

She and Herbert "owed" Ethel a show, Dorothy said. "Mermsy" and Dorothy were both dear friends and frequent collaborators. As such, Dorothy "knew [Merman's] every mood and every mannerism."[5] The notion of musicalizing the story of Annie Oakley may have come to Fields as quickly as she'd later describe it, but it's also possible that the idea had been ruminating, however subconsciously, since her brother Joseph had contributed to the screenplay for a 1935 film in which Barbara Stanwyck played the so-called "World's Greatest Rifle Shot." Regardless, she took the idea straight to Michael Todd. Dorothy and Herbert had an agreement to write another show with the eccentric producer. Generally a risk-taker, Todd was completely uninterested in the Annie Oakley idea, saying, as Dorothy paraphrased it, "Who cares about a girl who knows from nothing but guns?"[6] That same afternoon, Dorothy attended an ASCAP meeting. Oscar Hammerstein was there, as well. After the success of *Oklahoma*, he and Dorothy's longtime friend Richard Rodgers had started producing shows, as well as writing them. When she saw the man she called "Ockie," Dorothy took her shot. She asked, "What do you think about Ethel Merman as Annie Oakley?" Hammerstein replied, "We'll do it! Talk to Dick." She did. Rodgers also agreed to take on the project. Herbert and Dorothy would co-write the libretto, and Dorothy would write the lyrics. In a meeting with Rodgers and Hammerstein, the Fieldses agreed that Kern was the perfect person to pen the music. Convincing Kern to return to New York, however, was not an easy proposition. While working on the score for *Swing Time*, Kern had announced that he was quitting Broadway. "I believe that my future lies with the screen," he said.[7] As stubborn as he was gifted, it took some sweet talking from Rodgers and Kern's former collaborator Hammerstein to convince him to leave Whittier Drive for a suite at New York's St. Regis Hotel. Rodgers sent a telegram that said, "It would be one of the greatest honors of my life if you would consent to write the music for this show"; Hammerstein sweetened the deal by promising a revival of *Show Boat*.

Whether it was Rodgers's telegram, Hammerstein's *Show Boat* proposal, or the idea of writing again—for the first time since the 1940 film *One Night in the Tropics*—with Dorothy Fields, Kern agreed to take the job. The rest of the team was jubilant. All that was left was to convince Merman to take on the title role. That proved to be more complicated than anyone expected it to be. Merman had just delivered her second child, a son named Bobby; she'd promised her husband she'd take a year off to be with the baby and his big sister, Ethel. But Dorothy was resolved that Merman would take the role. The songwriter showed up at her friend's room in Doctor's Hospital and told Merman about the role. Merman said she'd think it over. When Dorothy offered the leading lady an astronomical $4,500 a week plus ten percent of the show's gross, Merman could not refuse. Regardless of what she'd promised her husband, she signed on for the job in August of 1945.

With their leading lady on board, work began in earnest for the show that would become *Annie Get Your Gun*. Dorothy and Herbert conducted their customary research, diving deeply into the lives of Annie Oakley and Frank Butler. They soon discovered that the two "were about the dullest people in the world. Annie Oakley in real life used to sit in her tent and knit, for God's sake!" Dorothy said.[8] Kern made his plans to return to New York. After a farewell party thrown in Beverly Hills, a happy Kern arrived in the city in early November. He and Eva had plans for dinner with Eli and Dorothy Fields Lahm the night after they arrived in town. Dorothy decided she'd like to see her friend Eva for lunch that day, as well. Early that morning, Dorothy rang the Kern suite at the St. Regis Hotel. Jerome answered, as Eva wasn't up yet. He took Dorothy's message and left a note for his wife written in soap on the bathroom mirror. "Meet Dorothy at 1 p.m.," it said. Kern had plans to shop for antiques while the ladies lunched. After lunch, Dorothy and Eva strolled down Fifth Avenue, browsing through Tiffany's before going their separate ways. Dorothy later arrived home to a message that she should get to City Hospital on Welfare Island. Jerome Kern was gravely ill.

Kern had gone antiquing, as planned. At the intersection of Park Avenue and Fifty-Seventh Street, he collapsed. Help quickly arrived, but none of the responders had any idea that the infirmed was one of the American theater's most significant figures. He carried no identification other than an ASCAP membership button. After Kern arrived at the pauper's hospital, he remained unconscious and was placed in a ward with other indigent patients. Because of the button, hospital staff contacted ASCAP, who alerted Hammerstein. Hammerstein and his personal physician, Dr. Harold Hyman, raced to City Hospital, but after examining Kern, Hyman told Hammerstein that Kern's condition was likely fatal. For the next several days—including after Kern had been transferred to Doctor's Hospital at his daughter Betty's insistence—Dorothy, Hammerstein, and Eva and Betty Kern kept a vigil by the Dean's bedside. Whether he ever regained consciousness is up for debate. Dorothy claimed that he did not, while Kern biographers Stephen Banfield and Geoffrey Holden Block suggest that he did, "but only intermittently and briefly."[9] Regardless, sixty-year-old Jerome Kern died on November 11; he was laid to rest the following day in a funeral attended by about fifty show business luminaries. Psalms 23 and 90 were read, and Oscar Hammerstein delivered the following eulogy:

> We all know in our hearts that these few minutes we devote to him now are small drops in the ocean of our affections. Our real tribute will be paid over many years of remembering, telling good stories about him, and thinking about him when we are by ourselves. We in this chapel will cherish our special knowledge of this world figure. We will remember a jaunty, happy man whose sixty years were crowded with success and fun and love. Let us thank whatever God we believe in that we shared some part of this good, bright life Jerry led on this earth.

Dorothy would call it "the worst week of my life."[10]

At lunch following the funeral, Dorothy, Herbert, Rodgers, and Hammerstein were discussing their Annie Oakley project. They were concerned that they might never find a composer as gifted as Kern to write the show's music. Rodgers made his suggestion carefully: "Irving," he floated, knowing to bring on Berlin, who wrote both music and lyrics, would mean Dorothy could no longer serve as lyricist. Outside of that, though, the idea made perfect sense. Berlin's bread-and-butter sound was the all-American anthem. Hit songs like "God Bless America," "Blue Skies," and "Alexander's Ragtime Band" headlined a career that had already stretched for nearly four decades. He was a perfect choice to tell the story of a Midwesterner. With her customary grace, Dorothy easily agreed to the change. "I have enough to do with the book," she said, but getting Berlin to join the team was as tricky as convincing Kern to come on board. Berlin liked to steer his own ship; he was known for maintaining control of every aspect of his productions—from writing the music and lyrics to publishing the sheet music.

Shared billing—particularly with names as well-known as his own—was not in his wheelhouse. He refused to do the show unless it was known as "Irving Berlin's *Annie Oakley*." On that, Dorothy pushed back. "We can't do that, Irving," she said. "It's our idea." Berlin asked for the weekend to think it over, refusing to even read Dorothy and Herbert's finished first act, lest it influence his decision.

According to Berlin biographer Laurence Bergreen, Berlin spent a few days going through the proposition in his mind. On the one hand, it'd be a great way to recoup some of the nearly ten million dollars he'd donated to the US Army in support of the recent war effort; on the other hand, he'd never written what he called "a situation musical" of the type Rodgers and Hammerstein had perfected. He wondered whether his work would measure up. At Rodgers's suggestion, Berlin took Dorothy and Herbert's half-finished book and went to Atlantic City. By the time he returned, he'd written six songs, including "Doin' What Comes Naturally" and "You Can't Get a Man with a Gun." He'd also written "There's No Business Like Show Business," a number that almost went the way of "The Way You Look Tonight." Berlin played the song for the creative team, which now included director Joshua Logan, and received an elated response. On a subsequent airing, he detected what he perceived as a lack of enthusiasm. The next time he played through the score, Berlin left the number out altogether, prompting Rodgers to ask why he'd taken it out. "Well, the last time I played the score . . . I looked at your face, and you weren't enjoying yourself . . . so I decided to cut it," Berlin said.[11] Rodgers, of course, insisted Berlin put it back in.

By May of 1946, *Annie Get Your Gun*, a name likely derived from a scrapped Fields/Cole Porter musical to be called *Jenny, Get Your Gun* (1942), was ready for its premiere. Dorothy called its creation "the easiest and happiest show I ever worked on,"[12] with the exception of one scene. In Act II, there was a scene that took place in the Brevoort Hotel. It had to be rewritten so many times that it became a joke among the creators. "Whenever somebody said to somebody else, 'What are you going to do tonight?' The answer was 'rewrite the Brevoort!'"[13] After its Boston tryout, *Annie Get Your Gun* opened at the Imperial Theatre on May 16, 1946. Its $6.60 tickets were the highest priced since *Oklahoma*'s in 1943. Dorothy's $450,000 brainchild, the show that Irving Berlin wasn't sure he wanted to sign on to, became the most successful of his illustrious career. It closed after an almost three-year run, having played more than 1,100 performances. With Dolores Gray in the title role, its run at the London Coliseum was even longer. The movie rights for *Annie Get Your Gun* were sold to MGM for an unprecedented $650,000. The resulting film featured Betty Hutton playing the title role opposite Howard Keel's Frank Butler. During filming, Hutton was brought in to replace Judy Garland, who was originally cast as Annie but whose health became problematic during production. After the 1946 production closed on Broadway, there were companies in twelve different foreign countries. Since then, *Annie* has played to packed houses on the community and educational theater circuits across the globe. It's also had two major Broadway revivals and a US telefilm. In its many iterations, the title role has been associated with such luminaries as Mary Martin, Barbara Eden, Debbie Reynolds, Bernadette Peters, Susan Lucci, and Reba McEntire, but the success all started in the mind of Dorothy Fields. Obviously thrilled with the success of *Annie Get Your Gun*, Dorothy did the only thing she knew to do: she went to work on another show.

The creative team of *Annie Get Your Gun* (front, left to right) Ray Middleton and Ethel Merman (rear, left to right) Joshua Logan, Irving Berlin, Richard Rodgers, Oscar Hammerstein, Dorothy Fields, and Herbert Fields. Photofest.

# Chapter 12
## "I Like It Here"

Just before the Boston tryout of *Annie Get Your Gun*, Dorothy Fields got a phone call. It was a real estate broker. She'd found a property Dorothy needed to see. As quickly as she could, Dorothy made her way from Boston to Brewster, New York, where she toured a 125-acre estate at 118 Federal Hill Road. Dorothy immediately knew this was the place for her. New York City would always be home, but as her children were growing, she wanted them to have room to roam. The house in Brewster, which had been owned by State Representative Benjamin J. Rabin of the Bronx, had that in spades. In addition to a spacious seventeen-room manor house, there were two brooks, a lake, a swimming pool, and a double tennis court. Just sixty miles north of New York, Dorothy, Eli, David, and Eliza could easily commute back and forth between the two; that's precisely what they did. Manhattan remained their permanent base, but their summers and holidays were spent in Brewster. Dorothy loved it there; it was so different from her experience with city life. "Everyone is so pleasant and so sweet," she said. "It is fascinating, too, to be a part of a growing community, and everyone who lives here seems to have his whole soul in the community's best interests."[1] Dorothy did too. Just as she gave of her time and talents to charities in New York, so did she open her country home to organizations like the Brewster Women's and Garden Clubs. She planned a dinner dance for the Chamber of Commerce, and when a 1947 fire damaged a section of the house, the consummate hostess showed her appreciation to the responding firemen by bringing them into the kitchen and, with the assistance of Herbert and Frances, serving them breakfast. Exchanges like these endeared Dorothy Fields to the people of Brewster. Through the years, she, Herbert, and others would meet there to do their work. For a time in the mid-1950s, the Lahm family would live there full time. Until then, the spacious retreat provided Dorothy with a welcome respite from her hectic life in New York.

Once *Annie Get Your Gun* had opened, Dorothy began her search for a new story to tell. The idea for what would, more than a decade later, become *Redhead* came to her sometime in 1946. She'd visited Madame Tussauds's wax museum and was fascinated, certain the setting was rife with potential for a musical. Then referred to as *The Works*, Dorothy imagined it as another project to be produced by Rodgers and Hammerstein. Canadian-born comedienne Bea Lillie would star. Dorothy and Herbert began their research but were put off of the idea when they found out Madame Tussaud lived in the eighteenth century; the two did not want to take on what Dorothy called a "short pants play, a powdered wig thing."[2] They decided instead to keep the idea of a waxworks—thus its original name *The Works*—but update the story and make it their own. Members of the Theatre Guild had another idea. The guild was founded in 1918 and aimed to produce non-commercial work. Since its inception, the guild had mounted plays by the likes of George Bernard Shaw, Eugene O'Neill, and Maxwell Anderson. They'd also presented musicals, like the original production of *Oklahoma*. They were hungry for another hit. Seeing the success of *Annie Get Your Gun*, the board of the guild asked Dorothy and Herbert to adapt a 1933 play called *The Pursuit of Happiness*. The play had been co-written by a guild founder, Lawrence Langer, and his wife, Armina Marshall (under the pseudonyms of Alan Child and Isabelle Loudon). Though not exactly a "powdered wig thing," the Revolutionary War setting of the story did call for several pairs of "short pants." Dorothy and Herbert accepted anyway. They tabled *The Works* and dug, instead, into the lives of Connecticut Yankees in 1776. Burton Lane, whose *Finian's Rainbow* was running on Broadway at the time, accepted the guild's offer to compose the piece. An early 1949 opening was planned.

The going was slow. The Fieldses, who'd always preferred developing their own shows to adapting them from other sources, were having a hard time with Langer and Marshall's material. There were disagreements with Lane as well on the direction the piece should take. After over a year at work on the adaptation, Lane left the project. Morton Gould replaced him. Gould, known for his incredible versatility as a composer of jazz, blues, gospel, and classical music, had worked on the music staffs of both Radio City Music Hall and NBC. He'd had his Broadway debut in 1945, writing the score for *Billion Dollar Baby* alongside up-and-coming lyric-writing duo Betty Comden and Adolph Green. *Arms and the Girl*, as the adaptation would be called at Richard Rodgers's suggestion (no relation to either the 1917 or 1935 films of the same name), gave him a chance to not only return to Broadway for the first time in five years but also to prove himself worthy of the illustrious company of Dorothy and Herbert Fields. The trio of Dorothy, Herbert, and Morton Gould frequently retreated to the house in Brewster to focus on their work; nevertheless, the Fieldses, typically known for how quickly they could complete a job, were stumped. The story of a Yankee-born tomboy who dreams of joining General Washington's cause was proving to be more trouble than it was worth, reminding the siblings why they preferred to start from scratch with stories.

The guild called in help. Rouben Mamoulian joined the team to both direct the show and to help Dorothy and Herbert get their arms around its libretto.

Russian born and raised, Mamoulian had studied acting in the famed Moscow Art Theatre. Better known as the conservatory operated by Constantin Stanislavski, the theater's work served as a major source of inspiration for the artists who'd founded New York's groundbreaking Group Theatre. Since emigrating to the United States, Mamoulian had made a name for himself by directing some of the most important pieces in the modern musical theater—*Porgy and Bess* (1935) and *Oklahoma!* (1943) among them. He'd also directed films like *Dr. Jekyll and Mr. Hyde* (1931) and *The Mark of Zorro* (1940). It was the guild's relationship with Mamoulian by way of *Oklahoma!*, though, that brought the director to *Arms and the Girl*. He'd been offered the project when it began but refused. Not wanting to burn the bridge between him and the Theatre Guild, he reversed course a year later. When the guild asked him to come in and salvage its $200,000, struggling show, Mamoulian diplomatically accepted the assignment.

Within months of working with Mamoulian, Dorothy and Herbert decided the story was in sufficiently good shape to try in front of an audience. The Forrest Theatre in Philadelphia and Shubert Theatre in Boston were booked for the tryouts. When it opened out of town, the story went like this: Jo Kirkland (played by Nanette Fabray) is a young lady in Ridgefield, Connecticut. Having had a rather unconventional upbringing with a somewhat warmongering father, Kirkland wants nothing more than to join the Revolutionary War effort. In the process, she ends up making a captive of a Hessian soldier named Franz (played by Georges Guetary) and blowing up bridges, which end up stifling the effort, instead of supporting it. Ultimately, General George Washington himself (played by Arthur Vinton) begs her to "keep the hell out of this Revolution."[3] Kirkland agrees, and, as is most often the case in pieces of musical theater, all's well that ends well by the time the final curtain closes. Dorothy, admitting it was "a long, tough job," was downright energized by how the libretto had turned out. Always passionate about her work, she could hardly contain her excitement when explaining the plot of the story to reporter Barbara L. Wilson of *The Philadelphia Inquirer*. Wilson described the scene like this:

> Her blonde hair . . . bobbed excitedly, and her eyes gleamed. Explaining the plot, Dorothy even did a little singing and acting. At one point, while describing a dueling scene, she leaped to her feet, thrusting out an imaginary rapier.[4]

Notices in both Philadelphia and Boston were relatively warm. Though the untrimmed production ran until nearly midnight on its first night in Philadelphia, the *Variety* reviewer in attendance said the show "adds up to an intelligent, artistically noteworthy evening in the theatre." The much-beleaguered book, he said,

> is by no means stodgy or heavy. Just when it starts to be, the authors start to spoof a bit. All the way through, the show is often satiric, sometimes very sentimental,

sometimes out and out farce . . . it's an intelligent, adult book and maintains the atmosphere and spirit of the times with remarkable fidelity, but it's still questionable as to just how audiences will take it.[5]

Of the show's stay in Boston, Cyrus Durgin wrote in the *Daily Boston Globe*, "The musical comedy business . . . is back on the gold standard with *Arms and the Girl*." He ended his review with, "You'll find it a consistently good show."[6] After more than a year of research and reworking, such positive feedback had to be even more gratifying than it usually was. Buoyed by a pair of successful tryouts, the producers set the date for the show's Broadway opening. February 2, 1950— nearly a year later than originally planned—was the date; the Forty-Sixth Street Theatre was the place. Between the positive out of town notices and the blue-chip team of the Fieldses and Mamoulian, the show opened with an advance sale of more than $450,000. Star Fabray—who'd worked with Dorothy and Herbert in *Let's Face It!*—received solid notices in her role as Jo Kirkland. Pearl Bailey, who played a runaway slave named Connecticut, did too. The reviews were not kind, however, to the book. Brooks Atkinson said in the *New York Times* that the story was "not conspicuous for originality, skill, or beauty."[7] He likened the show to the antiquated stylings of operetta and lamented that the libretto "never really

**Dorothy and Herbert Fields with *Arms and the Girl* collaborator Rouben Mamoulian, 1950.** Photofest.

triumphs over the meager humor of the skittish joke on which it is founded."[8] In his review for *The Billboard*, Bob Francis suggested that the problem was

> that Herbert and Dorothy Fields, plus Rouben Mamoulian, have followed a play pattern so closely in their musical book. There are laggard intervals and repetitious material which slow down a fast-running musical.

Still, Francis's overall take was that the show made for "a highly enjoyable evening."[9] Richard P. Cooke suggested in the *Wall Street Journal* that the stars of the show would endear the show to audiences.[10] In his review for the *New York Herald Tribune*, Howard Barnes agreed. He called *Arms and the Girl* "far better as a play," finding the "tunes and antics have been so unevenly distributed through the tedious and top-heavy plot that it takes a heap of acting to keep it ambling along."[11] Luckily for the show, its actors were more than capable of keeping it afloat throughout the spring. Fabray hit her stride in her first turn as a leading lady. Her delivery of songs, like "A Girl with a Flame," "He Will Tonight," and "You Kissed Me," was spot-on. Critics and audiences alike found her irresistible in the role. The same could be said for Bailey. In her role as a runaway slave, Bailey sang two of the most uproarious numbers of the night. "Nothin' for Nothin'" and "There Must Be Something Better Than Love," a song whose title and sentiment is very similar to *Sweet Charity*'s "There's Gotta Be Something Better Than This," for which Dorothy also wrote the lyrics, were bona fide showstoppers.

In spite of her success in the show, though, Bailey threatened to leave it, citing the fact that several company members used racial slurs in reference to her. According to the *Chicago Defender*, someone "called her 'honey chile,' talked to her in dialect and patronizingly pinched her cheeks." Another called her a "damn Eurasian."[12] Understandingly unwilling to work in these conditions, Bailey planned to walk away from the show. "I'd rather starve than go on taking it," she said.[13] She was convinced by its producers—and Mamoulian, who'd directed Bailey's Broadway debut in *St. Louis Woman* (1946) and for whom she had "deep respect"[14]—to remain. Appropriate apologies were made, and the show went on. It lasted through the spring and closed on May 27, 1950. *Arms and the Girl*, for the enormous amount of work required to get it off the ground, had played a disappointing 134 performances. Its score, littered with the kind of double entendre Dorothy had used so masterfully in songs like "A Fine Romance," is entirely forgettable outside of the context of the musical.

As usual, Dorothy had a number of other projects already lined up. This took some of the sting out of the failed *Arms and the Girl* experience. Some of this new work required her to return to Hollywood. Having sold her place on Arden Drive, Dorothy now rented a bungalow at the Beverly Hills Hotel whenever California came calling. For this trip, Dorothy had a lyric-writing assignment with Harry Warren ("I Only Have Eyes for You," "Jeepers Creepers," "That's Amore," "At Last," and others). Warren, who wrote primarily for film, was awarded the first gold record in history for his "Chattanooga Choo Choo." One of the most prolific film composers of his time, Warren wrote with Dorothy to create the music for *Texas Carnival* (1951). Dorothy had also been hired to write with Harold Arlen for a film called *Mr. Imperium*. Arlen, whose most notable success was the score for *The Wizard of Oz*, considered Dorothy to be one of his favorite people. She called him "Schnitter," a word she made up, because it sounded Yiddish. He dubbed her "the Red Arrow," owing to her ability to write so quickly. The pair collaborated on two films—*Mr. Imperium* (1951) and *The Farmer Takes a Wife* (1953), always writing in her bungalow. Arlen, writing with Ted Koehler, had replaced Dorothy and McHugh at the Cotton Club. By the 1950s, though, he maintained his full-time residence in Los Angeles. He and Dorothy maintained their friendship and their respect for the other's work across the miles. Arlen biographer Walter Rimler suggests that, in the years after the 1970 death of Arlen's wife, Dorothy expressed an interest in pursuing a romantic relationship with the "Over the Rainbow" writer. Dorothy had been widowed for more than a decade; Arlen's wife had been gone for a couple of years too. Rimler's suggestion is not at all beyond the realm of possibility; however, no corroboration one way or the other exists in the record of Dorothy's life.[15]

After a brief sojourn out West, Dorothy was ready to get back to New York. Arthur Schwartz, her partner for *Stars in Your Eyes*, was waiting there, as was the development of their new show. It was another adaptation. The pair was making a musical of Betty Smith's best-selling novel *A Tree Grows in Brooklyn*. This time, however, Dorothy had signed on to write the lyrics only. Smith herself was to write the libretto, an assignment she never imagined accepting. The idea for a story about a poor Brooklyn family at the turn of the twentieth century came to Smith when she was a student at the University of Michigan. Centered on the lives of Johnnie, Katie, and Frances Nolan, the play was called *Francie Nolan* and won the Avery Hopwood Award in Drama. For a while, Smith assumed that would be the end of her first full-length play. Socially conscious, "as was the style back in 1930," Francie Nolan was never produced or even remembered until a decade later when Smith decided to try her hand at writing a novel. In the ten years since she'd left college, Smith had become adept at writing one-act plays—she'd published seventy-five of them—but novel-writing was new to her. Since the story was originally written as a play, its structure was all dialogue. Smith spent two years converting her 800-page play into a 400-page tome. The result was *A Tree Grows in Brooklyn*, a semi-autobiographical novel split into four "books," each one telling of a different period in the Nolan family's life. Smith's 1943 publishing debut was a resounding success. The work sold more than five million copies and was adapted into a 1945 film, directed by Elia Kazan. Smith had no part in the creative process of the film, nor did she plan to play a part in the creative process of the musical when producers George Abbott and Robert Fryer purchased the rights in 1949. "I made it very plain to Helen Strauss, my agent, that I wouldn't work on the play under any circumstances," she wrote in an article for the *New York Times*. Immediately after meeting Abbott, the two began talking about the direction the musical might take. "Miss Strauss broke in to say, 'It is understood that Miss Smith does not wish to work on the play.' I looked at her blankly and said, 'But I am working on it.'"

That was that. After that 1949 meeting with Abbott, he and Smith spent ten months developing a working script. Abbott was pulling triple duty for the show.

**Dorothy Fields with legal pad and bright blue pencil in hand, ca. 1953.** Photofest.

One of Broadway's most prolific artists, he was *A Tree Grows in Brooklyn*'s co-librettist, director, and producer. In both 1934 and 1939, Abbott directed five different plays that opened on Broadway. By the end of his career—he died at age 107 in 1995—he had won five Tony Awards for shows like *The Pajama Game* (1955) and *Damn Yankees* (1956) and a Pulitzer Prize for his libretto to *Fiorello!* (1959). Smith called working with Abbott "one of the most amiable collaborations in dramatic history."[16] Once the script was in suitable shape, Schwartz and Dorothy came in to write the songs. Before long, the production was ready to get on its feet. Tryouts in both Philadelphia and New Haven preceded a New York opening at the Alvin Theatre on April 19, 1951. Almost without exception, critics and audiences alike embraced it as "one of those happy inspirations that the theatre dotes on."[17] John Chapman wrote,

> *A Tree Grows in Brooklyn* is a splendid musical—or two musicals. The first act is marvelously funny, with Shirley Booth giving the performance of her or almost any other comedienne's life. The second act is a very touching one as it completes the story of a Brooklyn Liliom, who is a wonderful fellow even if he is a rumpot and a failure. There has been nothing on the music-show stage which tugs so strongly at the heartstrings as this act does, since Evelyn Laye came over here in Noel Coward's *Bittersweet*.[18]

When the show opened, nearly a half million dollars in advance tickets had been sold. Immediately, the musicalized *A Tree Grows in Brooklyn* was as big a hit as the book on which it was based. Critics and audiences alike adored the "sweet and touching musical"[19] about turn-of-the-century life in a Brooklyn tenement district. Without a doubt, the star of the show was Shirley Booth in her role as Aunt Cissy. The creative team had insisted on securing Booth's services for their show. They'd delayed their opening until she'd returned from a tour of her Tony Award–winning turn in William Inge's first play *Come Back, Little Sheba* (1950). As it turned out, their insistence that Booth play the role of the "rowdy, juicy, and generous character, completely devoid of inhibitions"[20] was wise, as proven by reviewer John Beaufort, who suggested the performer was "the greatest single asset" to the show.[21] Aunt Cissy collects husbands both of the legal and common law variety and calls them all "Harry." In number after number, Booth gave "the performance of her or almost any other comedienne's life."[22] Her skills were best displayed by the song "He Had Refinement." In the number, Aunt Cissy sings about her first "Harry" in tongue-in-cheek terms far more condemning than complimentary. The song never failed to stop the show. Louis Sheaffer wrote in the *Brooklyn Daily Eagle* that "Without knowing her past achievements, I can't imagine that [Fields] has ever done anything much better than the words for" Aunt Cissy's three comedy songs, of which "He Had Refinement" was, without doubt, the most memorable.[23] In a list of songs he wishes he'd written, Stephen Sondheim includes this classic example of Dorothy's ability to write something sexual without *saying* something sexual.

Dorothy and Schwartz were understandably thrilled with the success of the show. After a lackluster outing with *Arms and the Girl*, Dorothy felt vindicated to be back on top. She and Schwartz worked well together. They couldn't help but compliment the other's work. In an interview that illustrates the kind of collaborator Dorothy was, Schwartz talked about how "inspired" her lyrics were, how they stayed so closely to the dialogue of the show. He noted how hard it was to capture the dialogue in rhythm as opposed to prose. Dorothy immediately turned the spotlight back onto the composer. She leaned in, the reporter noted, "to say that it was the lilt of Arthur's music that gave her prosaic words real meaning."[24] That she was so easy to work with—aside from those early morning wake-up calls—is one of the things that can be credited with the fact that so many of her collaborators wanted to work with her time and again. Schwartz, of course, was one of those. He was among Dorothy's most frequent collaborators. When *A Tree Grows in Brooklyn* closed in December of 1951, it had played 267 performances. Dorothy and Schwartz subsequently joined forces for another pair of projects. The first was the score for a film called *Excuse My Dust*. The second gave them another opportunity to work with the one and only Shirley Booth, who, by that time, had won three Tony Awards (out of four nominations) and an Oscar.

The project was called *By the Beautiful Sea*. The name of both the show and the boarding house operated by heroine Lottie Gibson (played by Booth), *By the Beautiful Sea* found its creators in the same idiom from which came *A Tree Grows in Brooklyn*. In addition to operating her boarding house, Gibson is also a vaudeville performer. She falls in love with a Shakespearean actor. Lottie convinces him to stay at her boarding house, only to learn he's a divorced father of a young lady who'll stop at nothing to put an end to his relationship with Lottie. What's interesting about the character of Lottie, though, is that she isn't willing to put up with that. Like most of the other female characters of her time, Lottie wants love, but unlike the others, she wants it on her terms. She's mature—a "sadder but wiser girl," perhaps—and she knows that love alone isn't worth losing everything else for. In her number "I'd Rather Wake Up by Myself," Lottie Gibson expresses what few other musical theater characters—male or female—had. Rather than settle for less than her "ideal," Gibson would "rather wake up by myself." Dorothy's unintentionally feminist lyric is an exquisite example of the unique way in which she approached character.

(VERSE)
This is the first man I've wanted to marry,
But it looks like it ain't gonna be.
All my life I appealed to the guys from left field
Who never appealed to me.
I've nibbled at offers of marriage,
But I wiggled myself off the hook,
And gee, am I glad I stayed single
When I think what I might have took.

(CHORUS)
That fresh air fiend was healthy but not too bright.
My wifely duties would've been very light.
Inhale, exhale, that's all we would do all night.
I'd rather wake up by myself.
My Latin lover had a disturbing whim.
When girls passed by, his eye went from limb to limb.
I know darn well if I had've married him,
I'd always wake up my myself.

(BRIDGE)
My cowboy friend was rugged
From top to bottom
Before I got him,
Some Injun shot him!

So if I feel I'll never get my ideal
Why should I rest my head with
Some big baboon I wouldn't be found dead with.
I'm sure I'd rather wake up by myself.

Joe made big dough.
His business, he said, was printin'
What Joe was printin'
Got him San Quintin.

So there's the list of husbands I'm glad I missed.
If I can't be the wife for
The only guy I'd risk my life for.
I know I'd rather wake up by myself.

*By the Beautiful Sea* played 270 Broadway performances. During its life span in New York, the show was housed at the Majestic Theatre and then the Imperial. It was clear from its tryout in Boston, though, that the show was in trouble. According to reviews, the biggest problems were with its book. One reviewer criticized the plot as "extremely slender."[25] Another suggested it was "going to require a massive dose of theatrical vitamins to put it on its feet,"[26] and, according to Brooks Atkinson, the problems weren't solved before the show hit Broadway. Dorothy and Herbert's libretto, he said, was "a perfunctory affair with as many loose ends as a session of Congress."[27] Perhaps the best assessment of *By the Beautiful Sea* came from Boston reviewer Cyrus Durgin, who noted, "Shirley Booth does a good deal more for *By the Beautiful Sea* than the show does for her."[28]

With composer Burton Lane, Dorothy's next assignment was a television musical called *Junior Miss*. It aired in 1957 and was part of the DuPont Show of the Month. The musical was adapted from a 1941 play Dorothy's brother Joseph had co-written with Jerome Chodorov. Once that project was done, Dorothy returned her focus to the project she and Herbert had been discussing since 1946. They were ready for *The Works*.

Members of the Songwriters Protective Association on the steps of federal court in September of 1956: (left to right, front row) Steve Allen, Oscar Hammerstein, Dick Adler, Dorothy Fields, Otto Harbach, and Leo Shull (left to right, rear) Arthur Schwartz, Bob Merr, Harold Rome, and Stanley Adams. Bettman/Getty Images.

# Chapter 13
## "Merely Marvelous"

In 1956, Dorothy Fields was in her early fifties. She showed no signs of slowing down. In addition to her work on stage, in television, and in film, she continued to make significant contributions of her time to a variety of charitable organizations in and around New York City. The Girl Scouts and the Federation of Jewish Philanthropies were the most frequent beneficiaries of her efforts. On their behalves, she helped to raise millions of dollars, impacting scores of lives in the doing of it. A letter from Dorothy to producer Leland Hayward (*South Pacific, Call Me Madam*, and later, *Gypsy* and *The Sound of Music*) reveals some of her motivation for her work with the Girl Scouts:

> On the leaflet, it says, "A growing force for freedom," and that's the story! It's a story of day and summer camps for them—after school recreation centers for them— opportunities to be with girls in their several age groups—no color or creed barred. You see, Girl Scouts don't hang out on street corners or wait in front of hotels and theaters for movie stars. They have other things on their minds, such as growing up to be a credit to all of us who are trying to help them. Please help us to help them, and we will all be mighty beholden to you.
>
> Love,
> Dorothy.

Dorothy was frequently recognized for this kind of work. When the Women's Division of the New York Guild for the Jewish Blind honored her at its sixth annual membership luncheon, Dorothy was given a citation noting that her "heart is as great as her talents." In 1956, Dorothy chaired an event called "Festival of Song." The luncheon, held at the Waldorf Astoria, was to aid the Federation of Jewish Philanthropies in its drive to raise $18 million for 116 different health and welfare agencies. Her dear friends "the Dorothys"—Mrs. Richard Rodgers and

**Dorothy Fields (second from left) with Dorothy Hammerstein, Evelyn Asinov, and Dorothy Rodgers at a 1950 event to benefit the Federation of Jewish Philanthropies of New York.** Photofest.

Mrs. Oscar Hammerstein—aided Dorothy Fields in hosting this event, where entertainers from Edward G. Robinson to a virtually unknown Julie Andrews took the stage. Also on the docket was a titian-haired, two-time Tony Award winner (she'd win a third the following year) named Gwen Verdon.

Verdon was a California-born dancing sensation who'd dabbled in film (including playing an uncredited role in *The Farmer Takes a Wife*, for which Dorothy and Harold Arlen had written the music) and worked as a choreographer before bursting onto the Broadway scene in Cole Porter's 1953 *Can-Can*. She "stole the show,"[1] earning herself the first of four Tony Awards. Her next role was as the leading lady in 1955's *Damn Yankees* (music by Richard Adler and Jerry Ross, book by Douglass Wallop and George Abbott, who'd been one of Dorothy's collaborators on *A Tree Grows in Brooklyn*). She played Lola, a part tailor-made for her many talents. In addition to winning Verdon her second Tony, the experience with *Damn Yankees* also solidified Verdon's relationship with the show's choreographer, Bob Fosse. The two had been aware of each other since their days as dancers at the MGM studio in Hollywood; they'd been officially introduced at a party hosted by fellow dancer/choreographer Michael Kidd, but *Damn Yankees* was the first time the two had interacted with each other in a prolonged and meaningful way. Their subsequent partnership, stormy as it was, would bring to Broadway some of its most iconic moments. After the premiere of their next shared endeavor, *New Girl in Town* (1957), Gwen Verdon was Broadway royalty. She had arrived as, according to one writer, "the kind of performer who can 'carry' a musical, whether or not her shoulders seem broad enough for the role."[2]

To have a star of Verdon's stature on the program for her luncheon was a boon to Dorothy's efforts and an indication of the high regard in which all of Broadway esteemed one of its premier lyricists and librettists. By now, she and Herbert were hard at work on *The Works*. Originally planned with Beatrice Lillie as its star, the show had been in the backs of their minds for more than a decade, but its creative team had been something of a revolving door. Rodgers and Hammerstein had agreed to produce it in the early 1950s but soon reversed course to develop a new show of their own. Lawrence Carr and Robert Fryer, who'd co-produced *By the Beautiful Sea*, signed on instead. As Dorothy found herself increasingly interested in focusing her work on the show's libretto, Dorothy and Herbert had invited Irving Berlin to write the music and lyrics. Berlin declined. Signing a star proved problematic as well. Over the years, the role was offered to Lillie, Ethel Merman, Mary Martin (*South Pacific* and *Peter Pan*), Celeste Holm (*Oklahoma!* and *The King and I*), and Gisele Mackenzie (Canadian-born singer best known at the time as a regular guest on television's *Your Hit Parade*). For whatever reason, no one was as interested in *The Works* as Herbert and Dorothy seemed to be. Though highly frustrated, the pair persevered. They completed their usual amount of fastidious research. Both Dorothy and Herbert were insistent that every detail of their shows be as accurate as possible. For this reason, they were also in frequent attendance at both rehearsals and performances of their productions.

They were elated when composer Albert Hague signed on to write the music for *The Works*. A relative newcomer, Hague had had moderate success as the composer for 1955's *Plain and Fancy,* a musical about a pair of sophisticates who find themselves in a rural Pennsylvania Amish community. Still earning his stripes on Broadway, Hague spent eight months composing the show on a "rickety card table with poor lighting." If nothing else, *Plain and Fancy* assured that he would never have to work in such circumstances again. "The first thing I did, after we were sure the show was a success, was to buy a beautiful, smooth substantial desk for further work," he said.[3] *Plain and Fancy*, which featured Barbara Cook in the role of Hilda Miller and Beatrice Arthur as an understudy, played for 461 performances. In the years following his collaboration with the Fieldses, Hague would play Professor Shorofsky in the film *Fame* and the television series it spawned. The three of them had nearly completed their work on the score and the book of *The Works* when Dorothy and Herbert received crushing news. Their friend and former producer Michael Todd had died in a plane crash while traveling to a banquet being held in his honor. Called "the most spectacular individual showman of the last few years," Todd had worked with the Fields siblings on *Something for the Boys*, *Mexican Hayride*, and *Up in Central Park*. He'd also been the one to reject Dorothy's idea for a musical made of the life of Annie Oakley, sending her instead to the Rodgers and Hammerstein Organization. As the theater world mourned his sudden loss, Dorothy was hit again. Just two days later, Herbert, with whom she'd collaborated on eight musicals and a screenplay, was dead of a heart attack. Dorothy was leveled. She'd later admit that she "didn't know how to go on without him."[4] Somehow, she mustered the energy to plow ahead. Four months later, she faced another tragedy.

Her husband, Eli, died as suddenly as Herbert had. Because he and Dorothy spent most of their time at the Brewster house by 1958, they were overnighting at what had been Herbert's East Sixty-Ninth Street apartment. Eli woke up in the middle of the late-July night. In his stupor, he'd knocked over a lamp, waking Dorothy. He went into the bathroom, where he vomited and collapsed. As his daughter Eliza described it to biographer Charlotte Greenspan, "It was horrible. He'd just been to the doctor about a week before and gotten a clean bill of health."[5] In a span of sixteen weeks, Dorothy had lost two of the people she loved the most, as well as a beloved colleague. Her grief was insurmountable, the loneliness paralyzing. "They all fulfilled a different part of my life," she admitted.[6] Dorothy found respite in two things: her work and her children. David, who'd spent years studying classical piano, was nearing college age; Eliza was thirteen and a budding artist. As usual, Dorothy busied herself by caring for them, but times were tough. The men who had been touchstones in her life both personally and professionally were gone, each of them taken unexpectedly and in an instant. Her son, in whom she took such great pride, was months away from leaving her too. He'd become, in his own words, a "fanatical jazz enthusiast." Weeks after his father's death, David would be off to Amherst College. There, he'd continue studying jazz and, eventually, graduate with a degree in English.

With her children requiring less and less of her time, Dorothy threw herself as vigorously as she could into her work. At the time, work was *The Works*. Just a few weeks before Eli's death, Dorothy and Hague set out to complete the project she and Herbert had begun more than a decade before. The first step was to complete its creative team. Above all else, they'd need a director and a star. David Hocker, agent to stars, like Leonard Bernstein, Jerome Robbins, and Dorothy Fields, set out to make this happen. He arranged a meeting between the show's producers (Robert Fryer and Lawrence Carr), its writers (Dorothy and Sidney Sheldon, who'd been brought in after Herbert's death), and another of Hocker's clients, Bob Fosse. Hocker saw the chance to facilitate a major casting coup, providing *The Works* both a director and a star in the one-two tandem of Broadway's new power couple, Bob Fosse and Gwen Verdon. There are different versions of how the meeting went. Some say Verdon went to Hague's apartment that night to hear the show's songs, as she was considering taking the lead role. Once there, Verdon insisted she'd only sign on if Fosse were brought in as director. Verdon herself disputed this, claiming she wasn't a big enough star to make demands like these. Others say producers offered Fosse the directing gig as an alternative to giving him the small part he'd requested. Whatever the content of the meeting, the outcome was a win for all involved. Fosse would direct, Verdon would star, and Dorothy and Herbert's book would need a significant overhaul. Gwen Verdon was a drastically different "type" than Beatrice Lillie, for whom the show had been written. David Shaw, a television writer with whom Verdon had worked in her early career, joined the team. He was tasked with cutting subplots to make room for more dance numbers for Verdon.

The resulting show had a new name; *Redhead* was a clear homage to its carrot-topped star. Just as problems had plagued Dorothy and Herbert in their twelve years of *The Works,* so were *Redhead*'s out-of-town tryouts rife with challenges. The show changed in each of its ten nights in New Haven. Jokes weren't working; songs were falling flat. The show's *Variety* review suggested *Redhead* was "headed in the right direction" but was "not at [its] peak as yet."[7] The book continued to be a source of great consternation. While Dorothy and Herbert's original idea had been to set the story in Madame Tussauds wax museum, that had changed, over time, for a couple of reasons. The first of these is that they didn't want to set the show in the late eighteenth and early nineteenth centuries, which is when Tussaud actually lived. Second, Tussaud's heirs were being tricky to work with; they were demanding approval rights over each draft of the script, and the Fieldses weren't willing to grant that. Their solution was to keep the idea of a waxworks but make it a fictional one, not linked to Tussauds. They'd also update the timeline, so that the action took place around the year 1900. Dorothy and Herbert were getting very comfortable working in the turn of the century milieu. Their two previous musicals (*A Tree Grows in Brooklyn* and *By the Beautiful Sea*) took place at the same time. Instead of the New York setting they'd been working in, however, *The Works* would be set in London. Still, the story ended up being very confusing. Essie Whimple (played by Verdon) works in the wax museum run by her two aunts. After a young American actress is murdered, the museum does an exhibit of the events surrounding her death. This brings Scotland Yard to the museum, as well as some of the deceased's fellow performers, including a strong man named Tom Baxter (played by Richard Kiley). Essie falls in love with Tom. The customary hijinks ensue, but the musical ultimately ends with Tom and Essie happily coupled.

Dorothy handled criticisms of her work in stride. With regards to the music, her rule was "Give it four performances. Monday, Tuesday, Wednesday matinee, and evening," she said. "If it hasn't worked by then, take it out."[8] Those songs that hadn't, they took out. She and Hague wrote two new songs after a New Year's Eve party one night: "Look Who's in Love" and "Back in Circulation" were the resulting numbers. Most of the songs in the show were typical of Fields's style. They were very character-specific with plain-spoken language. One particular number, though rooted in character, is another anomaly from the rest of Fields's catalog. "Erbie Fitch's Twitch" was written as a number for Verdon's character, Essie Whimple. She's fallen in love with the strong man of a vaudeville company, and in order for her to be near him, she attempts to join the company by auditioning with the only song and dance number she knows, a Cockney song her father used to perform in the music halls. The lyric not only tests the elocution of its performer—rhyming "twitch," "witch," and "Ipswitch" in a single line—but it also shows the versatility of its writer.

It's easy to wonder if Dorothy called upon the verbal acrobatics of her own vaudevillian-father when writing the number for the character of Essie. Wherever she received her inspiration, Dorothy had to be relieved that the project, so long in its development, was nearing an opening night. Dorothy always spoke very diplomatically about her collaborators—Verdon she called "fascinating and young and vibrant."[9] Still, it had to be frustrating for an established woman of the stage to have her work turned topsy-turvy by an upstart director, like Fosse. Whatever angst she may have felt, however, she kept to herself. After its troubled time out of town, the $216,000 musical opened on February 5, 1959, at the Forty-Sixth Street Theatre. It was a megahit. Audiences were once again smitten with Verdon, but critics were also bullish on Fields's lyrics. Brooks Atkinson called Dorothy "the bard of the evening." He noted her "excellent songs." He was confused, however, as most reviewers were, by the book. "[It's] as complicated as an income-tax return and just about as entertaining," was Atkinson's damning critique in the *New York Times*.[10] Perhaps the misguided libretto was a result of "too many cooks in the kitchen." It made no difference to audiences, though. They showed up in droves to see Verdon's latest. The show closed over a year later, having played more than 450 performances. When the show opened in Los Angeles in 1960, press reception was pretty much the same, Albert Goldberg wrote in the *Los Angeles Times* that the story is "not likely to cause any concern to the adjudicators of the Pulitzer Prize," but Verdon's charms could salvage even that. He continued, "It is a vehicle show concocted to exhibit thoroughly and at length the considerable dancing and comic talents . . . of a bright star with more than enough stamina to sustain the heavy chores put upon her."[11]

Though *Redhead* has never had a major revival nor was there a film adaptation made—some have suggested the show was too tailor-made to Verdon's talents for the musical to have a significant afterlife—its only Broadway production was successful enough to warrant six Tony Award nominations. In 1959, the Tony Awards were only thirteen years old. An outgrowth of the same organization that had underwritten the Stage Door Canteen, the Tonys were initially given each spring in ceremonies held in hotel ballrooms—generally at the Waldorf Astoria. *Redhead* beat out *La Plume de Ma Tanta* and *Flower Drum Song* for Best Musical. *Flower Drum Song*, with music and lyrics by Rodgers and Hammerstein, had a book by Hammerstein and Joseph Fields. Like Dorothy and Herbert, Joseph had found incredible success as a writer. At one point in 1943, he had three shows running concurrently on Broadway—*Doughgirls*, *My Sister Eileen* (the basis for the musical *Wonderful Town*), and *Junior Miss* (the basis for the 1957 television musical for which Dorothy and Burton Lane provided the music). Though they had never collaborated in the same way that Dorothy and Herbert had, Dorothy and Joseph remained close. They'd grow closer still in the spring of 1959 when their sister Frances died. In less than a year, Dorothy had lost two siblings and her husband. Meanwhile, she had just helped to create a Broadway show worthy of winning a Tony Award. With no other projects on the horizon—and no guaranteed collaborator with whom to work—Dorothy would enter her sixth decade completely unsure of what would come next.

# Chapter 14
## "After Forty, It's Patch, Patch, Patch"

During the run of *Redhead*, Dorothy Fields spent a week at Elizabeth Arden's Maine Chance luxury spa. Situated at the base of Camelback Mountain in Scottsdale, Arizona, the spa was modeled after Arden's rural farm spa in central Maine. There, women—most of whom returned year after year—pampered themselves with the latest in spa amenities. This included the use of machines to help reduce hip and thigh fat, regular massages, and a closely monitored nine hundred calories a day of spa cuisine. Guests were told not to leave the property during the week, lest they be tempted to cheat on the diet. Only open in the winter, notables from Ava Gardner to Mamie Eisenhower were among the spa's tony clientele. Exactly why Dorothy chose to visit the spa isn't known; she'd always been trim. Even in adulthood, she exercised daily; she watched what she ate and didn't snack between meals. It couldn't have been weight control that she went in search of. More likely, she retreated to Arizona to reflect on what would be her next step. The crushing loneliness that Dorothy Fields felt was related not only to the loss of those she loved; many of the collaborators and colleagues she'd known for decades were ending their careers—if not by death (like Kern, Todd, and Hammerstein), then by an inability to adapt to Broadway's changing sound. Dorothy insisted there were still songs and stories in her—"Listen, Honey. I've got songs coming out of me I haven't even thought about yet. I plan to write 'til I can no longer hold a pencil," she told Rex Reed in 1973[1]—but would anyone want to hear them?

Likewise, would anyone remember what she'd already done? Undoubtedly, the deaths of so many so close to her had made Dorothy examine her own mortality. There's evidence that the idea of "legacy" may have been weighing on her mind. She had an Academy Award and, after *Redhead*, a Tony. She had financial security that she'd built for herself and the loving respect of her peers. Her work was so highly regarded that, when her friend "Ockie" Hammerstein succumbed to stomach cancer in August of 1960, Dorothy was mentioned as his potential replacement in a *Variety* article headlined "Rodgers' New Collab?" Conversely, she had years of experiences of being unknown, the secret superstar in a universe populated by the likes of luminaries from Cole Porter to Irving Berlin. Dorothy, who was always self-deprecating, laughed this off. She told a story of meeting an older woman at a reception in Toronto. When introduced, the woman replied, "How nice to meet you, Mrs. Fielding." Another time, she was in Boston for the out-of-town tryout of *Let's Face It*. At intermission, she and Cole Porter went into the theater lobby to get a feel for the buzz about the show, which starred Danny Kaye. They heard one woman say to another, "Isn't that Danny Kaye a card? I don't know how he thinks of all those funny things to say, one right after the other," Dorothy relayed the story, adding, "Cole stuck his elbow in my ribs and said, 'See how famous you are, Dorothy?'"[2] Famed gossip monger Hedda Hopper even alluded to Dorothy's anonymity in her "Talk of Hollywood" column, writing, "If you've forgotten who wrote the lyrics for 'Sunny Side of the Street,' for which she rarely gets credit, it was Dorothy Fields."[3]

Though Dorothy joked about it, she was clearly bothered by her relative anonymity. It can't be known whether this had always been an issue or if it had just begun to bother her as she started to lose so many colleagues and family members. Maybe she wondered what would be remembered of her after she was gone. What is certain is that by May of 1959, Dorothy Fields had set out to do something about it: she hired a press agent. Before long, Dorothy found herself again the spotlight, just as she'd been on those 1933 WJZ radio broadcasts with Jimmy McHugh. Audiences could see for themselves the warm, witty, self-assured genius who'd written the words to tunes they'd been humming for decades. The publicist made quick work of spreading Dorothy's story: among other things, she was a guest on *The Perry Como Show*. She took part in a program called "Broadway, I Love You," broadcast from WCBS TV in New York, and when *Vogue* analyzed the handwriting of "Famous Americans," Dorothy's was included with that of Anne Bancroft, General Robert E. Lee, Walt Whitman, and others. The analysis of Dorothy's penmanship was spot-on:

> careful about words, details, likes to turn in a good job; the letters are well connected, revealing a logical mind. Free of flourishes, she dispenses with no essentials, but the wide spacing shows generosity, the hooks on "m" and "w" conventionality.[4]

Dorothy was so excited with the coverage that she kept the clipping in her personal files. About the *Perry Como* appearance, she said, "I talked about myself. It was terrific!"[5]

Having done something to preserve—and promote—her legacy, Dorothy set out to return to work. Among others, Dorothy invited Mary Rodgers, composer-daughter of Richard Rodgers, to collaborate. Mary's music had debuted on Broadway by way of her *Once Upon a Mattress* (1959). She declined Dorothy's invitation. "I remember thinking, 'She's a brilliant lyric-writer,' but I would feel uncomfortable unless I was working with a man," Mary said. "I'd grown up thinking that that's where the authority is."[6] Dorothy hadn't known such rejection since her days of pounding the pavement around Tin Pan Alley with J. Fred Coots. There were a handful of projects that would be announced in the trade papers, attention probably garnered by the press agent she'd hired. These would never get off the ground. There was a film adaptation of *By the Beautiful Sea* that would star Judy Garland; it was scrapped. Producer Ray Stark suggested Dorothy write the lyrics for Jule Styne's musical *Funny Girl*. The show, which told the story of vaudevillian Fanny Brice, would have been an excellent fit for Dorothy's skills and experience. Styne refused. He was "worried that a female star and female lyricist might gang up on him." Styne insisted Bob Merrill, a pop songwriter with no Broadway experience, write the lyrics.[7] The project most frequently mentioned was a musical about the nation's new Peace Corps. Having been long discussed in the halls of Congress, the Peace Corps finally came to fruition in the early days of President John F. Kennedy's administration. The program was instituted as a means of spreading assistance and goodwill to developing nations around the globe. The executive order that established the corps was issued in March of 1961 and authorized by Congress in September of that year. Remembering Irving Mills's directive to "hop on a current thing," Dorothy had an idea. She'd write a musical about the Peace Corps. In so doing, she'd not only spread awareness of the new organization, but she'd also give herself something to do, and she'd be doing it with another powerhouse woman of the American theater—Cheryl Crawford. Crawford would produce. A founding member of the Group Theatre, Crawford had also helped to launch The Actor's Studio in 1947. She had directed and produced on Broadway, as well, and had collected an impressive list of credits that included multiple revivals of *Porgy and Bess*, the original production of Tennessee Williams's *The Rose Tattoo* (1951), and a pair of musicals by Alan Jay Lerner and Frederick Loewe, *Brigadoon* (1947) and *Paint Your Wagon* (1951).

When Dorothy struggled to find a songwriting collaborator for the project, she had a solution for that as well. Crawford had received clearance to use seventy-five unpublished melodies written by Jerome Kern. Dorothy had been trying to use Kern's unpublished work since he died. His compositions felt like the perfect choice for Dorothy's Peace Corps project, which she'd tentatively titled *Side by Side*. Several months later, it was announced that producers Robert Fryer and Lawrence Carr were developing their own musical about the Corps. It had to feel like a double cross to Dorothy when they announced a new project so similar in content to one she'd been working on very publicly for months. When asked about the second show, Dorothy responded with her typical diplomacy: "Honey," she said, "I didn't copyright the Peace Corps." The Fryer/Carr collaboration was to be a satirical look at the new organization as seen through the eyes of a female member who "inadvertently complicates things."[8] Judy Holliday, Carol Burnett, and Rosalind Russell were floated as potential leading ladies. Mary Rodgers, daughter of Richard, would write the music and Martin Charnin the lyrics. For reasons that are unknown, both shows were scrapped. Dorothy's dream of "collaborating" again with Kern was never realized. She found herself, once again, a storyteller without a show—or a song—to write.

By now, she was comfortably installed at the Beresford, a chic pre-war apartment building at 211 Central Park West between Eighty-First and Eighty-Second Streets. She'd sold the Brewster property shortly after Eli's death. As much as she'd loved her family's thirteen years there, it was way more space than she needed with her children growing up and leaving home. The estate was purchased by the Episcopal Order of the Community of the Holy Spirit; it became a retreat for nuns who continue to use it today. Her eight-room apartment in the Beresford was more than adequate for her needs. The building was designed by Emery Roth, whose namesake architectural firm was responsible for more than a hundred New York City skyscrapers. Roth himself was no fan of the glass-and-steel style of modern architecture that would typify the work of the firm; he preferred masonry buildings with classical details. That's the aesthetic with which he built the Beresford in 1929. Having also designed the San Remo, onetime home of Herbert and Foxy Sondheim, Roth considered the Beresford to be one of his best designs. To this day, it stands as one of New York's most prestigious addresses. It was then too. Sharing the twenty-three story building with Dorothy were the likes of comedian Phil Silvers, actor Victor Moore, and broadcaster Hugh Downs. Adolph Green and his wife Phyllis Newman lived directly across the hall. With Betty Comden, Green had co-written the lyrics and librettos for shows like *On the Town* (1944), *Peter Pan* (1954), and *Bells Are Ringing* (1956),

**Dorothy Fields and others at the celebration of ASCAP's Fiftieth Anniversary in 1964 (from left) Dorothy Fields, Leroy Anderson, Noble Sissle, Richard Adler, Harold Arlen, Arthur Schwartz, Stanley Adams, and Morton Gould; Dorothy had previously collaborated with three of the men pictured.** Photofest.

and films like *Singin' in the Rain* (1952). The two apartments—Dorothy's and the Green family's—took up the entirety of the building's seventh floor.

One night in 1963, Dorothy was at the Beresford, playing another role in which she'd always excelled; she was hosting a group of songwriters. Among them was a young composer named Cy Coleman. Almost twenty-five years younger than Dorothy, Coleman was born just months after she was celebrating the success of *Blackbirds of 1928*. His New York upbringing looked more like that of the characters in *A Tree Grows in Brooklyn* than Dorothy's pampered childhood. From those inauspicious Bronx beginnings, Coleman was quickly noticed as a prodigy at the piano. His parents owned several tenement houses. As one renter was moving out, there was an object too big to relocate. It was a piano. Coleman's parents moved the instrument into their apartment, and four-year-old Cy—born Seymour—began to pick out tunes. "One day the milkman heard me and sent over his son's piano teacher," Coleman said. "She thought I was a real talent and said she'd give me two lessons for the price of one."[9] As a young child, he'd presented recitals at Town Hall, Carnegie Hall, and other high-tone Manhattan venues. His focus at the time was on classical music. As he grew, though, Coleman became increasingly interested in jazz. He worked as both a performer of it—as part of the Cy Coleman Trio—and, eventually, presenter. He owned his own club, the Playroom.

Before long, Cy had signed a publishing deal. Carolyn Leigh was one of the earliest lyricists with whom he wrote. Together, they produced standards like "The Best Is Yet to Come," "Witchcraft," and "Hey, Look Me Over." They also wrote two musicals together. *Wildcat*, starring Lucille Ball, opened in 1960; *Little Me* followed in 1962. With a book by Neil Simon, *Little Me* was a star turn for the inimitable Sid Caesar. In the show, Caesar played seven roles, each as hilarious as the other. Both shows were reasonably successful by the standard of the time. *Wildcat* ran for nearly two hundred performances; *Little Me* reached 257, but by the show's opening in November of 1962, it was clear that the collaboration between Coleman and Leigh could not continue. Their relationship was volatile at best. Leigh told a reporter, "It's the best way for us. He writes a song and plays it for me, and I don't like it, and I say, 'Cy, no. I won't write words for that.'" Conversely, Cy would respond to her lyrics with, "I've known you to do much better on a bad day . . . try again, Poet. Try again." When Leigh bought a home in East Hampton, Coleman followed suit, so that they could continue writing *Little Me* in person. "It made it easier to work together," Coleman said. "Snarling on a telephone is empty compared to insults face to face. Besides, on a phone, the other collaborator can always just hang up."[10] Clearly, Cy Coleman was in desperate need of someone new with whom to write. That's the position in which he found himself in 1963, as he walked into the home of one of the most successful lyric writers of all time. Full of the bravado of one who's known nothing but success, Coleman walked up to Dorothy and said, "I'm Cy Coleman."

"I know who you are," she responded.[11]

"How would you like to write a song?"[12]

# Chapter 15
## "If My Friends Could See Me Now"

Dorothy was elated by the request of the thirty-something composer standing in her luxurious apartment in New York's chic Beresford building. "I'd love it!" she responded. "Thank God you asked!" Coleman was surprised. "Don't a lot of people ask you?" "No," Dorothy said. "They're either intimidated or whatever."[1] By August of 1963, the news was in the trade papers: Dorothy Fields, one of Broadway's all-time great lyricists, would be working with Cy Coleman, one of its up-and-coming composers. Coleman had made the suggestion, assuming the two might write a song or two. He could never have imagined the opportunity that would eventually present itself. While they waited, Coleman headed for California, where he had plans to score a Cary Grant film called *Father Goose*. Dorothy went about with life as usual; there was her typical charity work to complete, David's graduation from Amherst to prepare for, and the birth of Gwen Verdon's new baby to celebrate. For all of their professional success, Verdon and Fosse's road to parenthood was a long one. Gwen had a teenaged son from a previous relationship; she was desperate to share a child with her new husband, Fosse. She and Fosse had married in April of 1960. Afterward, she'd decided to take time off to recuperate from the demands of a role like *Redhead* and to focus on having a second child. The process was long and hard. Fosse and Verdon availed themselves of every sort of fertility assistance available to them at the time. Finally, Verdon was pregnant. Nicole Providence Fosse was born in March of 1963. Both Fosse and Verdon were over the moon. Their baby girl's middle name was suggested by Dorothy. Knowing the trouble Verdon had had conceiving her, Dorothy thought Providence was the perfect way to celebrate the gift of the little girl. The new parents agreed.

During Verdon's time off, Fosse had continued to build his Broadway empire. After *Redhead*, he'd done the musical staging for Frank Loesser and Abe Burrows's Pulitzer Prize–winning *How to Succeed in Business without Really Trying*

(1961). He'd also directed and choreographed Cy Coleman, Carolyn Leigh, and Neil Simon's *Little Me*. When Verdon began to feel ready to return to work, Fosse started his hunt for the perfect show in which she could make her triumphant return. He found that to be a difficult proposition. Verdon was entering her late thirties at the time. Typical ingenue roles—like Holly Golightly in the stage adaptation of *Breakfast at Tiffany's*—were off the table.[2] At the same time, the role had to be significant enough to showcase Verdon's many talents. That's when Fosse remembered a foreign film he'd seen in 1962. *Nights of Cabiria* was a film by Italian moviemaker Federico Fellini. The film was the story of a prostitute (Cabiria) in Rome who longed for a life far away from the one in which she found herself trapped. She saved for a home of her own; she prayed for a husband, and in the end, she found herself jilted by a lover who'd stolen her savings and left her high and dry. The role was played by Italian actress Giulietta Masina. One reviewer referred to her as "the mischievous Masina, the pixy-with-the-pop-eyes and dimpled smile."[3] It's easy to see why Fosse thought the role might be right for Verdon.

He arranged for producers Carr and Fryer to screen the film. As Fosse biographer Sam Wasson notes in his *Fosse*, the director knew he had a hard sell on his hands. Heartbroken prostitutes were hardly the stuff that musicals were made of. Eventually, Fosse convinced the team to at least entertain his idea. He envisioned a pair of one-act musicals, one written by him and based on *Nights of Cabiria* (though with significant changes), the other written by playwright Elaine May. Together, the two would be called *Hearts and Flowers*. Fosse called his *Little Me* collaborator, Cy Coleman, to see if he might write the score. Coleman agreed, provided Dorothy write the lyrics. At last, the two had the opportunity they'd been looking for. They began their work on the music for *Sweet Charity*, much of which was written at their separate homes in the Hamptons. As development of the script went on, it became clear that Fosse would need more than one act to tell his adapted story of Cabiria. The original idea for *Hearts and Flowers* was scrapped in favor of fully focusing on a single story, a story that, Fosse was beginning to realize, was completely beyond his ability to write. He needed help for the project that had come to be called *Sweet Charity*. He knew just whom to call.

Neil Simon was one of Broadway's brightest lights. In addition to writing the gut-busting libretto of *Little Me*, Simon had penned a trio of plays—*Come Blow Your Horn* (1961), *Barefoot in the Park* (1963), and *The Odd Couple* (1965)—that had made him a sought-after commodity. After winning a Tony Award for *The Odd Couple*, Simon decided to take a vacation. He and his wife, Joan, took their two daughters to Italy. Not long after they'd arrived, Simon received a call from Fosse. He all but begged for Simon's help on the book of his new project: Fosse didn't think it was funny enough; assuming Simon was the perfect person to fix his problem, Fosse sent a copy of the script to Simon's rented home on the Appia Antica. Simon read the script as soon as it arrived. "Fosse was wrong," Simon said. "It didn't need humor. It *desperately* needed humor."[4] Simon went to work, doing a quick rewrite of a handful of lines and sending them back to Fosse. Fosse begged Simon, "Don't quit!" but Simon was in the middle of adapting his play *Barefoot in the Park* for film. Taking on another gig, particularly while on vacation, did not appeal to Simon in the least. Fosse, on the other hand, was desperate. Completely unbeknownst to Simon, Fosse showed up in Rome, bringing with him a recording of Dorothy and Coleman's score. Fosse played two numbers—"Hey, Big Spender" and "There's Gotta Be Something Better Than This"—for Simon and his wife, Joan. At the end of the second song, Joan turned to her husband and said, "If you don't do this show, you and I are through." Fosse asked, "You want to hear more?" Simon responded with characteristic sarcasm, "No. Who wants to sit here and listen to the best score I have ever heard. Turn it off."[5]

Needless to say, Simon accepted the gig. *Sweet Charity* started its rehearsals in August of 1965. The Broadway run was slated for the famed Palace Theatre at Broadway and Forty-Seventh Street, the first show in what would be a newly renovated space. The Palace had opened in March of 1913 and was operated by the Keith-Albee vaudeville circuit. With nearly 1,800 seats, the Palace was not only one of Broadway's biggest theaters, it was also one of its most opulent. Guests entered via an eleven-story office building that opened into a lobby forty-feet wide and covered in Italian marble. Ed Wynn had headlined the opening bill, but the Palace would later play host to a who's who of international entertainment. Sarah Bernhardt, Fanny Brice, the Marx Brothers, Weber and Fields, and Florence Mills were among the superstars who'd top the bills of the theater perceived to be "the Olympus of vaudeville to which every variety entertainer did aspire."[6] Charlie Chaplin made his first American appearance there. The Palace operated without a single day of darkness from September 1913 until the early 1930s. As the American appetite for entertainment shifted from the stage medium to film, the Palace Theatre *modus operandi* was unsustainable. It became an RKO movie house in November of 1932. In 1965, the Nederlander Organization bought the Palace from RKO for $1.6 million. Their intent was to restore it to its original use as a bastion of live entertainment. Topping the opening night bill of the new space would not be Ed Wynn but Gwen Verdon, who, according to notices from the show's out-of-town tryouts, was more than up to the occasion: "At last! A honey of a musical with a honey of a redhead, Gwen Verdon" (Ernest Schier, *Philadelphia Bulletin*), "The most enlivening first night in many seasons!" (Jerry Gaghan, *Philadelphia News*), "The musical show we've all been waiting for—the one with the songs and dances and the funny sayings, the one with the lovely people and the unfailing sense of humor, opened Monday. It has the faith and hope that theater lovers have been waiting for" (Henry Murdoch, *Philadelphia Inquirer*).[7] Because of demand at the box office, police had to be called in to maintain order around Philadelphia's Shubert Theatre.

Due to delays in the Palace Theatre's renovations, *Sweet Charity*'s opening was briefly postponed. This allowed the show the benefit of an unanticipated second tryout in Detroit's Nederlander-operated Fisher Theatre. Shortly after the show opened in Detroit, Dorothy and Coleman received a resounding endorsement from one of their peers: "Have just heard your demo and am joyously excited by it. This is the freshest and best scores to come to us in many years. Good luck and thanks to you both. Love, Dick Rodgers."[8] After six years of loneliness and professional stagnation, Dorothy was elated—and relieved!—to be working

**Rehearsal for the stage production *Annie Get Your Gun:* (clockwise from upper left) Richard Rodgers, Ethel Merman, Irving Berlin, and Dorothy Fields, 1966.** Photo by Friedman-Abeles ©The New York Public Library for the Performing Arts.

again and at as high a level as she ever had. Just as the Palace Theatre was being reborn on the February night that *Sweet Charity* finally opened, so, in a sense, was Dorothy Fields's career. She, whose work had been born in the Jazz Age and perfected in the Golden Age, was being made-over for the coming Age of Aquarius. The enormity of this fact was not at all lost on her. With the incredible success of *Sweet Charity*, Dorothy Fields was infused with an elation that eluded so many of her peers. Weeks after the show had opened, Dorothy sheepishly told reporter Martin Gershen, "It's nice to know you can still function in the idiom."[9] She was being modest, but the fact is, many of the former greats were struggling to make the change—transitioning from the "older" sound of Broadway to its new one—that Dorothy had just been able to make. As a Toronto reporter put it, "The sell-out business of *Sweet Charity* . . . indicates that her hand has not lost its cunning in making songs go."[10]

All told, *Sweet Charity* played for a year and a half, turning in more than six hundred performances. It was nominated for nine Tony Awards—including one for Coleman and Dorothy in the category of Best Composer and Lyricist—and won one (Best Choreography to Bob Fosse), having lost most of the major awards to *Man of La Mancha* by Mitch Leigh and Joe Darion. With the exception of the heartache of losing her brother Joseph just six weeks after its premiere at the Palace, Dorothy Fields was riding on a high she hadn't felt in years. Other "old guard" songwriters were beginning to hang it up. Ira Gershwin had quit writing in 1954. Richard Rodgers never returned to see the second act of *Hair*. Frustrated by the changing sound of Broadway, Rodgers said, "I don't pretend to understand."[11] Harry Warren called the new music "awful," and Irving Berlin, "The Father of American Popular Song," spent the last decades of his life as a recluse:

> It was as if I owned a store, and people no longer wanted to buy what I had to sell . . . everything changed. The world was a different place. The death of President Kennedy, the Vietnam war, the social protest. Music changed, too. The Beatles and other groups reached audiences. I couldn't. It was time to close up shop.[12]

That was not Dorothy's take. Where others saw the end of the game, Dorothy saw a beginning. In 1966, she had *Sweet Charity* running on Broadway; a twentieth-anniversary revival of *Annie Get Your Gun* would open later that same year. At one time, she'd run in the same circles as George Gershwin and Jerome Kern; now she found herself collaborating with the crew who would carry Broadway's mantle in to the next decades. Incredibly, they loved working with her as much as she loved working with them. In his 1996 memoir *Rewrites*, Simon recorded his remembrances of Dorothy:

> Working with [her] was a major joy and surprise for me. When I met her, she was in her sixties and reminded me a little of Lillian Hellman. She was tough, all business, and could meet a crisis with the best of them . . . what I didn't know about her was that she was fond of a drink at dinner. She was even fonder of two or three drinks

even without dinner. When she appeared at the theater every night for the evening performance, she was dressed in her Park Avenue best, always looking elegant. She didn't stand too well, however, as a result of a martini or two, and often leaned on a friendly arm or a bannister to give her balance, although she never lost her dignity. Be that as it may, at nine o'clock in the morning, she was fresh, alert, and had already written a new set of lyrics that would knock your socks off. Whether it was a ballad or a comedy song, she always delivered overnight and first-class. I'm sorry I only had one opportunity to work with her.[13]

The song "I'm a Brass Band" is an example of Dorothy's working "overnight and first-class." It was written in one morning during the Philadelphia tryout of *Sweet Charity*. The creators realized that they needed another song for Verdon. With nothing more than the title and the first line of the lyric in her head, Dorothy went from her suite at the Barclay Hotel to Coleman's at the Warwick. By that afternoon, the number was done. On the other hand, they had to cut a song called "Raincheck" in Detroit. Dorothy called it "a real stinker."[14] Over the weekend, she and Coleman wrote its replacement, a number called "The Rhythm of Life," which is one of the most recognized moments in the show. That she was capable of working quickly is not to say that she found it easy. Coleman recalled her struggling through "The Rhythm of Life" lyric. "She worked at it like a jigsaw puzzle and put the lyric together one phrase at a time," he said.[15] For a woman who had written the lyric for "I Feel a Song Coming On," Dorothy was the first to admit that the work was, at times, difficult:

> I wrote that, the words to "I Feel a Song Coming On," but I don't believe a word of it. A song just doesn't "come on." I've always had to tease it out, squeeze it out, and anyone that tells you a song is something that's an inspiration . . . has got to prove that one to me. It's hard, slave labor . . . and I love it.[16]

After the success of *Sweet Charity*, it wasn't a question of if Dorothy and Coleman would collaborate again, but when. Her 7 a.m. wake-up calls notwithstanding ("[They] drove me up a wall," Coleman said),[17] Coleman found working with her to be endlessly more agreeable than writing with Carolyn Leigh. He was committed to continuing the partnership; she was too. "The Coleman magic got this old gal to write the kind of contemporary words that settle so well in 'Doc,' as we called him, Simon's book," she said, adding: "Mr. Coleman, may I say, courtesy of Rodgers and Hammerstein, 'I'm in love; I'm in love; I'm in love; I'm in love; I'm in love with a wonderful Cy!'"[18] Their post-*Charity* assignments would include writing several new numbers for the 1969 film adaptation, in which Shirley MacLaine took on the title role. They also looked for new material to tackle together. A David Merrick–produced musical called *The Happy Time*, based on a 1949 comedy by Samuel Taylor, was announced. Dorothy and Coleman dropped out of the project when they found out that Yves Montand, for whom they'd been writing, wouldn't be available for two more years. Up-and-comers John Kander and Fred Ebb took over writing duties; the show, starring Robert Goulet, opened on Broadway in 1968. They turned down fifteen projects, waiting for the one about which they were both excited. As they waited, Dorothy took an assignment to write a lyric for record producer and songwriter Quincy Jones. Their "Where There Is Love" was the theme song for a 1968 film called *The Hell with Heroes*.

Finally, Dorothy and Coleman found their perfect project. The collaboration would continue.

**Dorothy Fields with composer Cy Coleman, 1973.** Photofest.

# Chapter 16
## "It's Not Where You Start, It's Where You Finish"

Where Dorothy Fields and Cy Coleman came up with the idea for a musical based on the courtship of Franklin D. and Eleanor Roosevelt isn't known. What's certain is that, by the end of 1969, the pair was well on its way to completing the score for their *Eleanor*. Jerome Coopersmith, who'd written the librettos for *Baker Street* and *The Apple Tree*, was on board to write the book. Morton DaCosta (*Auntie Mame*, *The Music Man*) would direct, and Alexander Cohen—the producer who, in 1967, had introduced the idea of a nationally televised Tony Awards broadcast—was initially announced as their producer. Coleman considered the score their finest collaboration. Time and again, though, the production was put off. It had been scheduled for an opening in the fall of 1970. Because of disagreements with Coopersmith—"the book writer didn't want anybody coming and changing anything," Coleman said[1]—*Eleanor* was shelved forever. Dorothy and Coleman were understandably disappointed; they were resolved, however, to team up again. The search began for a new project to which they could apply their combined skillset.

As they waited, Dorothy received a string of honors. First, she was elected to the Songwriter's Hall of Fame, the only woman in its first-ever class of honorees. The ceremony was held at the New York Hilton in May of 1971. Dorothy was voted on by the hall's 1,600 dues-paying members, who'd selected her from a slate of thirty nominees. Also inducted with her were Harold Arlen, Hoagy Carmichael, Duke Ellington, Rudolf Friml, Ira Gershwin, Alan Jay Lerner, Johnny Mercer, James Van Heusen, and Harry Warren. The inductees received miniature pianolas and were entertained by Frank Sinatra, who joked, "Without you, I would have been selling ties."[2] The next April, Dorothy took part in the Lyrics and Lyricists Series hosted by New York's 92nd Street Young Men's and Young Women's Hebrew Association (now the 92nd Street Y). She was the first woman to be honored with such a program. In his introduction, the host for the

129

evening announced that Dorothy's catalog of work was "the most important and significant of any woman writer ever in the history of ASCAP."[3] The program featured a slate of performers singing Dorothy's songs; she narrated, revealing autobiographical details with the same self-deprecating and disarming charm that had made her so appealing on stage in the 1920s and on the air in the 1930s. The event was such a hit that it was reprised later that year. As Dorothy summered at a Bridgehampton rental, which had been her tradition since selling the house in Brewster, East Hampton's Guild Hall presented an encore performance of the Lyrics and Lyricist's Series program. Critic Ted Strongin called it "a postgraduate course in lyric-writing."[4]

Dorothy, who'd always been so quick to shine the spotlight on others, was suddenly standing squarely under its warmth. The legacy with which she'd been concerned when she hired the press agent in 1959 was beginning to take its shape. While still reveling in the accolades, Dorothy found herself back at work with Coleman. It was announced on the front page of *Variety* that they would be musicalizing *Merton of the Movies*, a 1922 play by George S. Kaufman and Marc Connelly. That show was never written. What was written is an adaptation of William Gibson's 1958 play *Two for the Seesaw*. The play starred Henry Fonda and Anne Bancroft and played for an incredible 750 performances; it was then adapted into a 1962 film, starring Robert Mitchum and Shirley MacLaine. In it, a straitlaced Nebraska attorney (Jerry Ryan), who's going through a divorce, finds himself in New York City, where he crosses paths with a neurotic dancer named Gittel Mosca. The setup was tailor-made for a musical. The show's road to Broadway, however, was as bumpy as Gittel's relationship with Jerry. The problems began with its star. Lainie Kazan, who'd understudied Barbra Streisand in Broadway's *Funny Girl*, had known both Dorothy and Coleman for a while when their work on *Seesaw* was announced. Kazan lobbied—hard—for the role of Gittel. Eventually, her efforts paid off. Though the producers believed her to be overweight for the role of their leading lady, they nevertheless offered her the part with the understanding that she would lose forty pounds prior to the start of rehearsal. Tony Award winner Ken Howard (*Child's Play*) soon joined the cast as Jerry Ryan.

Kazan came to rehearsals completely unprepared. She hadn't lost the weight that she had agreed to in order to portray a dancer; secondly, she didn't know her lines. Finally, she and the director fought to the extent that Ken Howard felt like he was getting no help at all. Fed up, Coleman decided it was time for a change. They wouldn't just need a new star; they'd new a new director. Producers Joseph Kipness and Larry Kasha made the pitch to twenty-nine-year-old Michael Bennett. Bennett had started his career as a dancer and quickly risen through the ranks. Within a decade, he'd become a celebrated choreographer and worked on contemporary musicals like *Promises, Promises* (1968), *Company* (1970), and *Follies* (1971), which also marked his directorial debut. Bennett was not at all interested in the project. He was already beginning to ruminate on what would be

Clumsy — in life
" How to fail without really trying "
Misfire
strike out —
successless —
flummoxed —
Beat

*Im a Dame a Dozen — Dame*

unfit
miss fit
ass in a lion's skin —
square peg —
mismatch — mishmosh —
strictly —
I'm much Ado About Nothing
One big frustration
a Blight —
over-ripe banana
Defunct —
a Collapse
a Crash —
an over-drawn account
a rubber check
a bad check —
men of straw
default
a dispossess notice
I'm a swindle —
Drug on the market of life —
a slump — a painful mump —
a free day to a hangang —
I'm a Fire Sale
As the devils say — a Bum march
I'm a Dime a Dozen

**A page from Dorothy's legal pad that illustrates her method of brainstorming prior to writing.** Billy Rose Theatre Division, The New York Public Library for the Performing Arts.

his *magnum opus*—a musical called *A Chorus Line*, which would open in 1975 and change the face of Broadway forever. Kipness and Kasha wouldn't take no for an answer. They guilted Bennett into taking the show, telling the rising star that it was his duty to take the job, if he cared anything about the future of Broadway. In exchange, they'd cede to him complete creative control of the show. Bennett finally accepted. His first order of business was to call in help.

His friend Tommy Tune was a 6'6" Texan, who'd been dancing on Broadway since arriving in New York in 1965. He'd also worked in film. Tune had just wrapped a movie in England when he got the call from Bennett. Bennett told Tune to get to Detroit immediately. *Seesaw* was at the Nederlander's Fisher Theatre and in desperate need of any help he could give. With the help of a very willing pair of songwriters and Tune, who received $500 for each number that he reworked, Bennett overhauled the entire show; sets, costumes, orchestrations, nothing was left untouched. Coleman called it "the most radical change I ever went through."[5] When librettist Michael Stewart suddenly walked out, Neil Simon came in to complete significant rewrites on the libretto. Simon refused to take credit for the work, so producers asked Dorothy if she'd be willing to put her name on it. She wasn't: she wouldn't put her name on something she hadn't done. In the end, Bennett received credit for the book. He'd eventually be credited as the show's director, choreographer, and librettist.

While still in Detroit, Dorothy had an encounter with a young dancer that illustrates the depth of the songwriter's warmth and generosity. Dorothy noticed chorus member Amanda McBroom looking forlorn during rehearsal one day. She asked McBroom what was bothering her. The young performer, it turned out, was missing her boyfriend.

> [Dorothy] put down this enormous Louis Vuitton bag, which she always carried around, pulled out a pack of Camels, lit one up, pulled out a flask, took a drag, then pulled out her checkbook, wrote me a check for $300, handed it to me, and said, "You get him here. Romance is important."

In the years after making her Broadway debut in *Seesaw*, McBroom would become a lyricist herself. Her song "The Rose," written for Bette Midler's 1979 movie of the same name, sold more than a half million copies, hit number one on the Billboard Hot 100, and garnered a Grammy Award for Bette Midler. Country superstar Conway Twitty had similar success with the song, taking it to #1 on the country chart in 1983.

*Seesaw*'s breakup with Kazan was a bad one. They were able to replace her with the brilliantly talented Michele Lee, who'd starred in *How to Succeed in Business without Really Trying* on Broadway and in the Disney film *The Love Bug*, but the producers were legally bound to continue paying Kazan $3,000 a week for the run of the show.[6] That put the already struggling show into a financial chokehold. Having gone more than a half million dollars over the show's $750,000 budget, the creators were determined to make *Seesaw* work: Coleman and Fields deferred their royalties and put in $30,000 each. Kipness took a loss on one of his shares in the show to raise cash and pay bills. Bennett refused his $5,000 directing fee, saying, "We're not in this for the money. It must be love. Wasn't it Moss Hart who said, 'The theater is not an occupation; it's a disease.'"[7] Bennett personally paid the Nederlander Organization, who owned the show's Uris Theatre, a $15,000 fee to allow them to open on a Sunday. This would allow the show to run for a week before closing on the following Saturday, so that they didn't have to pay the next week's wages.

When *Seesaw* opened, it was met with modestly favorable reviews. Douglas Watt's assessment in the *New York Daily News* summarized them well. He called *Seesaw*

an intimate, bittersweet comedy and a big, brassy musical [which] exist side by side, independent of one another. Both shows have great points in their favor, but they never truly become one—two ends of a seesaw, if you like.[8]

In spite of its lackluster notices, *Seesaw*'s ticket sales surprised everyone. The show clicked with audiences; the characters felt familiar and interesting. By the second week of its run, *Seesaw* made $794 more than its $60,000 a week break-even point. The show would go on to shock everyone. It ran for most of 1973, closing in December having played nearly three hundred performances. The gratification felt by Dorothy, Coleman, and the others who'd battled to keep the *Seesaw* afloat, was significant. According to Coleman,

We had all worked so long and so hard. It seemed ridiculous to give up just because we needed more dough. Out of town, we had real problems—big problems—and we solved them. Why couldn't we solve this? *Seesaw* succeeded because . . . six weeks ago, a group of us banded together and worked with love and complete trust. No egos were involved. The behind-the-scenes story of *Seesaw* is terribly corny, like an MGM musical, circa 1948.[9]

Almost a year to the day after the opening of *Seesaw*, Dorothy was going about with life as usual. She'd woken up in her apartment at the Beresford around 7 a.m. and indulged in "breakfast" in bed. For her, concerned as she was with her weight, this generally meant a cup of coffee. She'd placed her daily call to Eliza. Now married and working as an artist, Eliza was the mother of a ten-month-old boy named David, on whom Dorothy doted. With her routine at home completed, Dorothy headed to the rehearsal studio. *Seesaw* had spawned a national tour. On that day, March 28, 1974, the company showed Dorothy its choreography for a song she'd written just for the road show. It was called "The Party's on Me." That afternoon, she received the news that *Seesaw*, the show she'd seen struggle its way into a successful Broadway run, had been nominated for seven Tony Awards, including one for her score. She called her son David to let him know the news. He wasn't home to take the call but received the message when he returned home that night. Not long after, David received another call. It was Bobbi Weinstein, who lived several floors above Dorothy at the Beresford. She was calling to say that his mother was gone. As she'd prepared to attend a benefit for the Young Adult Institute that evening, sixty-nine-year-old Dorothy had died as suddenly as her beloved Herbert and Eli had sixteen years before and just as unexpectedly.[10] Her housekeeper found her, dead of a heart attack. A Broadway giant had fallen, while standing as tall at the end of her fifty-year career as she had at its beginning.

News of her death quickly spread to a shocked Broadway. A funeral service was held at the Frank E. Campbell Funeral Chapel at Madison Avenue and Eighty-First Street. The chapel was—and still is—known for facilitating celebrity funerals, including those of Irving Berlin, Jacqueline Kennedy Onassis, Judy Garland, John Lennon, and many others. The funeral wasn't enough, though. Those who knew and loved Dorothy wanted to honor her in a more significant way. "Right after she died, a group of us talked about doing a Memorial to Dorothy," said Coleman. "It evolved into . . . a kind of birthday party that would raise funds for one of her pet charities, [East Hampton, NY arts and entertainment center] Guild Hall. Once the word got out, we were practically besieged, even by people who never worked with her."[11] The idea behind the so-called "Tribute to Dorothy Fields" was a great one. Each year since Dorothy had started summering in Bridgehampton, her friends who were also in the area would join her to celebrate her July 15th birthday. The "tribute" that Coleman and company imagined would be an extension of that, open to the public with ticket sales benefiting an East Hampton performance venue. Dorothy, whose hospitality was as boundless as her charity, would have been pleased: her legacy was secure, and it lives on in a catalog of shows and songs that play as freshly today as in the time they were written. Wrote Rex Reed,

> From the beginning, Dorothy Fields's songs were laced with vinegar and gin. Soft as a powder puff was "Remind Me," but there was scar tissue around the heart in "I'll Pay the Check." These were tough songs written by a tough lady, who knew the way to live was to take as well as give, and through the world-weariness, the songs emerged entirely young and fresh . . . and she wrote all kinds of songs with many points of view, and it's a tribute to her intelligence and foresight that none of them seems dated today.[12]

**Dorothy Fields and other songwriters in a 1983 drawing by Al Hirschfeld, "Smithsonian: Great Songwriters."** © The Al Hirschfeld Foundation. www.AlHirschfeldFoundation.org.

# Conclusion

Dorothy Fields had the kind of career that most people only dream of. From beginning to end, she was at the top of her game. Part of this was owing to her top-level talent. She had an incredible way with words and an insightful ear for expressing both character and sentiment. Another part of Dorothy's success, though, was the time at which she entered the field. As music historian Artis Wodehouse noted in the 1998 documentary *Yours for a Song: The Women of Tin Pan Alley*, the 1920s and '30s were as hospitable to women songwriters as many of the decades since have been. There were 178 women who joined ASCAP between the years of 1920 and 1949.[1] On the list, of course, were some of those mentioned by Dorothy in her conversation with Henry Kane—Dana Suesse, Kay Swift, and others. What's shocking is to look through the ranks of Broadway creative teams in the late 1920s and early 1930s and see how many women are represented. Though many of their names have been, sadly, forgotten, women composers, lyricists, or librettists were on the creative teams for nearly thirty percent of the musicals that opened in the same season as *Blackbirds of 1928* (1927–1928). Jo Trent. Ida Hoyt Chamberlain. Gertrude Purcell. There are so many more. The following season (1928–1929), the percentage dropped, but it remained surprisingly high at a remarkable twenty-five percent. Agnes Morgan. Grace Henry. Fanny Todd Mitchell. These percentages seem even higher when considered in light of the number of shows that opened in those seasons: 1927–1928 saw 282 openings; fifty-four of them were of musicals. In 1928–1929, there were 250 openings; forty-four were musicals. Women writers, though by no means in the majority, were, nonetheless, represented on the Jazz Age stage in a surprisingly significant way. Muriel Pollock. Irene Franklin. Rida Johnson Young.

The same sort of analysis on current Broadway rosters is just as shocking. In the seasons from 2009–2019, there were 417 shows that opened; 151 of them were musicals—about fifteen a year. Thirty-three of the 151 had a female composer,

137

lyricist, or librettist. Of the fifteen or so musicals that premiered each year, this works out to an average of three shows per season with at least one female creator. Three. Twenty percent. One in five. In the twenty-first century. Lynn Ahrens. Irene Sankoff. Brenda Russell. The decade before is even more surprising. From 1999–2008, roughly twelve new musicals opened each season. Two, on average, had at least one female on its writing team. Quiara Alegria Hudes. Nell Benjamin. Lisa Lambert. In other words, women are more meagerly represented on Broadway in 2019 than they were in 1929. Composer Dana Suesse, a contemporary of Dorothy's, once said, "In the early days of ASCAP, I remember looking around the room and seeing that the entire meeting was full of men and maybe a half-dozen women, including me."[2] In a 2008 essay, Jennifer Jones Cavenaugh noted that composer Jeanine Tesori (*Thoroughly Modern Millie, Fun Home*) has said she is "often the only woman in musical production meetings."[3] I don't have an answer for why this is; I just have data. I also have surprise that it was the 2015–2016 season before Broadway had enough female representation (by way of *Waitress* and *Eclipsed*'s all-female creative teams) to warrant a pair of *New York Times* reporters considering it a "year of women."[4] Finally, I have Dorothy Fields's opinion. When Henry Kane asked the Tony Award–winning, Academy Award–winning, Songwriter's Hall of Fame inductee if she thought more women should be interested in songwriting, Dorothy Fields responded, "Yes. Emphatically, I do."[5]

# Appendix A
## Song List

*Most of this list (through 1959) is compiled from one in Dorothy's Personal Papers at the New York Public Library. Any omissions are accidental.*

| TITLE | YEAR | COMPOSER |
|---|---|---|
| I'm a Broken-Hearted Blackbird | 1927 | Jimmy McHugh |
| | | |
| Collegiana | 1928 | Jimmy McHugh |
| Bon-Soir—Cherie | 1928 | Jimmy McHugh |
| Harlem River Quiver | 1928 | Jimmy McHugh |
| | | |
| (**Blackbirds of 1928**, Broadway) | | |
| I Can't Give You Anything but Love | 1928 | Jimmy McHugh |
| Porgy (aka Blues for Porgy) | 1928 | Jimmy McHugh |
| I Must Have That Man | 1928 | Jimmy McHugh |
| Diga Diga Do | 1928 | Jimmy McHugh |
| Doin' the New Low Down | 1928 | Jimmy McHugh |
| Shuffle Your Feet and Just Roll Along | 1928 | Jimmy McHugh |
| Bandanna Babies | 1928 | Jimmy McHugh |
| Here Comes My Blackbird | 1928 | Jimmy McHugh |
| Dixie | 1928 | Jimmy McHugh |
| Baby | 1928 | Jimmy McHugh |
| Magnolia's Wedding Day | 1928 | Jimmy McHugh |
| | | |
| (**Hello, Daddy**, Broadway) | | |
| Out Where the Blues Begin | 1928 | Jimmy McHugh |
| Futuristic Rhythm | 1928 | Jimmy McHugh |
| In a Great Big Way | 1928 | Jimmy McHugh |
| Your Disposition Is Mine | 1928 | Jimmy McHugh |
| Let's Sit and Talk about You | 1928 | Jimmy McHugh |

*(continued)*

| TITLE | YEAR | COMPOSER |
|---|---|---|
| As Long as We Are in Love | 1928 | Jimmy McHugh |
| Hot Chocolate | 1929 | Jimmy McHugh |
| Hottentot Tot | 1929 | Jimmy McHugh |
| Freeze an' Melt | 1929 | Jimmy McHugh |
| A Japanese Dream | 1929 | Jimmy McHugh |
| Think of You, Think of Me in the Moonlight | 1929 | Jimmy McHugh |
| Let Me Sing before Breakfast | 1929 | Jimmy McHugh |
| | | |
| (**Ziegfeld's Midnight Frolic**, Broadway) | | |
| Looking for Love | 1929 | Jimmy McHugh |
| Raisin' the Roof | 1929 | Jimmy McHugh |
| | | |
| (**International Revue**, Broadway) | | |
| Exactly Like You | 1930 | Jimmy McHugh |
| I'm Feelin' Blue 'Cause I've Got Nobody | 1930 | Jimmy McHugh |
| On the Sunny Side of the Street | 1930 | Jimmy McHugh |
| Keys to Your Heart | 1930 | Jimmy McHugh |
| Cinderella Brown | 1930 | Jimmy McHugh |
| I've Got a Bug in My Head | 1930 | Jimmy McHugh |
| | | |
| (**Kelly's Vacation**, Film) | | |
| Any One Else | 1930 | Jimmy McHugh |
| Dreaming | 1930 | Jimmy McHugh |
| Do I Know Why? | 1930 | Jimmy McHugh |
| Wearin' of the Green | 1930 | Jimmy McHugh |
| A Man on Earth Is Worth a Half a Dozen on the Moon | 1930 | Jimmy McHugh |
| | | |
| (**Love in the Rough**, Film) | | |
| One More Waltz | 1930 | Jimmy McHugh |
| Go Home and Tell Your Mother | 1930 | Jimmy McHugh |
| I'm Doin' That Thing | 1930 | Jimmy McHugh |
| Like Kelly Can | 1930 | Jimmy McHugh |
| I'm Learning a Lot from You | 1930 | Jimmy McHugh |
| Spring Fever | 1930 | Jimmy McHugh |
| Dance Fool Dance | 1930 | Jimmy McHugh |
| Topsy and Eva | 1930 | Jimmy McHugh |
| Rosalie | 1930 | Jimmy McHugh |
| There's a Kick in the Old Girl Yet | 1930 | Jimmy McHugh |
| | | |
| (**March of Time**, Film) | | |
| Isn't Nature Wonderful (A Social Success) | 1930 | Jimmy McHugh |
| | | |
| (**Vanderbilt Revue**, Broadway) | | |
| Blue Again | 1930 | Jimmy McHugh |
| Button Up Your Heart | 1930 | Jimmy McHugh |

*(continued)*

| TITLE | YEAR | COMPOSER |
|---|---|---|
| (**Shoot the Works**, Broadway) | | |
| How's Your Uncle | 1931 | Jimmy McHugh |
| | | |
| (**Singin' the Blues**, Broadway) | | |
| It's the Darn'dest Thing | 1931 | Jimmy McHugh |
| Singin' the Blues | 1931 | Jimmy McHugh |
| | | |
| (**Flying High**, Film) | | |
| We'll Dance until the Dawn | 1931 | Jimmy McHugh |
| I'll Make a Happy Landing the Lucky Day I Land You | 1931 | Jimmy McHugh |
| | | |
| (**The Cuban Love Song**, Film) | | |
| Cuban Love Song | 1931 | Jimmy McHugh/ Herbert Stothart |
| Tramps at Sea | 1931 | Jimmy McHugh/ Herbert Stothart |
| I'm Full of the Devil | 1932 | Jimmy McHugh |
| Hey, Young Fella; Close Your Old Umbrella | 1932 | Jimmy McHugh |
| Happy Times | 1932 | Jimmy McHugh |
| Don't Blame Me | 1932 | Jimmy McHugh |
| Then You Went and Changed Your Mind | 1932 | Jimmy McHugh |
| Ain't It the Truth | 1932 | Jimmy McHugh |
| Good-Bye Blues | 1932 | Jimmy McHugh/ Arthur Johnston |
| | | |
| (**Meet the Baron**, Film) | | |
| Clean as a Whistle | 1933 | Jimmy McHugh |
| I Love Gardenias | 1933 | Jimmy McHugh |
| Tell Me | 1933 | Jimmy McHugh |
| Thank You for a Lovely Evening | 1933 | Jimmy McHugh |
| Lost in a Fog | 1933 | Jimmy McHugh |
| Who Said That Dreams Don't Come True | 1933 | Jimmy McHugh |
| | | |
| (**The Prizefighter and the Lady**, Film) | | |
| Lucky Fella | 1933 | Jimmy McHugh |
| | | |
| (**Dancing Lady**, Film) | | |
| My Dancing Lady | 1933 | Jimmy McHugh |
| In the Little White Church on the Hill | 1933 | Jimmy McHugh |
| With a Feather in Your Cap | 1933 | Jimmy McHugh |
| I've Got a Roof over My Head | 1933 | Jimmy McHugh |
| Dinner at Eight | 1933 | Jimmy McHugh |
| | | |
| Serenade for a Wealthy Widow | 1934 | Reginald Foresythe |
| | | |
| Harlem at Its Best | 1935 | Jimmy McHugh |

*(continued)*

| TITLE | YEAR | COMPOSER |
|---|---|---|
| Every Little Moment | 1935 | Jimmy McHugh |
| | | |
| (**Roberta**, Film) | | |
| I Won't Dance | 1935 | Jerome Kern |
| Lovely to Look At | 1935 | Jerome Kern |
| | | |
| (**The Nitwits**, Film) | | |
| Music in My Heart | 1935 | Jimmy McHugh |
| | | |
| (**Hooray for Love**, Film) | | |
| I'm in Love All Over Again | 1935 | Jimmy McHugh |
| Hooray for Love | 1935 | Jimmy McHugh |
| You're an Angel | 1935 | Jimmy McHugh |
| Palsie Walsie | 1935 | Jimmy McHugh |
| I'm Livin' in a Great Big Way | 1935 | Jimmy McHugh |
| | | |
| (**Every Night at Eight**, Film) | | |
| I Feel a Song Comin' On | 1935 | Jimmy McHugh |
| I'm in the Mood for Love | 1935 | Jimmy McHugh |
| Take It Easy | 1935 | Jimmy McHugh |
| Speaking Confidentially | 1935 | Jimmy McHugh |
| Every Night at Eight | 1935 | Jimmy McHugh |
| That's the Hollywood Lowdown | 1935 | Jimmy McHugh |
| | | |
| (**Alice Adams**, Film) | | |
| I Can't Waltz Alone | 1935 | Max Steiner |
| | | |
| (**In Person**, Film) | | |
| Out of Sight, Out of Mind | 1935 | Oscar Levant |
| Got a New Lease on Life | 1935 | Oscar Levant |
| Don't Mention Love to Me | 1935 | Oscar Levant |
| | | |
| (**I Dream Too Much**, Film) | | |
| I Dream Too Much | 1935 | Jerome Kern |
| The Jockey on the Carousel | 1935 | Jerome Kern |
| I Got Love | 1935 | Jerome Kern |
| I'm the Echo; You're the Song That I Sing | 1935 | Jerome Kern |
| | | |
| It's Not in the Cards | 1936 | Jerome Kern |
| | | |
| (**The King Steps Out**, Film) | | |
| Madly in Love | 1936 | Fritz Kreisler |
| Stars in My Eyes | 1936 | Fritz Kreisler |
| Learn How to Lose | 1936 | Fritz Kreisler |
| What Shall Remain | 1936 | Fritz Kreisler |

*(continued)*

| TITLE | YEAR | COMPOSER |
|---|---|---|
| (***Swing Time***, Film) | | |
| The Way You Look Tonight | 1936 | Jerome Kern |
| Bojangles of Harlem | 1936 | Jerome Kern |
| The Waltz in Swingtime | 1936 | Jerome Kern |
| A Fine Romance | 1936 | Jerome Kern |
| Pick Yourself Up | 1936 | Jerome Kern |
| Never Gonna Dance | 1936 | Jerome Kern |
| | | |
| (***When You're in Love***, Film) | | |
| Our Song | 1937 | Jerome Kern |
| The Whistling Boy | 1937 | Jerome Kern |
| | | |
| (***Joy of Loving***, Film) | | |
| Heavenly Party | 1938 | Jerome Kern |
| Just Let Me Look at You | 1938 | Jerome Kern |
| What's Good about Goodnight | 1938 | Jerome Kern |
| You Couldn't Be Cuter | 1938 | Jerome Kern |
| | | |
| (***Stars in Your Eyes***, Film) | | |
| Just a Little Bit More | 1939 | Arthur Schwartz |
| This Is It | 1939 | Arthur Schwartz |
| It's All Yours | 1939 | Arthur Schwartz |
| Terribly Attractive | 1939 | Arthur Schwartz |
| All the Time | 1939 | Arthur Schwartz |
| Lady Needs Change | 1939 | Arthur Schwartz |
| One Brief Moment | 1939 | Arthur Schwartz |
| Self-Made Man | 1939 | Arthur Schwartz |
| I'll Pay the Check | 1939 | Arthur Schwartz |
| Goin' Home | 1939 | Arthur Schwartz |
| | | |
| (***One Night in the Tropics***, Film) | | |
| Back in My Shell | 1940 | Jerome Kern |
| You and Your Kiss | 1940 | Jerome Kern |
| Remind Me | 1940 | Jerome Kern |
| Farandola | 1940 | Jerome Kern |
| | | |
| (***Up in Central Park***, Broadway) | | |
| Currier and Ives | 1944 | Sigmund Romberg |
| Rip Van Winkle | 1944 | Sigmund Romberg |
| April Snow | 1944 | Sigmund Romberg |
| The Fireman's Bride | 1944 | Sigmund Romberg |
| It Doesn't Cost You Anything to Dream | 1944 | Sigmund Romberg |
| Close as Pages in a Book | 1944 | Sigmund Romberg |
| The Big Back Yard | 1944 | Sigmund Romberg |
| Carousel in the Park | 1944 | Sigmund Romberg |
| You Can't Get Over the Wall | 1944 | Sigmund Romberg |

*(continued)*

| TITLE | YEAR | COMPOSER |
|---|---|---|
| When You Walk in the Room | 1945 | Sigmund Romberg |
| Sergeant Housewife | 1945 | Joseph Meyer |
| | | |
| (**Arms and the Girl**, Broadway) | | |
| That's My Fella | 1950 | Morton Gould |
| You Kissed Me | 1950 | Morton Gould |
| A Cow and a Plough and a Frau | 1950 | Morton Gould |
| Don't Talk | 1950 | Morton Gould |
| Nothin' for Nothin' | 1950 | Morton Gould |
| There Must Be Somethin' Better Than Love | 1950 | Morton Gould |
| A Girl with a Flame | 1950 | Morton Gould |
| That's What I Told Him Last Night | 1950 | Morton Gould |
| I Like It Here | 1950 | Morton Gould |
| He Will Tonight | 1950 | Morton Gould |
| Little Old Cabin Door | 1950 | Morton Gould |
| I'll Never Learn | 1950 | Morton Gould |
| She's Exciting | 1950 | Morton Gould |
| Mister Washington, Uncle George | 1950 | Morton Gould |
| | | |
| (**Mr. Imperium**, Film) | | |
| Let Me Look at You | 1951 | Harold Arlen |
| Andiamo | 1951 | Harold Arlen |
| My Love an' My Mule | 1951 | Harold Arlen |
| | | |
| (**A Tree Grows in Brooklyn**, Broadway) | | |
| Pay Day | 1951 | Arthur Schwartz |
| The Bride Wore Something Old | 1951 | Arthur Schwartz |
| He Had Refinement | 1951 | Arthur Schwartz |
| Mine Till Monday | 1951 | Arthur Schwartz |
| That's How It Goes | 1951 | Arthur Schwartz |
| Is That My Prince | 1951 | Arthur Schwartz |
| Look Who's Dancing | 1951 | Arthur Schwartz |
| I'm Like a New Broom | 1951 | Arthur Schwartz |
| Love Is the Reason | 1951 | Arthur Schwartz |
| Make the Man Love Me | 1951 | Arthur Schwartz |
| Growing Pains | 1951 | Arthur Schwartz |
| I'll Buy You a Star | 1951 | Arthur Schwartz |
| If You Haven't Got a Sweetheart | 1951 | Arthur Schwartz |
| Don't Be Afraid | 1951 | Arthur Schwartz |
| | | |
| (**Excuse My Dust**, Film) | | |
| Get a Horse | 1951 | Arthur Schwartz |
| Spring Has Sprung | 1951 | Arthur Schwartz |
| Goin' Steady | 1951 | Arthur Schwartz |
| Lorelei Brown | 1951 | Arthur Schwartz |
| That's for Children | 1951 | Arthur Schwartz |

*(continued)*

| TITLE | YEAR | COMPOSER |
|---|---|---|
| I'd Like to Take You Out Dreaming | 1951 | Arthur Schwartz |
| Where Can I Run from You | 1951 | Arthur Schwartz |
| One More You | 1951 | Arthur Schwartz |
| It Couldn't Happen to Two Nicer People | 1951 | Arthur Schwartz |
| | | |
| (**Texas Carnival**, Film) | | |
| Whoa, Emma | 1951 | Harry Warren |
| Cornie's Pitch | 1951 | Harry Warren |
| It's Dynamite | 1951 | Harry Warren |
| Love Is a Lovely Word | 1951 | Harry Warren |
| A Face Full of Wonderful Things | 1951 | Harry Warren |
| Schnapps | 1951 | Harry Warren |
| Young Folks Should Get Married | 1951 | Harry Warren |
| Tuscaloosa | 1951 | Arthur Schwartz |
| | | |
| (**Lovely to Look At**, Film) | | |
| The Most Exciting Night | 1952 | Jerome Kern |
| Lafayette | 1952 | Jerome Kern |
| Opening Night | 1952 | Jerome Kern |
| | | |
| (**The Farmer Takes a Wife**, Film) | | |
| When I Close My Door | 1953 | Harold Arlen |
| Today, I Love Everybody | 1953 | Harold Arlen |
| Can You Spell Schenectady? | 1953 | Harold Arlen |
| I Could Cook | 1953 | Harold Arlen |
| The Erie Canal | 1953 | Harold Arlen |
| We're Doin' It for the Natives in Jamaica | 1953 | Harold Arlen |
| With the Sun Warm upon Me | 1953 | Harold Arlen |
| We're in Business | 1953 | Harold Arlen |
| Look Who's Been Dreaming | 1953 | Harold Arlen |
| Something Real Special | 1953 | Harold Arlen |
| | | |
| (**By the Beautiful Sea**, Broadway) | | |
| Hooray for George the Third | 1954 | Arthur Schwartz |
| Happy Habit | 1954 | Arthur Schwartz |
| Good Time Charley | 1954 | Arthur Schwartz |
| Coney Island Boat | 1954 | Arthur Schwartz |
| The Sea Song | 1954 | Arthur Schwartz |
| Alone Too Long | 1954 | Arthur Schwartz |
| It's Up to You | 1954 | Arthur Schwartz |
| Hang Up | 1954 | Arthur Schwartz |
| Please Don't Send Me Down a Baby Brother | 1954 | Arthur Schwartz |
| More Love Than Your Love | 1954 | Arthur Schwartz |
| I'd Rather Wake Up by Myself | 1954 | Arthur Schwartz |
| Old Enough to Love | 1954 | Arthur Schwartz |
| Mona from Arizona | 1954 | Arthur Schwartz |

*(continued)*

| TITLE | YEAR | COMPOSER |
|-------|------|----------|
| Throw the Anchor Away | 1954 | Arthur Schwartz |
| Finale | 1954 | Arthur Schwartz |
| Me and Pollyanna | 1954 | Arthur Schwartz |
| It's Not Where You Start | 1954 | Arthur Schwartz |
| | | |
| April Fooled Me | 1956 | Jerome Kern |
| Introduce Me | 1956 | Jerome Kern |
| Nice to Be Near | 1956 | Jerome Kern |
| | | |
| (**Junior Miss**, Film-TV) | | |
| Let's Make It Christmas All Year 'Round | 1957 | Burton Lane |
| Junior Miss | 1957 | Burton Lane |
| I'll Buy It | 1957 | Burton Lane |
| Have Feet Will Dance | 1957 | Burton Lane |
| The Happy Heart | 1957 | Burton Lane |
| A Male Is an Animal | 1957 | Burton Lane |
| It's Just What I Wanted | 1957 | Burton Lane |
| | | |
| (**Redhead**, Broadway) | | |
| Behave Yourself | 1959 | Albert Hague |
| Erbie Fitch's Twitch | 1959 | Albert Hague |
| Going Solo | 1959 | Albert Hague |
| I'll Try | 1959 | Albert Hague |
| The Right Finger of Me Left Hand | 1959 | Albert Hague |
| The Simpson Sister's Door | 1959 | Albert Hague |
| We Loves Ye, Jimey | 1959 | Albert Hague |
| Uncle Sam Rag | 1959 | Albert Hague |
| You Might Be Next | 1959 | Albert Hague |
| It Doesn't Take a Minute | 1959 | Albert Hague |
| Two Faces in the Dark | 1959 | Albert Hague |
| Just for Once | 1959 | Albert Hague |
| I Feel Merely Marvelous | 1959 | Albert Hague |
| My Girl Is Just Enough Woman for Me | 1959 | Albert Hague |
| Look Who's in Love | 1959 | Albert Hague |
| I'm Back in Circulation | 1959 | Albert Hague |
| Chase and Finale | 1959 | Albert Hague |
| | | |
| (**Sweet Charity**, Broadway) | | |
| Baby, Dream Your Dream | 1966 | Cy Coleman |
| Big Spender | 1966 | Cy Coleman |
| Charity's Soliloquy | 1966 | Cy Coleman |
| Did You Ever Look at You (cut) | 1966 | Cy Coleman |
| Free Thought in Action Class (cut) | 1966 | Cy Coleman |
| Gimme a Raincheck (cut) | 1966 | Cy Coleman |
| A Good Impression (cut) | 1966 | Cy Coleman |
| I Can't Let You Down (cut) | 1966 | Cy Coleman |

*(continued)*

| TITLE | YEAR | COMPOSER |
|---|---|---|
| I Love to Cry at Weddings | 1966 | Cy Coleman |
| I'll Take Any Man (cut) | 1966 | Cy Coleman |
| I'm Way Ahead (cut) | 1966 | Cy Coleman |
| I'm a Brass Band | 1966 | Cy Coleman |
| I'm the Bravest Individual | 1966 | Cy Coleman |
| I've Tried Everything (cut) | 1966 | Cy Coleman |
| If My Friends Could See Me Now | 1966 | Cy Coleman |
| Keep It in the Family (cut) | 1966 | Cy Coleman |
| Pink Taffeta Sample Size Ten (cut) | 1966 | Cy Coleman |
| Poor Everybody Else | 1966 | Cy Coleman |
| The Rhythm of Life | 1966 | Cy Coleman |
| Sweet Charity | 1966 | Cy Coleman |
| There's Gotta Be Something Better Than This | 1966 | Cy Coleman |
| Too Many Tomorrows | 1966 | Cy Coleman |
| When Did You Know? (cut) | 1966 | Cy Coleman |
| Where Am I Going? | 1966 | Cy Coleman |
| You Can't Lose 'Em All | 1966 | Cy Coleman |
| You Should See Yourself | 1966 | Cy Coleman |
| You Wanna Bet (cut) | 1966 | Cy Coleman |
| | | |
| (**The Hell with Heroes**, Film) | | |
| Where There Is Love | 1968 | Quincy Jones |
| | | |
| (**Sweet Charity**, film) | | |
| It's a Nice Face | 1969 | Cy Coleman |
| My Personal Property | 1969 | Cy Coleman |
| Sweet Charity | 1969 | Cy Coleman |
| Five O'Clock Sky | 1969 | David Lahm |
| | | |
| (**Eleanor**, unproduced) | | |
| After Forty, It's Patch, Patch, Patch | 1970 | Cy Coleman |
| Charge | 1970 | Cy Coleman |
| A Good Impression | 1970 | Cy Coleman |
| I Can't Let You Go | 1970 | Cy Coleman |
| I Struck Out | 1970 | Cy Coleman |
| Keep It in the Family | 1970 | Cy Coleman |
| Love and Logic | 1970 | Cy Coleman |
| Meat and Potatoes | 1970 | Cy Coleman |
| The Old Kitchen Sink | 1970 | Cy Coleman |
| Red Hot Tomatoes | 1970 | Cy Coleman |
| Sixty Percent of the Accidents | 1970 | Cy Coleman |
| So What Now? | 1970 | Cy Coleman |
| What Do I Do? | 1970 | Cy Coleman |
| When Did You Know? | 1970 | Cy Coleman |
| Whisper on the Wind | 1970 | Cy Coleman |

*(continued)*

| TITLE | YEAR | COMPOSER |
|---|---|---|
| (**Seesaw**, Broadway) | | |
| Big Fat Heart (cut) | 1973 | Cy Coleman |
| Chapter 54, Number 1909 | 1973 | Cy Coleman |
| Did You Ever Look at You? (cut) | 1973 | Cy Coleman |
| He's Good for Me | 1973 | Cy Coleman |
| Hospitality (cut) | 1973 | Cy Coleman |
| I'm Way Ahead | 1973 | Cy Coleman |
| I'm in a Highly Emotional State | 1973 | Cy Coleman |
| In Tune | 1973 | Cy Coleman |
| It's Not Where You Start | 1973 | Cy Coleman |
| More People Like You (cut) | 1973 | Cy Coleman |
| My City | 1973 | Cy Coleman |
| Nobody Does It Like Me | 1973 | Cy Coleman |
| The Party's on Me (added for tour) | 1973 | Cy Coleman |
| Pick Up the Pieces (cut) | 1973 | Cy Coleman |
| Poor Everybody Else | 1973 | Cy Coleman |
| Ride Out the Storm | 1973 | Cy Coleman |
| Salt (cut) | 1973 | Cy Coleman |
| Seesaw | 1973 | Cy Coleman |
| Spanglish | 1973 | Cy Coleman |
| Tutu and Tights (cut) | 1973 | Cy Coleman |
| Visitors (cut) | 1973 | Cy Coleman |
| We've Got It | 1973 | Cy Coleman |
| Welcome to the Holiday Inn | 1973 | Cy Coleman |
| You're a Lovable Lunatic | 1973 | Cy Coleman |

# Appendix B
## Composer List

*This list is chronological by year.*

J. Fred Coots
      Popular Songs (*music unpublished*)
Jimmy McHugh
      Popular Songs
      Cotton Club Revues (1927–1930)
      *Blackbirds of 1928* (1928, Broadway)
      *Hello, Daddy* (1928, Broadway)
      *Ziegfeld's Midnight Frolic* (1929, Broadway)
      *Kelly's Vacation* (1930, film)
      *Love in the Rough* (1930, film)
      *Vanderbilt Revue* (1930, Broadway)
      *International Revue* (1930, Broadway)
      *Singin' the Blues* (1931, Broadway)
      *Shoot the Works* (1931, Broadway)
      *The Cuban Love Song* (1931, film)
      *Flying High* (1931, film)
      *Rhapsody in Black* (1931, Broadway)
      *Dancing Lady* (1933, film)
      *The Prizefighter and the Lady* (1933, film)
      *Meet the Baron* (1933, film)
      *The Nitwits* (1935, film)
      *Hooray for Love* (1935, film)
      *Every Night at Eight* (1935, film)
Reginald Foresythe
      Popular Song

Max Steiner
        *Alice Adams* (1935, film)
Jerome Kern
        *Roberta* (1935, film)
        *I Dream Too Much* (1935, film)
        *Swing Time* (1936, film)
        *When You're in Love* (1937, film)
        *Joy of Loving* (1938, film)
        *One Night in the Tropics* (1940, film)
        *Lovely to Look At* (1952, film)
Oscar Levant
        *In Person* (1935, film)
Fritz Kreisler
        *The King Steps Out* (1936, film)
Arthur Schwartz
        *Stars in Your Eyes* (1939, Broadway)
        *A Tree Grows in Brooklyn* (1951, Broadway)
        *Excuse My Dust* (1951, film)
        *By the Beautiful Sea* (1954, Broadway)
Sigmund Romberg
        *Up in Central Park* (1944, Broadway)
Joseph Meyer
        Popular Song
Morton Gould
        *Arms and the Girl* (1950, Broadway)
Harold Arlen
        *Mr. Imperium* (1951, film)
        *The Farmer Takes a Wife* (1953, film)
Harry Warren
        *Texas Carnival* (1951, film)
Burton Lane
        *Junior Miss* (1957, TV film)
Albert Hague
        *Redhead* (1959, Broadway)
Cy Coleman
        *Sweet Charity* (1966, Broadway)
Quincy Jones
        *The Hell with Heroes* (1968, film)
David Lahm
        Popular Song

# Appendix C
## Project List

*This chronological list excludes Popular Songs that were not written as part of a film or show.*

| SHOW | YEAR | COMPOSER | PLACE |
|---|---|---|---|
| Blackbirds of 1928 | 1928 | Jimmy McHugh | Broadway |
| Hello, Daddy | 1928 | Jimmy McHugh | Broadway |
| Ziegfeld's Midnight Frolic | 1929 | Jimmy McHugh | Broadway |
| International Revue | 1930 | Jimmy McHugh | Broadway |
| Kelly's Vacation | 1930 | Jimmy McHugh | Film |
| Love in the Rough | 1930 | Jimmy McHugh | Film |
| March of Time | 1930 | Jimmy McHugh | Film |
| Vanderbilt Revue | 1930 | Jimmy McHugh | Broadway |
| Shoot the Works | 1931 | Jimmy McHugh | Broadway |
| Singin' the Blues | 1931 | Jimmy McHugh | Broadway |
| Flying High | 1931 | Jimmy McHugh | Film |
| The Cuban Love Song | 1931 | Jimmy McHugh | Film |
| Meet the Baron | 1933 | Jimmy McHugh | Film |
| The Prizefighter and the Lady | 1933 | Jimmy McHugh | Film |
| Dancing Lady | 1933 | Jimmy McHugh | Film |
| Roberta | 1935 | Jerome Kern | Film |
| The Nitwits | 1935 | Jimmy McHugh | Film |
| Hooray for Love | 1935 | Jimmy McHugh | Film |
| Every Night at Eight | 1935 | Jimmy McHugh | Film |
| Alice Adams | 1935 | Max Steiner | Film |
| In Person | 1935 | Oscar Levant | Film |
| I Dream Too Much | 1935 | Jerome Kern | Film |
| The King Steps Out | 1936 | Fritz Kreisler | Film |
| Swing Time | 1936 | Jerome Kern | Film |

*(continued)*

| SHOW | YEAR | COMPOSER | PLACE |
|------|------|----------|-------|
| *When You're in Love* | 1937 | Jerome Kern | Film |
| *Joy of Loving* | 1938 | Jerome Kern | Film |
| *Stars in Your Eyes* | 1939 | Arthur Schwartz | Broadway |
| *One Night in the Tropics* | 1940 | Jerome Kern | Film |
| *Let's Face It! | 1941 | n/a; libretto | Broadway |
| *Something for the Boys* | 1943 | n/a; libretto | Broadway |
| *Mexican Hayride* | 1944 | n/a; libretto | Broadway |
| *Up in Central Park* | 1944 | Sigmund Romberg | Broadway |
| *Annie Get Your Gun* | 1946 | n/a; libretto | Broadway |
| *Arms and the Girl* | 1950 | Morton Gould | Broadway |
| *Mr. Imperium* | 1951 | Harold Arlen | Film |
| *A Tree Grows in Brooklyn* | 1951 | Arthur Schwartz | Broadway |
| *Excuse My Dust* | 1951 | Arthur Schwartz | Film |
| *Texas Carnival* | 1951 | Harry Warren | Film |
| *Lovely to Look At* | 1952 | Jerome Kern | Film |
| *The Farmer Takes a Wife* | 1953 | Harold Arlen | Film |
| *By the Beautiful Sea* | 1954 | Arthur Schwartz | Broadway |
| *Junior Miss* | 1957 | Burton Lane | Film (TV) |
| *Redhead* | 1959 | Albert Hague | Broadway |
| *Sweet Charity* | 1966 | Cy Coleman | Broadway |
| *The Hell with Heroes* | 1968 | Quincy Jones | Film |
| *Sweet Charity* | 1969 | Cy Coleman | Film |
| *Eleanor* | 1970 | Cy Coleman | unproduced |
| *Seesaw* | 1973 | Cy Coleman | Broadway |

*Indicates shows for which Dorothy Fields co-wrote the librettos with her brother, Herbert.

# Notes

## INTRODUCTION

1. Henry Kane, *How to Write a Song, as Told to Henry Kane* (New York: Macmillan, 1962), 175.

2. "The Honor Roll of Popular Songwriters," *The Billboard* (New York, NY), May 19, 1951, 39.

3. "'35 Pop Sales Topped '34," *Variety* (New York, NY), September 2, 1936, 41.

4. Gary Trust, "Happy Birthday, Billboard Charts! On July 27, 1940, the First Song Sales Chart Debuted," *Chart Beat* (blog), entry posted July 27, 2017, accessed July 17, 2019.

5. Deborah Grace Winer, *On the Sunny Side of the Street: The Life and Lyrics of Dorothy Fields* (New York: Schirmer Books, 1998), ix.

6. Michael Whorf, *American Popular Song Composers: Oral Histories, 1920s–1950s* (Jefferson, NC: McFarland & Company, Inc. Publishers, 2012), 200.

7. *An Evening with Dorothy Fields*, DRG Records, 1972, compact disc, recorded April 9, 1972.

## CHAPTER 1 "Hello Daddy"

1. "Reminiscences of Dorothy Fields (1958)," *Popular Arts Project*, Oral History Archives at Columbia, Rare Book & Manuscript Library, Columbia University in the City of New York.

2. Martin Gottfried, "A Single and Great Performance," *Women's Wear Daily* (New York, NY), July 24, 1974, 45.

3. Caryl Flinn, *Brass Diva: The Life and Legends of Ethel Merman* (Berkeley, CA: University of California Press, 2007), 155.

4. "A Tribute to Dorothy Fields," *New York Times* (New York, NY), July 21, 1974, 87.

5. "Fairy Scene at Allenhurst Inn," *Asbury Park Press* (Asbury Park, NJ), June 13, 1901, 1.

6. The Gombach Group, "Allenhurst Residential Historic District," Living Places, accessed August 1, 2019, https://www.livingplaces.com/NJ/Monmouth_County/Allenhurst _Borough/ Allenhurst_Residential_HIstoric_District.html.

7. "Allenhurst: From Lake to Ocean," advertisement, *Asbury Park Press*, August 14, 1896, 2.

8. "In the Limelight: Lew Fields," *The Billboard*, November 4, 1911, 2.

9. Armond Fields and L. Marc Fields, *From the Bowery to Broadway: Lew Fields and the Roots of American Popular Theater* (New York: Oxford University Press, 1993), 12–27.

10. Ripley D. Saunders, "Happy Reunion of Weber & Fields Came at Psychological Moment on American Stage," *St. Louis Post-Dispatch* (St. Louis, MO), May 26, 1912, 9.

11. "Golden Jubilee of a Famous Team," *New York Times*, September 4, 1932, 8–13.

12. "Lew Fields Dies: Noted Comedian, 74," *New York Times*, July 22, 1941, 19.

13. Fields and Fields, *From the Bowery*, 20.

14. Greg Young and Tom Meyers, *The Bowery Boys: Adventures in Old New York* (Berkeley, CA: Ulysses Press, 2016), 180.

15. "Golden Jubilee," 8–13.

16. "In the Limelight," 2.

17. "Golden Jubilee," 8–13.

18. "Lew Fields Rites Held on Coast; Weber at Bedside as He Died," *New York Herald Tribune* (New York, NY), July 22, 1941, 13.

19. Trav S. D., *No Applause—Just Throw Money* (New York: Farrar, Straus, and Giroux, 2006), 51.

20. "Weber & Fields Died Hoping Hollywood Would Film-Biog Them," *Variety*, May 13, 1942, 2, 54.

21. Ibid.

22. "Lew Fields Rites," 13.

23. Max Wilk, *They're Playing Our Song: Conversations with America's Classic Songwriters*, 5th ed. (Westport, CT: Easton Studio Press, 2007), 36.

24. Emery Lewis, "Her Words Are Legend," *The Record* (Hackensack, NJ), May 27, 1973.

25. Dorothy Fields's birth year is often listed as 1905; however, her birth certificate lists the year as 1904. There is also record of her birth in the *New York Tribune* dated July 16, 1904. It is likely that the notion of Fields's being born in 1905 started with Fields herself. In her discussion with interviewers for the Columbia University Oral History Project, Fields misspoke and said she was born in 1905. The historical record, however, affirms that she was actually born the year before.

26. "Broadway Congratulates Fields on the Birth of a Daughter," *New York Tribune* (New York, NY), July 16, 1904, 7.

27. Karl Shriftgiesser, "Amazing Fields Family," *New York Times*, January 17, 1943.

28. Fields and Fields, *From the Bowery*, 278.

29. Ibid., 228.

30. Frank Short, "A Talk with Lew Fields," *Christian Science Monitor* (Boston, MA), June 24, 1924.

31. Joan Adams, "Fertile Fields: Striking It Rich in the Theater after Disobeying Their Father's Injunction," *Everybody's Weekly*, March 28, 1943.

32. Joseph Kaye, "Father Was Wrong: Lew Fields Gang Proves It," *The Cincinnati Enquirer* (Cincinnati, OH), January 4, 1942.

33. Fred F. Schrader, "Another Typical Fields Production: Big Upheaval at the New Theater," *The Washington Post* (Washington, DC), February 12, 1911.

34. Mae Tinee, "She Finds Lew Fields One of the Busiest Men in Town," *The Chicago Sunday Tribune* (Chicago, IL), November 5, 1911.

## CHAPTER 2 "Growing Pains"

1. Saunders, "Happy Reunion."
2. "Broadway Welcomes Weber & Fields Back," *The Hartford Courant* (Hartford, CT), February 10, 1912.
3. "At Lyceum," *The Times Tribune* (Scranton, PA), May 16, 1912.
4. Fields and Fields, *From the Bowery*, 306.
5. "Reminiscences of Dorothy Fields."
6. Ibid.
7. "$500,000 Jubilee Ended," *New York Tribune*, June 14, 1912.
8. "Reminiscences of Dorothy Fields."
9. Wilk, *They're Playing Our Song*, 43.
10. Fields and Fields, *From the Bowery*, 307.
11. Kane, *How to Write a Song*, 168.
12. "Romantic Miss Fields' Slapstick Dilemma," *Tampa Tribune* (Tampa, FL), April 25, 1926.
13. Adams, "Fertile Fields."
14. Kaye, "Father Was Wrong."
15. Fields and Fields, *From the Bowery*, 289.
16. "*Miss 1917* Makes Debut at Century," *The Sun* (New York, NY), November 6, 1917.
17. "The Theater: *A Lonely Romeo*," *The Brooklyn Eagle* (Brooklyn, NY), June 11, 1919.
18. "A Lonely Romeo," advertisement, *New York Times*, August 19, 1919.
19. Unmarked newspaper clipping, Richard Rodgers's Scrapbook #1 at the New York Public Library for Performing Arts, Billy Rose Theatre Collection.
20. Richard Rodgers, *Musical Stages: An Autobiography*, 2nd ed. (Cambridge, MA: De Capo Press, 2002), 29.
21. Ibid, 30.
22. "Reminiscences of Richard C. Rodgers (1968)," *Popular Arts Project*, Oral History Archives at Columbia, Rare Book and Manuscript Library, Columbia University in the City of New York.
23. David Ewen, *Richard Rodgers* (New York: Henry Holt and Company, 1957), 78.
24. Rex Reed, "Column: Rex Reed," *Minneapolis Tribune* (Minneapolis, MN), May 20, 1973.
25. "Children Give Show," *Theatre World*, March 1920.
26. *Say Mama!* (New York: Akron Club, 1921).

27. "Broadway Seeks 'First Love' Stars," *New York Evening Mail* (New York, NY), February 14, 1921.

28. "Lew Fields Believes Youth a Greater Asset Than Too Much Stage Experience," *New York Tribune*, September 5, 1920.

29. Rex Reed, "*Seesaw* Score Is Something to Sing About," *The Courier Journal* (Louisville, KY), May 6, 1973.

## CHAPTER 3 "I Feel a Song Coming On"

1. "Lew Fields Believes."

2. Undated clipping from the *Columbia Spectator* in Richard Rodgers's Scrapbook.

3. Mary McBride, "It's 'Just One Song after Another' for Lew Fields' Talented Daughter," *Austin American* (Austin, TX), April 8, 1934.

4. Kane, *How to Write a Song*, 171.

5. Ibid.

6. Jake Falstaff, "Pippins and Cheese," *Akron Beacon Journal* (Akron, OH), March 8, 1926.

7. "Romantic Miss Fields."

8. "Lake Placid: Adirondacks," advertisement, *New York Tribune*, June 16, 1914.

9. "Romantic Miss Fields."

10. Different articles list different dates. According to press clippings of the day, they were married on either March 8 or 9, 1925.

11. Adams, "Fertile Fields," 10.

12. Whorf, *American Popular Song Composers*, 61.

13. *An Evening with Dorothy Fields*.

14. "How Music 'Publishers' Prospered," *The Topeka Daily Capital* (Topeka, KS), February 13, 1908.

15. "'Tin Pan Alley?' Why It's the Place Where Popular Songs Come From," *St. Louis Post-Dispatch*, May 10, 1903.

16. Whorf, *American Popular Song Composers*, 61.

17. Ibid.

18. Alyn Shipton, *I Feel a Song Coming On: The Life of Jimmy McHugh* (Urbana, IL: The University of Illinois Press, 2009), 81.

19. Kane, *How to Write a Song*, 173.

20. Shipton, *I Feel a Song Coming On*, 81.

21. Kane, *How to Write a Song*, 173.

## CHAPTER 4 "I'm Doin' That Thing"

1. Kane, *How to Write a Song*, 174.

2. "Formally Open 'House That Jack Built,'" *The Music Trades*, September 15, 1923.

3. Shipton, *I Feel a Song Coming On*, 80.

4. *An Evening with Dorothy Fields*.

5. Jimmy McHugh, interview by Joan Franklin and Robert Franklin, New York, 1959.

6. Ibid.

7. Wilk, *They're Playing Our Song*, 38.

8. Martin Gershen, "Another Musical Hit," *Baltimore Sun* (Baltimore, MD), March 28, 1966, 16.

9. *An Evening with Dorothy Fields*.

10. Ann Corio and Joseph DiMona, *This Was Burlesque* (New York: Madison Square Press, 1968).

11. "Cotton Club Draws Color Lines," *The New York Age* (New York, NY), February 21, 1925.

12. Lewis, "Her Words Are Legend."

13. "Night Club Reviews: Cotton Club," *Variety*, December 7, 1927.

14. Milt Freudenheim, "Dot Fields Dislikes 'Ghosted' Biographies," *Cincinnati Enquirer*, May 2, 1966.

15. *An Evening with Dorothy Fields*.

16. Freudenheim, "Dot Fields Dislikes."

17. Lewis, "Her Words Are Legend."

18. "Silhouette," *Brooklyn Daily Eagle* (Brooklyn, NY), April 3, 1929.

19. "Reminiscences of Dorothy Fields."

## CHAPTER 5 "Here Comes My Blackbird"

1. Shipton, *I Feel a Song Coming On*, 82.

2. "*Delmar's Revels* Coming to Shubert Theatre," *Jewish Exponent* (Philadelphia, PA), March 2, 1928.

3. "Harry Delmar's *Revels*," *Brooklyn Times Union* (Brooklyn, NY), November 22, 1927.

4. "*The Plantation Revue* Pleases at 48th Street," *The Standard Union* (Brooklyn, NY), July 18, 1922.

5. "Dixie to Broadway," advertisement, *Daily News* (New York, NY), November 30, 1924.

6. Burns Mantle, "*Dixie to Broadway* Is a Colored Riot," *Daily News*, October 31, 1924.

7. It was widely reported at the time that Mills died from complications of an appendectomy; however, it has since been suggested that an infection related to tuberculosis was the culprit.

8 "Florence Mills Real Service to Her Race," *The Morning Herald* (Uniontown, PA), November 14, 1927.

9. Shipton, *I Feel a Song Coming On*, 86.

10. "Story of Late Song Hit's Discovery Reads like a Modern Fairy Tale," *Pittsburgh Courier* (Pittsburgh, PA), November 17, 1928.

11. "The Theatre: An Ethiopian Revue," *Wall Street Journal* (New York, NY), May 11, 1928.

12. "Joseph Fields, 71, Dies on Coast; Co-Author of *My Sister Eileen*," *New York Times*, March 5, 1966.

13. Burns Mantle, "Bojangles Robinson's Dancing Featured in *Blackbirds of 1928*," *The New York Age*, May 19, 1928.

14. "*Blackbirds of 1928*," *Variety*, May 16, 1928.

15. "Leslie's New Revue One of the Best of Its Kind Ever Presented Even on B'way," *The New York Amsterdam News* (New York, NY), May 23, 1928.

16. *An Evening with Dorothy Fields*.

## CHAPTER 6 "Raisin' the Roof"

1. "Midnight Shows Popular," *The Brooklyn Citizen* (Brooklyn, NY), September 16, 1928.

2. "Reminiscences of Jimmy McHugh (1959)," *Popular Arts Project*, Oral History Archives at Columbia, Rare Book & Manuscript Library, Columbia University in the City of New York.

3. Only Irving Berlin, with four decades, was better represented on the list than Dorothy and McHugh. Richard Rodgers and Oscar Hammerstein are the only other songwriters to be listed in three decades.

4. "Reminiscences of Oscar Hammerstein II (1959)," *Popular Arts Project*, Oral History Archives at Columbia, Rare Book & Manuscript Library, Columbia University in the City of New York.

5. Rowland Field, "The New Play: *Hello, Daddy*," *The Times Union* (Brooklyn, NY), December 27, 1928.

6. Burns Mantle, "*Hello, Daddy* a Fields Family Hit," *New York Daily News* (New York, NY), December 28, 1928.

7. Field, "The New Play: *Hello, Daddy*."

8. Donald Mulhern, "The New Play: Lew Fields and Some Pleasing Playmates Arrive in *Hello, Daddy*," *The Standard Union*, December 27, 1928.

9. Nimisha Bhat, "The Ziegfeld Midnight Frolic," *MCNY Blog: New York Stories*, entry posted July 1, 2014, accessed August 24, 2019, https://blog.mcny.org/2014/07/01/the-ziegfeld-midnight-frolic/.

10. "Ziegfeld to Close His Midnight Frolic," *New York Times*, May 18, 1921.

11. Betty Longacre, "Gossip of the Theatre," *The Standard Union*, September 20, 1928.

## CHAPTER 7 "I'm Livin' in a Great Big Way"

1. James Wierzbicki, *Film Music: A History* (New York: Routledge, 2009), 94.

2. Irene Thirer, "*The Jazz Singer* Moves Audience; Al's Own Voice on Vitaphone," *New York Daily News*, October 7, 1927.

3. Edwin Schallert, "*Jazz Singer* Is Landmark," *Los Angeles Times* (Los Angeles, CA), December 30, 1927.

4. Miles Krueger, ed., *The Movie Musical from Vitaphone to 42nd Street* (New York: Dover Publications, 1975).

5. Mayme Ober Peak, "Tin Pan Alley Extends to the Pacific Coast Now," *Variety*, May 8, 1929.

6. Florabel Muir, "Tin Pan Alley Goes West En Masse," *New York Daily News*, June 23, 1929.

7. William Collier, "From Weber and Fields to Hollywood," *The China Press* (Shanghai).

8. "Reminiscences of Dorothy Fields."

9. Shipton, *I Feel a Song Coming On*, 100.

10. Flinn, *Brass Diva*, 33, 37.

11. Rowland Field, "Lew Leslie Presents *International Revue* Crowded with Stars," *Brooklyn Times Union*, February 26, 1930.

12. *An Evening with Dorothy Fields*.

13. *"Vanderbilt Revue* Debut Postponed," *The News Journal* (Wilmington, DE), October 18, 1930.

14. *"Vanderbilt Revue," Variety*, October 22, 1930.

15. Rowland Field, "The New Play: *Vanderbilt Revue*, a New Song and Dance Entertainment," *Brooklyn Times Union*, November 6, 1930.

16. *"Vanderbilt Revue," Variety*, November 12, 1930.

17. "Lew Fields."

18. *New York Times*, "Bank of U.S. Closes; State Takes Over Affairs; Aid Offered to Depositors," December 12, 1930, 1.

## CHAPTER 8 "Every Night at Eight"

1. *"Clowns in Clover* Fair Summer Show," *The Billboard*, July 9, 1932.

2. Len G. Shaw, "The Theater," *Detroit Free Press* (Detroit, MI), June 20, 1932.

3. Bernard Sobel, "Smut Kills Stage Revues, according to Lew Leslie, Broadway Producer," *Pittsburgh Courier*, October 29, 1932.

4. "New York Society Throngs to Opening of Music Hall," *Cincinnati Enquirer*, December 28, 1932.

5. "Radio City Premiere Is a Notable Event," *New York Times*, December 28, 1932.

6. Kane, *How to Write a Song*, 177.

7. Winer, *On the Sunny Side of the Street*, 100.

8. "Radio City Premieres: Music Hall," *Variety*, January 3, 1933.

9. "Dorothy Fields Made Pro at $1500 Weekly at Musical Hall-No Confusion," *Variety*, January 10, 1933.

10. "Dorothy Fields and Jimmy McHugh," *Variety*, March 21, 1933.

11. Mark Barron, "New Yorker at Large," *Washington Court House Herald* (Washington Court House, OH), May 17, 1933.

12. Dorothy was on the December 22, 1932, episode of the so-called "Fleischmann Hour."

13. *Friday with Garroway*, NBC, April 29, 1955, performed by Dorothy Fields.

14. *An Evening with Dorothy Fields*.

15. "Reminiscences of Dorothy Fields."

16. Wilk, *They're Playing Our Song*, 171.

17. Ray Peacock, "Lew Fields's Children Carry on Traditions," *The Daily News-Journal* (Murfreesboro, TN), January 25, 1942.

18. "Reminiscences of Dorothy Fields."

19. Winer, *On the Sunny Side of the Street*, 83.

20. Shipton, *I Feel a Song Coming On*, 103.

21. "Reminiscences of Jimmy McHugh."
22. Wilk, *They're Playing Our Song*, 39.

## CHAPTER 9 "You Couldn't Be Cuter"

1. "Reminiscences of Dorothy Fields."
2. *Biography in Sound*, "Jerome Kern, the Man and the Music," NBC, November 29, 1955, narrated by Kenneth Banghart.
3. Reed, "Column: Rex Reed."
4. Kane, *How to Write a Song*, 162.
5. "Tribute to Dorothy Fields," *Napa Valley Register*, April 17, 1975, 15.
6. Kane, *How to Write a Song*, 161.
7. Andrew S. Hughes, "Acorn to Offer Songs of Gifted Lyricist," *The South Bend Tribune* (South Bend, IN), August 20, 2004, D3.
8. Kane, *How to Write a Song*, 161.
9. Wilk, *They're Playing Our Song*, 41.
10. Andre Sennwald, "The Screen: Lily Pons Makes Her Debut in *I Dream Too Much*," *New York Times*, November 29, 1935.
11. Clarke Wales, "Reviews of the New Films: *Swing Time*," *Detroit Free Press*, September 6, 1936.
12. "Dot Fields, Johnston Teaming for Song," *Variety*, September 22, 1937.

## CHAPTER 10 "A Lady Needs Change"

1. *An Evening with Dorothy Fields*.
2. Arthur Schwartz, "The Evolution of a Gay Musical: Collaborators Hardly Know It," *New York Herald*, February 12, 1939.
3. Brooks Atkinson, "The Play: Ethel Merman and Jimmy Durante in *Stars in Your Eyes* with Tunes and a Hollywood Accent," *New York Times*, February 10, 1939.
4. Brooks Atkinson, "'Red, Hot, and Blue,' with Ethel Merman, Jimmy Durante, Bob Hope, and a Musical Show," *New York Times*, October 30, 1936, 26.
5. Ethan Mordden, *Sing for Your Supper: The Broadway Musical in the 1930s* (New York: Macmillan, 2005).
6. "Divorce Granted to Comedian's Daughter," *The Corpus Christi Caller Times* (Corpus Christi, TX), June 29, 1939.
7. Alice Hughes, "Four Children of Lew Fields Make Good Writing for the Stage," *Akron Beacon Journal*, December 23, 1941.
8. Dorothy's lyric to "He Had Refinement," a number in *A Tree Grows in Brooklyn* (1951), is on the list of songs Sondheim says he wishes he'd written.
9. "Lew Fields' Kids, Herbert and Dorothy, Collaborate at Last," *Brooklyn Daily Eagle*, November 23, 1941.
10. Irving Drutman, "Lew Fields Left behind Him a Talented Family," *New York Herald Tribune*, December 14, 1941.
11. Kane, *How to Write a Song*, 170.

12. "Reminiscences of Dorothy Fields."

13. Alice Hughes, "A Woman's New York," *Poughkeepsie Eagle-News* (Poughkeepsie, NY), December 23, 1941.

14. "At the Palace," *New York Times*, September 5, 1941.

15. Mae Tinee, "*Father Takes a Wife* Lively, Clever Picture," *Chicago Daily Tribune* (Chicago, IL), September 21, 1941.

16. "The Stage: Shubert Theatre, *Something for the Boys*," *Daily Boston Globe* (Boston, MA), December 19, 1942, 8.

17. Richard P. Cooke, "The Theatre: *Something for the Boys*," *Wall Street Journal*, January 9, 1943.

18. Burns Mantle, "The Hot Mikado Burns Up All the Colored Show Records," *New York Daily News*, March 23, 1939, 215.

19. Bert McCord, "Entrances and Exits: 'Michael Todd's Staff Presents,' Not Just Michael Todd, and Thereby Hangs a Tale," *New York Herald Tribune*, April 30, 1944, C1.

20. Dorothy Kilgallen, "Michael Todd Thinks Navy Will Let Him Use Telephone, Will Continue as Producer," *Fort Worth Star-Telegram*, March 26, 1944, 21.

21. Kane, *How to Write a Song*, 167. This interview was conducted a handful of years after the death of Eli, which likely explains her omission of her husband in her list of interests.

22. Kane, *How to Write a Song*, 169.

23. Hughes, "Acorn to Offer," D3.

24. "Story Inspires Music, Says Jerome Kern," *Los Angeles Times*, October 3, 1936.

## CHAPTER 11 "Close as Pages in a Book"

1. David Shirey, "Art: Currier and Ives Revisited," *New York Times*, January 23, 1977, 340.

2. Kelcey Allen, "The New Musical," *Women's Wear Daily*, January 29, 1945.

3. Dorothy told this story two different ways. In *An Evening with Dorothy Fields*, she said that she talked directly to the lady from Traveler's Aid. In her interview with Max Wilk, Dorothy said that Eli, who volunteered with Traveler's Aid, had spoken with the lady, and Dorothy got the idea when he told her about the encounter.

4. *An Evening with Dorothy Fields*.

5. "The Lyrical Life of Dorothy Fields Goes On and On," *The Globe and Mail* (Toronto, ON), May 14, 1955.

6. *An Evening with Dorothy Fields*.

7. "Kern Quits Broadway," *Detroit Free Press*, July 22, 1936. In spite of this announcement, Kern and Hammerstein did collaborate on *Very Warm for May* in 1939.

8. Flinn, *Brass Diva*, 153.

9. Stephen Banfield and Geoffrey Holden Block, *Jerome Kern* (New Haven, CT: Yale Press, 2006).

10. Laurence Bergreen, *As Thousands Cheer: The Life of Irving Berlin* (New York: Viking, 1990), 449.

11. Bergreen, *As Thousands Cheer*, 453.

12. Rex Reed, "Dorothy Fields: Tin Pan Alley Is Her Turf," *Los Angeles Times*, April 29, 1973.

13. Wilk, *They're Playing Our Song*, 366.

## CHAPTER 12 "I Like It Here"

1. James Moore, "Songs of Quality Certain to Last, Says Top Lyricist," *Chappaqua Sun* (Chappaqua, NY), January 5, 1956.
2. "Reminiscences of Dorothy Fields."
3. Cyrus Durgin, "New Musical, 'Arms and the Girl,' Opens at Shubert," *Daily Boston Globe*, January 18, 1950, 24.
4. Barbara L. Wilson, "A Bundle of Mirth and Melody," *The Philadelphia Inquirer* (Philadelphia, PA), January 8, 1950.
5. "Plays Out of Town: *Arms and the Girl*," *Variety*, January 4, 1950, 274.
6. Durgin, "New Musical," 25.
7. Brooks Atkinson, "*Arms and the Girl*, a Musical Show about Colonial Times, Put on by Theatre Guild," *New York Times*, February 3, 1950.
8. Ibid.
9. Bob Francis, "Arms and the Girl," *The Billboard*, February 11, 1950, 51.
10. Richard P. Cooke, "The Theatre: Bundling to Music," *Wall Street Journal*, February 6, 1950, 10.
11. Howard Barnes, "Actors Save the Day in Two New Shows," *New York Herald Tribune*, February 12, 1950, C1.
12. "Pearl Bailey Gets Dander Up over Race Slurs," *The Chicago Defender* (Chicago, IL), February 18, 1950, 1.
13. "Singer Angered by Anti-Negro Talk to Quit Show," *Louisville Courier-Journal* (Louisville, KY), February 12, 1950, sec. 1, 13.
14. "Pearl Bailey Gets Dander Up," 1.
15. Walter Rimler, *The Man That Got Away: The Life and Songs of Harold Arlen* (Urbana, IL: University of Illinois Press, 2015).
16. "That 'Tree' Keeps Growing," *New York Times*, April 15, 1951, 99.
17. Brooks Atkinson, "First Night at the Theatre: *A Tree Grows in Brooklyn* Made into an Affable Musical Drama," *New York Times*, April 20, 1951, 24.
18. John Chapman, "'Tree in Brooklyn' a Double Hit; It's Very Funny and Sentimental," *New York Daily News*, April 21, 1951, 33.
19. Alice Hughes, "A Woman's New York," *The Journal Herald* (Dayton, OH), April 27, 1941.
20. "Two Sparkling Musicals Present Two New Stars," *The Courier Journal* (Louisville, KY), April 29, 1951.
21. John Beaufort, "*A Tree Grows in Brooklyn* Presented as Musical Show: Greatest Asset Tender Moments Pell-Mell Speed," *The Christian Science Monitor*, April 28, 1951, 8.
22. Chapman, "Tree in Brooklyn," 33.
23. Louis Sheaffer, "Curtain Time: 'Tree in Brooklyn' Enjoyably Transplanted in Broadway Show," *The Brooklyn Daily Eagle*, May 6, 1951, 31.
24. Marion Kelly, "Songwriters Collaborate in Musical," *The Philadelphia Inquirer*, April 1, 1951.
25. Edwin F. Melvin, "*By the Beautiful Sea* on Stage," *The Christian Science Monitor*, February 24, 1954.
26. Cyrus Durgin, "The Stage: *By the Beautiful Sea* Could Take Livening," *Daily Boston Globe*, February 24, 1954, 9.

27. Brooks Atkinson, "Magnetic Lady: *By the Beautiful Sea* Stars Miss Booth," *New York Times*, April 18, 1954, X1.

28. Durgin, "The Stage," 9.

## CHAPTER 13 "Merely Marvelous"

1. John Chapman, "*Can-Can* an Opulent Music Show with a Fine Cast and a Slow Book," *New York Daily News*, May 9, 1953.

2. Irving Kolodin, "*New Girl* Is Big Star Now," *Tucson Citizen* (Tucson, AZ), June 15, 1957.

3. Katherine Skogstad, "*Plain and Fancy* Music Written on Card Table," *The Atlanta Constitution* (Atlanta, GA), July 7, 1957, 2C.

4. *An Evening with Dorothy Fields.*

5. Charlotte Greenspan, *Pick Yourself Up: Dorothy Fields and the American Musical* (New York: Oxford University Press, 2010), 204.

6. Ward Morehouse, "Lyric Writing Fascinates Dorothy Fields," *Pittsburgh Press* (Pittsburgh, PA), July 5, 1959.

7. "Show Out of Town – Redhead," *Variety* (Los Angeles, CA), December 24, 1958, 48.

8. Wilk, *They're Playing Our Song*, 45.

9. "Reminiscences of Dorothy Fields."

10. Brooks Atkinson, "The Theatre: *Redhead*," *New York Times*, February 6, 1959.

11. Albert Goldberg, "Gwen Verdon Sparkles at *Redhead* Opening," *Los Angeles Times*, April 26, 1960, 41.

## CHAPTER 14 "After Forty, It's Patch, Patch, Patch"

1. Rex Reed, "*Seesaw* Score."

2. "The Lyrical Life of Dorothy Fields Goes On and On," *The Globe and Mail* (Toronto, ON), May 14, 1966.

3. Hedda Hopper, "Talk of Hollywood," *The Evening Sun* (Baltimore, MD), August 16, 1962.

4. Dorothy Sara, "Clues in the Handwriting of Great Americans," *Vogue*, February 1, 1961.

5. "The Lyrical Life of Dorothy Fields."

6. Mary Rodgers, "Sisters Gershwin: Where Are the Women Composers and Lyricists" (lecture, New York Public Library for Performing Arts, New York, March 24, 1997). Along these same lines, Mary Rodgers also wrote a 1958 show called *Three to Make Music* to teach children about the role of the orchestra. She wrote, "It takes three to make music . . . the man who writes it, the men who play it, and the folks they're playing it for."

7. Gerald Nachman, *Showstoppers: The Surprising Backstage Stories of Broadway's Most Remarkable Songs* (Chicago: Chicago Review Press, 2015), 219.

8. Sam Zolotow, "Second Show Is Due on Peace Corps," *New York Times*, March 21, 1962.

9. Rex Reed, "Fame Eludes Cy Coleman, but Now There's *I Love My Wife*," *The Baltimore Sun*, May 15, 1977.

10. Whitney Bolton, "Glancing Sideways," *Cumberland Evening Times* (Cumberland, MD), September 28, 1962.

11. Andy Propst, *You Fascinate Me So* (Milwaukee, WI: Applause Theatre and Cinema Books, 2015), 156.

12. Cy Coleman, "Cy Coleman," *Atlanta Constitution* (Atlanta, GA), August 29, 1965.

## CHAPTER 15 "If My Friends Could See Me Now"

1. Propst, *You Fascinate Me So*, 156.

2. Sam Wasson, *Fosse* (Boston: Mariner Books, 2013).

3. Les Wedman, "You'll Be Happy to Meet Cabiria," *Vancouver Sun* (Vancouver, BC), March 28, 1962.

4. Neil Simon, *Rewrites* (New York: Simon & Schuster, 1996).

5. Ibid., 216.

6. "No More Parades at the Palace," *New York Times*, October 16, 1932.

7. "Philly Critics Applaud Gwen's *Sweet Charity*," *Detroit Free Press*, December 8, 1965.

8. Dorothy Fields's papers, New York Public Library for the Performing Arts.

9. Martin Gershen, "People Keep Singing Dorothy Fields's Songs," *Asbury Park Press*, March 19, 1966.

10. "The Lyrical Life of Dorothy Fields."

11. "Reminiscences of Richard Rodgers."

12. Robert Kimball and Linda Emmet, *The Complete Lyrics of Irving Berlin* (New York: Alfred A. Knopf, 2001), xix.

13. Simon, *Rewrites*, 227–28.

14. Wilk, *They're Playing Our Song*, 46.

15. Propst, *You Fascinate Me So*, 168.

16. *An Evening with Dorothy Fields*.

17. "Composer Cy Coleman Has a Habit of Teaming Up with Sundry Companions for Words to Fit Tunes," *The Register*, September 18, 1977.

18. *An Evening with Dorothy Fields*.

## CHAPTER 16 "It's Not Where You Start, It's Where You Finish"

1. Al Kasha and Joel Hirschhorn, *Notes on Broadway: Conversations with the Great Songwriters* (Chicago: Contemporary Books, 1985).

2. "10 Elected to New Hall of Fame for Songwriters," *New York Times*, March 10, 1971.

3. John S. Wilson, "Miss Fields Views 47 Years of Song," *New York Times*, April 11, 1972.

4. Ted Strongin, "Previews and Postscripts," *The East Hampton Star* (East Hampton, NY), August 3, 1972.

5. Rex Reed, "Who Is Cy Coleman? Any Singer Can Tell You," *Independent Press Telegram*, May 15, 1977.

6. When Kazan won another role, the rate was reduced to $1,500 a week.

7. Patricia Bosworth, "The Fight to Save *Seesaw*," *New York Times*, April 8, 1973.

8. Douglas Watt, "*Seesaw* Is Comedy and Musical," *New York Daily News*, March 20, 1973.

9. Bosworth, "The Fight to Save *Seesaw*."

10. Greenspan, *Pick Yourself Up*, 223.

11. "A Tribute to Dorothy Fields."

12. Rex Reed, "Signoret and Fields Keep Winning Hearts," *New York Daily News*, December 2, 1978, 49.

## CONCLUSION

1. *Yours for a Song: The Women of Tin Pan Alley*, interview with Artis Wodehouse, Fox Lorber, 1998.

2. Whorf, *American Popular Song Composers*, 200.

3. Jennifer Jones Cavenaugh, *Women in American Musical Theatre: Essays on Composers, Lyricists, Librettists, Arrangers, Choreographers, Designers, Directors, Producers, and Performance Artists*, ed. Bud Coleman and Judith Sebesta (Jefferson, NC: McFarland & Co, Inc, 2008), 80.

4. Laura Collins-Hughes and Alexis Soloski, "Broadway May Not Be So White, but Is It Woman Enough?" *New York Times*, May 31, 2016.

5. Kane, *How to Write a Song*, 176.

# Bibliography

Adams, Joan. "Fertile Fields: Striking It Rich in the Theater after Disobeying Their Father's Injunction." *Everybody's Weekly*, March 28, 1943.

Allen, Kelcey. "The New Musical." *Women's Wear Daily* (New York, NY), January 29, 1945.

*Asbury Park Daily Press* (Asbury Park, NJ). "Marvelous Allenhurst: Two Years Ago Today It Was Started." August 10, 1897, 1.

*Asbury Park Press*. "Allenhurst: From Lake to Ocean." Advertisement. August 14, 1896, 2.

———. "Fairy Scene at Allenhurst Inn." June 13, 1901.

Atkinson, Brooks. "*Arms and the Girl*, a Musical Show about Colonial Times, Put on by Theatre Guild." *New York Times* (New York, NY), February 3, 1950.

———. "First Night at the Theatre: *A Tree Grows in Brooklyn* Made into an Affable Musical Drama." *New York Times*, April 20, 1951.

———. "Magnetic Lady: *By the Beautiful Sea* Stars Miss Booth." *New York Times*, April 18, 1954.

———. "The Play: Ethel Merman and Jimmy Durante in *Stars in Your Eyes* with Tunes and a Hollywood Accent." *New York Times*, February 10, 1939.

————. "'Red, Hot, and Blue,' with Ethel Merman, Jimmy Durante, Bob Hope, and a Musical Show." *New York Times*, October 30, 1936, 26.

————. "The Theatre: *Redhead*." *New York Times*, February 6, 1959.

*Austin Statesman* (Austin, TX). "More Lyrics for Dorothy." April 14, 1968.

*The Baltimore Sun* (Baltimore, MD). "Producer Mike Todd Is in the Money." February 28, 1943.

Banfield, Stephen, and Geoffrey Holden Block. *Jerome Kern*. New Haven, CT: Yale Press, 2006.

Barnes, Howard. "Actors Save the Day in Two New Shows." *New York Herald Tribune* (New York, NY), February 12, 1950.

Barron, Mark. "New Yorker at Large." *Washington Court House Herald* (Washington Court House, OH), May 17, 1933.

Beaufort, John. "*A Tree Grows in Brooklyn* Presented as Musical Show: Greatest Asset Tender Moments Pell-Mell Speed." *The Christian Science Monitor* (Boston, MA), April 28, 1951.

Bergreen, Laurence. *As Thousands Cheer: The Life of Irving Berlin*. New York: Viking, 1990.

Bhat, Nimisha. "The Ziegfeld Midnight Frolic." *MCNY Blog: New York Stories*. Entry posted July 1, 2014. Accessed August 24, 2019. https://blog.mcny.org /2014/07/01/the-ziegfeld-midnight-frolic/.

*The Billboard* (New York, NY). "*Clowns in Clover* Fair Summer Show." July 9, 1932.

*Biography in Sound*. "Jerome Kern, the Man and the Music." NBC. November 29, 1955. Narrated by Kenneth Banghart.

Bolton, Whitney. "Glancing Sideways." *Cumberland Evening Times* (Cumberland, MD), September 28, 1962.

Bosworth, Patricia. "The Fight to Save *Seesaw*." *New York Times*, April 8, 1973.

*The Brooklyn Citizen* (Brooklyn, NY). "Midnight Shows Popular." September 16, 1928.

*Brooklyn Daily Eagle* (Brooklyn, NY). "'Blithe Spirit' at Flatbush." May 31, 1944.

————. "Lew Fields' Kids, Herbert and Dorothy, Collaborate at Last." November 23, 1941.

————. "Silhouette." April 3, 1929.

*The Brooklyn Eagle* (Brooklyn, NY). "The Theater: *A Lonely Romeo*." June 11, 1919.

*Brooklyn Times Union* (Brooklyn, NY). "Harry *Delmar's Revels*." November 22, 1927.

Brown, James E. "Projected into Role of Humorist, Will Rogers Quickly Became the Greatest Monologist on the Stage; Mind Alert, and Wit Always Keen." *The Bristol Daily Courier* (Bristol, PA), August 22, 1935.

Calta, Louis. "Premiere Tonight for New Musical: 'Arms and the Girl,' Bowing at 46th Street Theatre, Has $453,766 Advance Sale." *New York Times*, February 2, 1950.

Canby, Vincent. "The Palace: From Ed Wynn to Gwen Verdon." *New York Times*, January 23, 1966.

Cavenaugh, Jennifer Jones. *Women in American Musical Theatre: Essays on Composers, Lyricists, Librettists, Arrangers, Choreographers, Designers, Directors, Producers, and Performance Artists*. Edited by Bud Coleman and Judith Sebesta. Jefferson, NC: McFarland & Co, Inc., 2008.

Chapman, John. "*By the Beautiful Sea* Gets Soggy." *New York Daily News* (New York, NY), April 9, 1954.

————. "*Can-Can* an Opulent Music Show with a Fine Cast and a Slow Book." *New York Daily News*, May 9, 1953.

————. "Tree in Brooklyn a Double Hit; It's Very Funny and Sentimental." *New York Daily News*, April 21, 1951.

*The Chicago Defender* (Chicago, IL). "Pearl Bailey Gets Dander Up over Race Slurs." February 18, 1950.

"Children Give Show." *Theatre World*, March 1920.

*Cincinnati Enquirer* (Cincinnati, OH). "Musical Show and Jury Romance Bring Robinson and Hayes Here." February 25, 1940.

———. "New York Society Throngs to Opening of Music Hall." December 28, 1932.

Coleman, Cy. "Cy Coleman." *Atlanta Constitution* (Atlanta, GA), August 29, 1965.

Collier, William. "From Weber and Fields to Hollywood." *The China Press* (Shanghai).

Collins-Hughes, Laura, and Alexis Soloski. "Broadway May Not Be So White, but Is It Woman Enough?" *New York Times*, May 31, 2016.

*Columbia Spectator* (New York, NY), 1920.

Cooke, Richard P. "The Theatre: Bundling to Music." *Wall Street Journal* (New York, NY), February 6, 1950.

———. "The Theatre: *Something for the Boys*." *Wall Street Journal*, January 9, 1943.

Corey, Herbert. "Beyond the Bridge." *The Brooklyn Daily Times* (Brooklyn, NY), June 15, 1929.

Corio, Ann, and Joseph DiMona. *This Was Burlesque*. New York: Madison Square Press, 1968.

*The Corpus Christi Caller Times* (Corpus Christi, TX). "Divorce Granted to Comedian's Daughter." June 29, 1939.

*The Courier Journal* (Louisville, KY). "Two Sparkling Musicals Present Two New Stars." April 29, 1951.

*Daily Boston Globe* (Boston, MA). "The Stage: Shubert Theatre, *Something for the Boys*." December 19, 1942.

*Daily News* (New York, NY). "Dixie to Broadway." Advertisement. November 30, 1924.

*Detroit Free Press* (Detroit, MI). "Kern Quits Broadway." July 22, 1936.

————. "Philly Critics Applaud Gwen's *Sweet Charity.*" December 8, 1965.

Drutman, Irving. "Lew Fields Left behind Him a Talented Family." *New York Herald Tribune*, December 14, 1941.

Durgin, Cyrus. "New Musical, 'Arms and the Girl,' Opens at Shubert." *Daily Boston Globe*, January 18, 1950.

————. "The Stage: *By the Beautiful Sea* Could Take Livening." *Daily Boston Globe*, February 24, 1954.

*An Evening with Dorothy Fields*. DRG Records, 1972, compact disc. Recorded April 9, 1972.

Ewen, David. *Richard Rodgers*. New York: Henry Holt and Company, 1957.

Falstaff, Jake. "Pippins and Cheese." *Akron Beacon Journal* (Akron, OH), March 8, 1926.

Field, Rowland. "Lew Leslie Presents *International Revue* Crowded with Stars." *Brooklyn Times Union* (Brooklyn, NY), February 26, 1930.

————. "The New Play: *Hello, Daddy.*" *The Times Union* (Brooklyn, NY), December 27, 1928.

————. "The New Play: *Vanderbilt Revue*, a New Song and Dance Entertainment." *Brooklyn Times Union* (Brooklyn, NY), November 6, 1930.

Fields, Armond, and L. Marc Fields. *From the Bowery to Broadway: Lew Fields and the Roots of American Popular Theater*. New York: Oxford University Press, 1993.

Fields, Dorothy. Interview by Joan Franklin and Robert Franklin. New York. November 1958.

Flinn, Caryl. *Brass Diva: The Life and Legends of Ethel Merman*. Berkeley, CA: University of California Press, 2007.

"Formally Open 'House That Jack Built.'" *The Music Trades*, September 15, 1923.

Francis, Bob. "Arms and the Girl." *The Billboard*, February 11, 1950.

Freudenheim, Milt. "Dot Fields Dislikes 'Ghosted' Biographies." *Cincinnati Enquirer*, May 2, 1966.

*Friday with Garroway*. NBC. April 29, 1955. Performed by Dorothy Fields.

Furia, Philip. *The Poets of Tin Pan Alley: A History of America's Great Lyricists*. New York: Oxford, 1990.

Gershen, Martin. "Another Musical Hit." *Baltimore Sun*, March 28, 1966.

———. "People Keep Singing Dorothy Fields's Songs." *Asbury Park Press*, March 19, 1966.

*The Globe and Mail* (Toronto, ON). "The Lyrical Life of Dorothy Fields Goes On and On." May 14, 1966.

Goldberg, Albert. "Gwen Verdon Sparkles at *Redhead* Opening." *Los Angeles Times* (Los Angeles, CA), April 26, 1960.

Goldberger, Paul. "Design Notebook." *New York Times*, February 16, 1978.

The Gombach Group. "Allenhurst Residential Historic District." Living Places. Accessed August 1, 2019. https://www.livingplaces.com/NJ/Monmouth_County /Allenhurst_Borough/Allenhurst_Residential_Historic_District.html.

Gottfried, Martin. "A Single and Great Performance." *Women's Wear Daily*, July 24, 1974, 45.

Greenspan, Charlotte. *Pick Yourself Up: Dorothy Fields and the American Musical*. New York: Oxford University Press, 2010.

*The Hartford Courant* (Hartford, CT). "Broadway Welcomes Weber & Fields Back." February 10, 1912.

———. "New Musical Presented at Shubert." December 23, 1958.

Haskins, Jim. *The Cotton Club*. New York: Hippocrene Books, 1994.

*The Hollywood Reporter* (Hollywood, CA). "'Something for the Boys' Has Advance of $120,000." January 12, 1943.

"The Honor Roll of Popular Songwriters: Mabel Wayne." *The Billboard*, May 19, 1951, 39.

Hopper, Hedda. "Talk of Hollywood." *The Evening Sun* (Baltimore, MD), August 16, 1962.

Hughes, Alice. "Four Children of Lew Fields Make Good Writing for the Stage." *Akron Beacon Journal* (Akron, OH), December 23, 1941.

————. "Melody Songs Replacing Rock and Roll Selections." *Poughkeepsie Journal* (Poughkeepsie, NY), January 22, 1963.

————. "A Woman's New York." *The Journal Herald* (Dayton, OH), April 27, 1941.

————. "A Woman's New York." *Poughkeepsie Eagle-News* (Poughkeepsie, NY), December 23, 1941.

Hughes, Andrew. "Acorn to Offer Songs of Gifted Lyricist." *The South Bend Tribune* (South Bend, IN), August 20, 2004.

Hyland, William G. *The Song Is Ended: Songwriters and American Music, 1900–1950*. New York: Oxford University Press, 1995.

"In the Limelight: Lew Fields." *The Billboard*, November 4, 1911, 2.

*Jewish Exponent* (Philadelphia, PA). "*Delmar's Revels* Coming to Shubert Theatre." March 2, 1928.

Kane, Henry. *How to Write a Song, as Told to Henry Kane*. New York: Macmillan, 1962.

Kasha, Al, and Joel Hirschhorn. *Notes on Broadway: Conversations with the Great Songwriters*. Chicago: Contemporary Books, 1985.

Kaye, Joseph. "Father Was Wrong: Lew Fields Gang Proves It." *The Cincinnati Enquirer*, January 4, 1942.

Kelly, Kevin. "New Reign for Old Vaudeville Queen." *The Boston Globe* (Boston, MA), January 30, 1966.

Kelly, Marion. "Songwriters Collaborate in Musical." *The Philadelphia Inquirer* (Philadelphia, PA), April 1, 1951.

Kilgallen, Dorothy. "Michael Todd Thinks Navy Will Let Him Use Telephone; Will Continue as Producer." *Fort Worth-Star Telegram* (Fort Worth, Texas), March 26, 1944.

Kimball, Robert, and Linda Emmet. *The Complete Lyrics of Irving Berlin*. New York: Alfred A. Knopf, 2001.

Kolodin, Irving. "*New Girl* Is Big Star Now." *Tucson Citizen* (Tucson, AZ), June 15, 1957.

Krueger, Miles, ed. *The Movie Musical from Vitaphone to 42nd Street*. New York: Dover Publications, 1975.

Lewis, Emery. "Her Words Are Legend." *The Record* (Hackensack, NJ), May 27, 1973.

Longacre, Betty. "Gossip of the Theatre." *The Standard Union* (Brooklyn, NY), September 20, 1928.

———. "Gossip of the Theatre: *Midnight Frolic* to Be Revived by Florenz Ziegfeld." *The Standard Union*, October 13, 1928.

*Los Angeles Times* (Los Angeles, CA). "Story Inspires Music, Says Jerome Kern." October 3, 1936.

*Louisville Courier-Journal* (Louisville, KY). "Singer Angered by Anti-Negro Talk to Quit Show." February 12, 1950.

Luhrssen, David. *Mamoulian: Life on Stage and Screen*. Lexington, KY: University of Kentucky Press, 2013.

Lyons, Leonard. "The Lyon's Den." *Salt Lake Tribune*. September 23, 1944.

Mantle, Burns. "Bojangles Robinson's Dancing Featured in *Blackbirds of 1928*." *The New York Age* (New York, NY), May 19, 1928.

———. "British Little Theater Takes Belasco Prize." *The Tampa Tribune* (Tampa, FL), May 20, 1928.

———. "*Dixie to Broadway* Is a Colored Riot." *Daily News* (New York, NY), October 31, 1924.

———. "*Hello, Daddy* a Fields Family Hit." *New York Daily News*, December 28, 1928.

———. "*The Hot Mikado* Burns Up All the Colored Show Records." *New York Daily News*, March 23, 1939.

———. "Mr. Ziegfeld Reopens the Roof." *New York Daily News*, February 8, 1929.

McBride, Mary. "It's 'Just One Song after Another' for Lew Fields' Talented Daughter." *Austin American* (Austin, TX), April 8, 1934.

McCord, Bert. "Entrances and Exits: 'Michael Todd's Staff Presents,' Not Just Michael Todd, and Thereby Hangs a Tale." *New York Herald Tribune*, April 30, 1944, C1.

McHugh, Jimmy. Interview by Joan Franklin and Robert Franklin. New York. 1959.

Melvin, Edwin F. "*By the Beautiful Sea* on Stage." *Christian Science Monitor*, February 24, 1954.

Moore, James. "Songs of Quality Certain to Last, Says Top Lyricist." *Chappaqua Sun* (Chappaqua, NY), January 5, 1956.

Mordden, Ethan. *Sing for Your Supper: The Broadway Musical in the 1930s*. New York: Macmillan, 2005.

Morehouse, Ward. "Lyric Writing Fascinates Dorothy Fields." *Pittsburgh Press* (Pittsburgh, PA), July 5, 1959.

*The Morning Herald* (Uniontown, PA). "Florence Mills Real Service to Her Race." November 14, 1927.

Muir, Florabel. "Tin Pan Alley Goes West En Masse." *New York Daily News*, June 23, 1929.

Mulhern, Donald. "The New Play: Lew Fields and Some Pleasing Playmates Arrive in *Hello, Daddy*." *The Standard Union*, December 27, 1928.

Nachman, Gerald. *Showstoppers: The Surprising Backstage Stories of Broadway's Most Remarkable Songs*. Chicago: Chicago Review Press, 2015.

*The News Journal* (Wilmington, DE). "*Vanderbilt Revue* Debut Postponed." October 18, 1930.

*The New York Age* (New York, NY). "Blackbirds Is Now the Hit of Broadway." September 29, 1928.

————. "Cotton Club Draws Color Lines." February 21, 1925.

*The New York Amsterdam News* (New York, NY). "Leslie's New Revue One of the Best of Its Kind Ever Presented Even on B'way." May 23, 1928.

*New York Daily News*. "Audition Singers." November 8, 1944.

*New York Evening Mail* (New York, NY). "Broadway Seeks 'First Love' Stars." February 14, 1921.

*New York Herald Tribune*. "Currier and Ives Pictures Bring \$20,332 at Auction." January 23, 1930.

————. "Lew Fields Rites Held on Coast; Weber at Bedside as He Died." July 22, 1941, 13.

————. "Michael Todd Is in Navy, Will Report in 21 Days." March 9, 1944.

*New York Times* (New York, NY). "Apologies Made to Pearl Bailey." February 12, 1950.

————. "10 Elected to New Hall of Fame for Songwriters." March 10, 1971.

————. "\$500,000 Jubilee Ended." June 14, 1912.

————. "A Few Notes about the Hot Michael Todd." October 8, 1939.

————. "A Lonely Romeo." Advertisement. August 19, 1919.

————. "A Tribute to Dorothy Fields." July 21, 1974, 87.

————. "At the Palace." September 5, 1941.

————. "Bank of U.S. Closes; State Takes Over Affairs; Aid Offered to Depositors." December 12, 1930, 1.

————. "Benny Goodman, King of Swing, Is Dead." June 14, 1986.

————. "Golden Jubilee of a Famous Team." September 4, 1932, 8–13.

————. "Joseph Fields, 71, Dies on Coast; Co-Author of *My Sister Eileen*." March 5, 1966.

———. "Leases Former Kahn Club." December 20, 1927.

———. "Lew Fields Dies: Noted Comedian, 74." July 22, 1941, 19.

———. "No More Parades at the Palace." October 16, 1932.

———. "Palace Opens Today." March 24, 1913.

———. "Radio City Premiere Is a Notable Event." December 28, 1932.

———. "Shubert Sees New Shows." July 16, 1911.

———. "That 'Tree' Keeps Growing," April 15, 1951.

———. "Ziegfeld to Close His Midnight Frolic." May 18, 1921.

*New York Tribune* (New York, NY). "Broadway Congratulates Fields on the Birth of a Daughter." July 16, 1904.

———. "Lake Placid: Adirondacks." Advertisement. June 16, 1914.

———. "Lew Fields Believes Youth a Greater Asset Than Too Much Stage Experience." September 5, 1920.

———. "Walter Luttgen Estate Parts with House in 75th Street Owned for Many Years." September 21, 1922.

*The Owensboro Messenger* (Owensboro, KY). "Club with Mirror for Dance Floor Is Opened." November 7, 1927.

*Passaic Daily News* (Passaic, NJ). "150,000 View Mills Funeral: Harlem Pays Heart-Throbbing Tribute to Dead Negress Musical Comedy Star." November 7, 1927.

Peacock, Ray. "Lew Fields's Children Carry on Traditions." *The Daily News-Journal* (Murfreesboro, TN), January 25, 1942.

Peak, Mayme Ober. "Tin Pan Alley Extends to the Pacific Coast Now." *Variety* (New York, NY), May 8, 1929.

*Pittsburgh Courier* (Pittsburgh, PA). "Story of Late Song Hit's Discovery Reads like a Modern Fairy Tale." November 17, 1928.

Propst, Andy. *You Fascinate Me So*. Milwaukee, WI: Applause Theatre and Cinema Books, 2015.

Reed, Rex. "Column: Rex Reed." *Minneapolis Tribune* (Minneapolis, MN), May 20, 1973.

————. "Dorothy Fields: Tin Pan Alley Is Her Turf." *Los Angeles Times*, April 29, 1973.

————. "Fame Eludes Cy Coleman, but Now There's *I Love My Wife*." *The Baltimore Sun* (Baltimore, MD), May 15, 1977.

————. "*Seesaw* Score Is Something to Sing About." *The Courier Journal* (Louisville, KY), May 6, 1973.

————. "Signoret & Fields Keep Winning Hearts." *New York Daily News*, December 2, 1978.

————. "Who Is Cy Coleman? Any Singer Can Tell You." *Independent Press Telegram*, May 15, 1977.

*The Register*. "Composer Cy Coleman Has a Habit of Teaming Up with Sundry Companions for Words to Fit Tunes." September 18, 1977.

"Reminiscences of Dorothy Fields (1958)," Popular Arts Project, Oral History Archives at Columbia, Rare Book & Manuscript Library, Columbia University in the City of New York.

"Reminiscences of Jimmy McHugh (1959)," Popular Arts Project, Oral History Archives at Columbia, Rare Book & Manuscript Library, Columbia University in the City of New York.

"Reminiscences of Oscar Hammerstein II (1959)," Popular Arts Project, Oral History Archives at Columbia, Rare Book & Manuscript Library, Columbia University in the City of New York.

"Reminiscences of Richard C. Rodgers (1968)," Popular Arts Project, Oral History Archives at Columbia, Rare Book and Manuscript Library, Columbia University in the City of New York. Rimler, Walter. *The Man That Got Away: The Life and Songs of Harold Arlen*. Urbana, IL: University of Illinois Press, 2015.

Rodgers, Mary. "Sisters Gershwin: Where Are the Women Composers and Lyricists." Lecture, New York Public Library for Performing Arts, New York, NY, March 24, 1997.

Rodgers, Richard. *Musical Stages: An Autobiography*. 2nd ed. Cambridge, MA: De Capo Press, 2002.

Rodgers, Richard C. Interview by Kenneth W. Leish. New York. 1968.

Ross, Don. "The Fields Family Recalls Papa Lew." *New York Herald Tribune*, June 7, 1959.

Sara, Dorothy. "Clues in the Handwriting of Great Americans." *Vogue*, February 1, 1961.

Saunders, Ripley D. "Happy Reunion of Weber & Fields Came at Psychological Moment on American Stage." *St. Louis Post-Dispatch* (St. Louis, MO), May 26, 1912, 9.

Savoy, Maggie. "Playgoers Are Smart and Always Demand the Best." *The Arizona Republic* (Phoenix, AZ), February 15, 1960.

*Say Mama!* New York: Akron Club, 1921.

Schallert, Edwin. "*Jazz Singer* Is Landmark." *Los Angeles Times*, December 30, 1927.

Schrader, Fred F. "Another Typical Fields Production: Big Upheaval at the New Theater." *The Washington Post* (Washington, DC), February 12, 1911.

Schwartz, Arthur. "The Evolution of a Gay Musical: Collaborators Hardly Know It." *New York Herald*, February 12, 1939.

*The Scranton Times* (Scranton, PA). "Lew Fields Gets Back on Job Next Monday." August 3, 1911.

S. D., Trav. *No Applause—Just Throw Money*. New York: Farrar, Straus, and Giroux, 2006.

Sennwald, Andre. "The Screen: Lily Pons Makes Her Debut in *I Dream Too Much*." *New York Times*, November 29, 1935.

Shackleford, W. H. "Happenings among Colored People." *The Tennessean* (Nashville, TN), November 13, 1927.

Shaw, Arnold. *The Jazz Age: Popular Music in the 1920s*. New York: Oxford University Press, 1987.

Shaw, Len G. "The Theater." *Detroit Free Press* (Detroit, MI), June 20, 1932.

Sheaffer, Louis. "Curtain Time: 'Tree in Brooklyn' Enjoyably Transplanted in Broadway Show." *Brooklyn Daily Eagle*, May 6, 1951.

Shelley, Peter. *Gwen Verdon: A Life on Stage and Screen*. Jefferson, NC: McFarland & Company Publishers, 2015.

Shipton, Alyn. *I Feel a Song Coming On: The Life of Jimmy McHugh*. Urbana, IL: The University of Illinois Press, 2009.

Shirey, David. "Art: Currier and Ives Revisited." *New York Times*, January 23, 1977.

Short, Frank. "A Talk with Lew Fields." *Christian Science Monitor* (Boston, MA), June 24, 1924.

Shriftgiesser, Karl. "Amazing Fields Family." *New York Times*, January 17, 1943.

Simon, Neil. *Rewrites*. New York: Simon & Schuster, 1996.

Skogstad, Katherine. "*Plain and Fancy* Music Written on Card Table." *The Atlanta Constitution* (Atlanta, GA), July 7, 1957.

Smith, Betty. "That 'Tree' Keeps Growing." *New York Times*, April 15, 1951.

Sobel, Bernard. "Smut Kills Stage Revues, according to Lew Leslie, Broadway Producer." *Pittsburgh Courier* (Pittsburgh, PA), October 29, 1932.

*The Standard Union* (Brooklyn, NY). "*The Plantation Revue* Pleases at 48th Street." July 18, 1922.

*St. Louis Post-Dispatch* (St. Louis, MO). "Musical Gold Rush Seems to Be Definitely Through." July 27, 1930.

———. "'Tin Pan Alley?' Why It's the Place Where Popular Songs Come From." May 10, 1903.

Ste. Claire, Dana. "Currier and Ives Created Image of America's Past." *Orlando Sentinel* (Orlando, FL). September 4, 1994. Volusia Edition.

Strongin, Ted. "Previews and Postscripts." *The East Hampton Star* (East Hampton, NY), August 3, 1972.

*The Sun* (New York, NY). "Lew Fields's Daughter Bride at Delmonico's." August 25, 1914.

———. "Lillian Russell Weds but Not in Church." June 13, 1912.

———. "*Miss 1917* Makes Debut at Century." November 6, 1917.

*Tampa Tribune* (Tampa, FL). "Romantic Miss Fields' Slapstick Dilemma." April 25, 1926.

Thirer, Irene. "*The Jazz Singer* Moves Audience; Al's Own Voice on Vitaphone." *New York Daily News*, October 7, 1927.

"'35 Pop Sales Topped '34." *Variety*, September 2, 1936, 41.

*The Times Tribune* (Scranton, PA). "At Lyceum." May 16, 1912.

Tinee, Mae. "*Father Takes a Wife* Lively, Clever Picture." *Chicago Daily Tribune* (Chicago, IL), September 21, 1941.

———. "She Finds Lew Fields One of the Busiest Men in Town." *Chicago Sunday Tribune* (Chicago, IL), November 5, 1911.

*The Topeka Daily Capital* (Topeka, KS). "How Music 'Publishers' Prospered." February 13, 1908.

"Tribute to Dorothy Fields." *Napa Valley Register* (Napa, CA), April 17, 1975.

Trust, Gary. "Happy Birthday, Billboard Charts! On July 27, 1940, the First Song Sales Chart Debuted." *Chart Beat* (blog). Entry posted July 27, 2017. Accessed July 17, 2019. https://www.billboard.com/articles/columns/chart-beat/7874034 /happy-birthday-billboard-charts-july-27-1940-song-sales.

*Variety* (New York, NY). "*Blackbirds of 1928*." May 16, 1928.

———. "*Delmar's Revels*." December 7, 1927.

———. "Dorothy Fields and Jimmy McHugh." March 21, 1933.

———. "Dorothy Fields Made Pro at $1500 Weekly at Musical Hall-No Confusion." January 10, 1933.

———. "Dot Fields, Johnston Teaming for Songs." September 22, 1937.

———. "Fields-Coleman Collab on Musicalized 'Merton.'" December 20, 1972.

———. "Metro Cuts Off Writers and Music Dept." November 5, 1930.

———. "Night Club Reviews: Cotton Club." December 7, 1927.

———. "Plays Out of Town: *Arms and the Girl.*" January 4, 1950.

———. "Radio City Premieres: Music Hall." January 3, 1933.

———. "Rodgers' New Collab?" August 31, 1960.

———. "Show Out of Town – *Redhead.*" December 24, 1958.

———. "Studios Anxious as 'Show-Me' Execs from East Start Trek Coast-ward." November 12, 1930.

———. "Vanderbilt Revue." November 12, 1930.

———. "Vanderbilt Revue." October 22, 1930.

———. "Weber & Fields Died Hoping Hollywood Would Film-Biog Them," May 13, 1942.

Wales, Clarke. "Reviews of the New Films: *Swing Time.*" *Detroit Free Press* (Detroit, MI), September 6, 1936.

*Wall Street Journal* (New York, NY). "The Theatre: An Ethiopian Revue." May 11, 1928.

*The Washington Post* (Washington, DC). "Astaire-Rogers World Premier Next Thursday." August 21, 1936.

Wasson, Sam. *Fosse.* Boston: Mariner Books, 2013.

Watt, Douglas. "*Seesaw* Is Comedy and Musical." *New York Daily News*, March 20, 1973.

Watts, Richard, Jr. "Delmar's Revels Is Pleasant Revue with Little Novelty." *New York Herald Tribune*, November 29, 1927.

"Weber & Fields Died Hoping Hollywood Would Film-Biog Them." *Variety*, May 13, 1942.

Wedman, Les. "You'll Be Happy to Meet Cabiria." *Vancouver Sun* (Vancouver, BC), March 28, 1962.

Whorf, Michael. *American Popular Song Composers: Oral Histories, 1920s–1950s*. Jefferson, NC: McFarland & Company, Inc. Publishers, 2012.

Wierzbicki, James. *Film Music: A History*. New York: Routledge, 2009.

Wilk, Max. *They're Playing Our Song: Conversations with America's Classic Songwriters*. 5th ed. Westport, CT: Easton Studio Press, 2007.

Wilson, Barbara L. "A Bundle of Mirth and Melody." *The Philadelphia Inquirer* (Philadelphia, PA), January 8, 1950.

Wilson, John S. "Miss Fields Views 47 Years of Song." *New York Times*, April 11, 1972.

Winer, Deborah Grace. *On the Sunny Side of the Street: The Life and Lyrics of Dorothy Fields*. New York: Schirmer Books, 1998.

Young, Greg, and Tom Meyers. *The Bowery Boys: Adventures in Old New York*. Berkeley, CA: Ulysses Press, 2016.

*Yours for a Song: The Women of Tin Pan Alley*. Interview with Artis Wodehouse. Fox Lorber, 1998.

Zolotow, Sam. "Musical Planned on Peace Corps." *New York Times*, November 6, 1961.

———. "Second Show Is Due on Peace Corps." *New York Times*, March 21, 1962.

# Index

# Lyric Credits

**Exactly Like You**
Words by Dorothy Fields
Music by Jimmy McHugh
Copyright © 1930 Cotton Club Publishing and Shapiro Bernstein & Co., Inc.,
  New York
Copyright Renewed
All Rights for Cotton Club Publishing Administered by Sony/ATV Music
  Publishing LLC, 424 Church Street, Suite 1200, Nashville, TN 37219
International Copyright Secured All Rights Reserved
Used by Permission
*Reprinted by Permission of Hal Leonard LLC*

**A Fine Romance**
from SWING TIME
Words by Dorothy Fields
Music by Jerome Kern
Copyright © 1936 UNIVERSAL-POLYGRAM INTERNATIONAL
  PUBLISHING, INC. and ALDI MUSIC
Copyright Renewed
Print Rights for ALDI MUSIC in the U.S. Controlled and Administered by
  HAPPY ASPEN MUSIC LLC c/o SHAPIRO, BERNSTEIN & CO., INC.
All Rights Reserved Used by Permission
*Reprinted by Permission of Hal Leonard LLC*

**I Can't Give You Anything But Love**
from BLACKBIRDS OF 1928
Words and Music by Jimmy McHugh and Dorothy Fields

**I'd Rather Wake Up By Myself**
from BY THE BEAUTIFUL SEA
Words by Dorothy Fields
Music by Arthur Schwartz

**Lovely To Look At**
from ROBERTA
Words and Music by Jimmy McHugh, Dorothy Fields and Jerome Kern

**On The Sunny Side Of The Street**
Lyric by Dorothy Fields
Music by Jimmy McHugh

**The Way You Look Tonight**
from SWING TIME
featured in the TriStar Motion Picture MY BEST FRIEND'S WEDDING
Words by Dorothy Fields
Music by Jerome Kern

**BLUE AGAIN**
Words by DOROTHY FIELDS
Music by JIMMY MCHUGH

**Blue Again**
Words by Dorothy Fields
Music by Jimmy McHugh

**HEY YOUNG FELLA (CLOSE YOUR OLD UMBRELLA)**
Words by DOROTHY FIELDS
Music by JIMMY MCHUGH

**Hey, Young Fella**
Words by Dorothy Fields
Music by Jimmy McHugh

# About the Author

**Kristin Stultz Pressley** is an author, speaker, and nationally recognized musical theater historian and teaching artist. She lives with her husband and their two sons in the mountains of North Carolina. Learn more about her work at DrBroadway. com or by following @DrBway on Twitter and Instagram.